Joseph Olshan

A Warmer Season

Pavanne
published by Pan Books

First published in Great Britain 1987 by Bloomsbury Publishing Ltd
This Pavanne edition published 1988 by Pan Books Ltd
Cavaye Place, London SW10 9PG
9 8 7 6 5 4 3 2 1
© Joseph Olshan 1987
ISBN 0 330 30121 7
Printed and bound in Great Britain by
Collins, Glasgow

FOR MY GRANDMOTHER, ROSE SANFORD

One pushes upward into an empty city.

—*The I Ching (46)*

ACKNOWLEDGMENTS

The author would like to express his gratitude to the following people, whose support made the completion of this book possible:

My father, Marvin Olshan, for his great generosity; Elisabeth Jakab, who believed in it from the beginning and made some wonderful suggestions along the way; Liz Calder, who also made some wonderful suggestions and endorsed me on the previous book; Melody Bell for stylistic interpretation; Ellen Resch for her guidance and advice; Martin McNamara, who told me to just do it; and to John Hawkins, who stood behind me and tried very hard at a time when the odds were not exactly in my favor.

1

"*Remember, Danny*, how you used to write all those beautiful poems in Italian," his mother said. "Remember when Camilla was getting married in Vicenza and we were late getting there because we were waiting for you to finish your marriage ode?"

"Rhyming is easier in Italian," Daniel reminded her. "Besides, in Italy, you write poems. In America you write poison pen letters."

The two of them and Daniel's sister, Alexis, were standing outside a small butcher shop. Ever since they had moved back to New York, his mother had wanted to explore the Italian neighborhood. This was their first excursion. Although most housewives preferred the conveniences of Shopwell and Finast, Irene had figured a better quality of product could be found at the "specialty shop," where she assumed one could get better bargains by speaking Italian.

"Please, Danny, go in there and order in Italian for me," she said.

"You order, Mom. You know what to say." Daniel and Alexis exchanged looks of exasperation.

Irene shrugged and strolled into the shop ahead of them, the rickety wooden door slamming behind her. Looking like a typical Italian urbanite, she was dressed in a white silk blouse and loose-fitting pants belted tightly at the waist. She was wearing a scarf around her taut, smooth throat, her dark auburn hair kept in a hacked, tastefully disheveled manner. She had never wanted to move back to America, and when his father had announced that his accounting firm was transferring them to New York, she had unsuccessfully lobbied Daniel and Alexis to remain in Italy. Irene had loved Padua. Padua was close to Venice—most of her friends lived in Venice—and besides, she had virtually forgotten she was an American. Daniel, on the other hand, had spent the first twelve years of his life in Italy, and took his native country for granted. He was curious about living in America, considered himself American.

This assumption lasted until the family finally settled in this suburb of New York City and he entered school, where he discovered that he was actually more Italian. His schoolmates were undemonstrative with their hands and stood far apart when they spoke to one another, sharing talk about a whole tradition of hit singles and movies Daniel had never heard or seen. People vied for popularity and played foolish dating games like "post office" and "spin the bottle." Feeling conspicuous and foreign, Daniel began stifling his knowledge of Italian and even Italian culture.

His Italian had always been a source of pride to his parents, who had never quite mastered the language themselves. By refusing to speak it, Daniel knew that he was adding to the frustrations his mother was facing in her native country. For one thing she had trouble meeting people; suburbanites were a far cry from her flamboyant artistic and intellectual Italian friends. Suburban social life centered around a tightly knit network of couples who played tennis and golf and did volunteer work. And then, soon after moving in, the Fells had discovered that their town was divided into two main constituencies: Jewish and Italian—they were Jewish.

When Alexis and Daniel finally went inside the shop, they found Irene struggling with her Italian in an attempt to place a meat order. The dark-eyed proprietress was squinting and brooding, repeating Irene's ungrammatical sentences in proper Italian as dutifully as a parent correcting a child. The woman eventually began speaking in broken English, as if to suggest that more would be accomplished in that language. This annoyed Irene, who lost her nerve and forgot the phrase for butterflied lamb.

When she saw Daniel she elbowed him to finish placing their order.

He turned to her, scowling. She knew he didn't like speaking Italian any longer, so why was she forcing him? "Just speak in English," he told her.

"No, let her think we're European," Irene whispered fiercely. Then she smiled, half embarrassed at her own insistence.

"Mom, what are you trying to prove?" he asked.

"Just do what I say, Daniel." She spoke behind a frantic smile.

With a sigh, Daniel took over the ordering. He told the shop-keeper that his family was newly arrived from Padua—but that his mother was born in Latvia; that's why her Italian was accented and hard to understand. Alexis was smart. She kept quiet the entire time and looked bored. As soon as Daniel opened his mouth, the woman was charmed and her Italian turned rapid and lilting. She shyly complimented him on his perfect accent and insisted on charging the Fells fifty cents less per pound than the advertised price.

They went home with the choicest cuts of lamb and Irene boasted to his father how she was monitoring costs. Harold was suitably impressed. But when, a few days later, a bill came in for a $500 dress she had charged in White Plains, Harold angrily pointed out the irony of cutting costs at the market after squan-dering money on designer clothing. As the years went by Irene forgot more and more of her Italian. And although she never became a typical suburbanite, she did settle into shopping at su-permarkets.

PART ONE

2

The slaughter of helpless zoo animals is a misdeed difficult to forget. When it occurred one night at the children's park in Houghton, the news was picked up by several wire services and transmitted all over the United States and even through parts of Europe. Some hoodlums had hurdled the Cyclone fence that surrounded the small verdant park and, with a wire cutter, had clipped the diamond mesh of metal that protected the animals. Using blunt kitchen knives, they massacred frightened lambs, chased down and decapitated two dozen chickens and cut open the soft bellies of rabbits. Although the culprits had yet to be identified, the high school students whispered among themselves that the Polanno brothers were responsible for the crime.

The Polanno brothers ruled over the youth of Houghton with an invisible hand; their reputation always preceded them. Between one and three years past high school age, they had not yet graduated. Their stints in youth prisons had interrupted their scholastic careers. In between these stints they attended school fairly regularly. They managed to pass their courses without doing a stitch of work, either by intimidating other students into making copies of their homework assignments or by procuring the answers to multiple choice Regents exams. Vito, twenty years old, was a senior. He had a lanky build, hawk eyes and a face riddled with acne. Mario, nineteen, was in eleventh grade, a pudgy fellow who would undoubtedly grow obese by the time he reached his middle twenties. Mickey, the good-looking one of the three, was eighteen and in tenth grade.

The Polannos were inseparable; Daniel never saw them apart. Indeed, he rarely saw them outside their black Trans Am. Their strength seemed to be in their triumvirate. The windows of the Trans Am were tinted with carbon, and when anyone saw the car careering through the high school parking lot, it was difficult if not impossible to detect anyone behind the window glass. This tended to give the impression that the Polannos were a single person rather than a threesome.

When the news first spread through the town how the throats of the animals had been slit and their bodies disemboweled, the police went through the usual motions of questioning certain kids whom they considered to be pivotal to the comings and goings of the Polanno brothers. But no one who knew anything—such as where the Polannos were the night of the incident—would divulge it. Quite simply everybody was afraid of having the Polannos after them, which meant getting beaten up long after you were made aware that they were after you. For several weeks before they actually descended upon a particular person, the Polannos used their intermediaries to stir up anxiety. You would be constantly reminded, "Oh man, the Polannos are looking for your ass," and then repeatedly questioned, "So, did they get you yet or wha?"

The autumn the animals were slaughtered Daniel had reached his last year of high school. He was still a virgin, a condition that had become increasingly burdensome to him. What if he ended up going to college without any real sexual experience? Houghton was a fairly conventional town and all of the girls he had dated refused to go all the way. They were virgins, too. While this explained their reluctance, Daniel worried whether there was something unsexy about him. Plenty of his acquaintances claimed to have gotten their virginal girlfriends to make love—so why couldn't he? He didn't think it was a physical hindrance, unless being "blond and stocky" precluded the ability to attract women more strongly. Once a girl told him he had a cute bod. What did that mean? Was a cute bod something to dally with but not indulge in? Other boys he knew had been fortunate enough to date girls who had already given up their virginity. Did his problem have

anything to do with growing up in Italy? Did he lack some kind
of necessary American gusto?

But then in late October, Julietta Polanno, the first cousin of
the Polanno brothers, took a fancy to him. He had heard she was
experienced. Julietta had first seen Daniel practicing with the
soccer team. She and her group of tough girlfriends liked to perch
along the limed sidelines, making catcalls. They all wore tight
blue jeans with flared cuffs and green bomber jackets, and stood
in close formation with their hips cocked. Julietta had a lovely
slim body and her buttocks were heart-shaped. She had a small
mole in the middle of her forehead, which, however, did not
detract from the sharp prettiness of her face. Her complexion was
dark and grainy like her cousin Vito's, and her eyes frequently
narrowed to slits whenever she grew anxious or fervent.

"Ever see a blond Jew?" Daniel heard Julietta intone to one of
her tough-girl minions as he dribbled the ball past them. "Long
hair looks good on him, don't it?" She added. At first Daniel was
unsure whether or not Julietta was trying to insult him; he had
had limited contact with anti-Semitism. "Look at those muscle
legs. Baby, you're cute," Julietta told him in her tough-girl's voice.

"Then you have good taste," Daniel forced himself to call back
as he passed the soccer ball. It was difficult to break through a
barrier of shyness that seemed to grow around him as Julietta
acted more and more aggressively. But he forced himself to.

The next thing Daniel knew, Julietta had learned his class
schedule from one of her Polanno connections who worked in the
high school office. That semester his chemistry class coincided
with one of her study halls, and he often found Julietta loitering
near the door of the chemistry lab. She would glance at him
suggestively. "Fancy seeing you here," Daniel would say. "Small
world, ain't it?" Julietta would remark. Whenever he saw her he
couldn't help first zeroing in on her tiny mole. But then he was
looking from the neck down and knew she was a "piece," as people
said, hanging on the *s* sound. The inner turmoil caused by Julietta's
attention kept Daniel aroused halfway through his class. And
when he would look up at the diagrams of molecules carefully
scrawled on the blackboard, they appeared as incomprehensible
to him as the calculus equations left over from the honors group
that used the schoolroom during the prior class period.

Despite his strong attraction to Julietta, Daniel was afraid to get involved with a Polanno. He imagined himself making some kind of blunder in pursuing Julietta that would only bring misery into his life. Given the natural animosity that existed between Jews and Italians in the town of Houghton, he figured that the Polanno brothers would relish any opportunity to fell a Jew. He pictured himself lying senseless in a gutter.

The Jews in Houghton were mostly upper-middle class and lived in the hills and ridges on one side of the town. They commuted to jobs in Manhattan. The Italians were middle and lower-middle class and lived in the flatter areas around the downtown section that was divided from the Jewish neighborhood by the railroad tracks. Most of the Italians lived in two-family homes and made up the local merchants, political officials and police force. The two factions rarely mixed, much less condoned cross-dating or intermarriage.

"What about a kiss, honey," Julietta began whispering to him when they passed in the hallways. He got flustered under the weight of her compliments. "Oh, do I love to see him blush." Strangely, when Julietta spoke affectionately, she sounded like an older, more experienced woman.

Daniel and Julietta had their first encounter on a Friday evening at a bar called the Oaks, which was located at the north end of town. The Oaks was the only bar in Westchester County that never bothered to ask its patrons for proof of age (the drinking age was then eighteen). If anyone was sixteen or seventeen and had a few mustache whiskers—girls had the leverage of applying heavy makeup to make themselves appear older—the bartender, who was the brother of the chief of police, didn't look twice. The walls were made of darkly stained shingles; errant cigarette burns left by nervous smokers actually enhanced the decor. On a Friday night the place gushed from portal to portal with beer and was packed with a cross section of the high school: the jocks, the computer geeks and of course the Polannos, who kept rearing in and out of the smoke-filled place like a three-headed hydra.

Daniel had gone to the Oaks with his friend, Patrick Riordan. Although Patrick was the class whiz in math and science, he did not have the goody-goody personality of a computer geek. They were in the midst of sharing their second pitcher of beer when Patrick asked Daniel if he had ever talked to Gianni Scaravento.

He was indicating a dark, curly-headed Italian boy of massive build whom Daniel knew as the quarterback of the football team, a distinction that commanded respect from all factions, even from people like the Polanno brothers. Over six feet tall, Gianni was standing at the bar, talking to Julietta. Just that day a rumor had reached the ears of Patrick and Daniel that Gianni and Julietta had been flirting with each other.

"You know," Daniel said to Patrick, "I've never seen her with any guy before. I mean, it's like she's all catcalls."

Patrick turned to him with a sardonic light in his gray eyes, which were glazed over from the vast quantity of beer they had already drunk. "I thought you understood, Danny," he said.

"Understood what?"

"Nobody wants to lay a finger on her . . ." Patrick broke off, searching the crowded room. But among the swell of underage high school students, the Polannos, the only ones whose presence in this bar was actually legal, could not be found.

"Nobody but Scaravento," Daniel grumbled.

"They wouldn't dare touch Scaravento," Patrick said snidely and left it at that. After all, Gianni *was* the quarterback who still had half a season left. The Polannos might commit carnage, but they wouldn't tamper with the local quarterback's throwing arm, not to mention a football schedule. Then they saw Gianni's tongue flick out, probe and finally enter Julietta's mouth. His tongue looked thick and rough and hungry. "Jesus," Patrick said. Daniel was fascinated that Gianni would dare to make out with Julietta under the watchful eyes of Polanno minions. Julietta, meanwhile, provisionally accepted his tongue. However, just as she did so, her glance shifted and caught Daniel's eyes. She jumped back and took a swipe at Gianni. Her hand glanced off his rugged face and then hit the counter, knocking over two beer glasses that ended up shattering on the floor.

"You fuck!" Gianni cried out, his large, dark eyes brimming with tears of anger. As he stalked toward the door, he glowered at Daniel. It was as though some instinct told Gianni that here was the presence that cooled Julietta's affections. His cheeks shone with wet as he walked out into the cold night.

"Gianni Scaravento." Patrick's voice broke the puzzled silence that was blanketing the Oaks.

Daniel turned to him. "It means something, Scaravento."

Patrick smiled, waiting for the pearl while Daniel suddenly felt on the verge of something ominous. "*Scaraventare* in Italian means to hurl," he said softly.

"But his name is Scaravento," Patrick said.

Daniel shrugged. "But when you say *Mi scaravento* in Italian it means I hurl myself."

3

Seconded by her friend Brenda, Julietta stood outside the Oaks. They were leaning against the Polannos' Trans Am. Looking seductive, Julietta had squeezed herself into a pair of snug black jeans and frizzed out her hair. Patrick and Daniel squinted at the car to see if the brothers were sitting inside it.

"They ain't here," Julietta said, her raspy voice knifing the cold darkness. Her eyes locked on them. "How ya doin', Danny?" she said.

Daniel glanced at Patrick, who grinned back at him goofily. Daniel peered down at the street that was glittering beer bottle shards under a buzzing lamplight. "I'm all right."

"Come over here," Julietta said. "I wanna talk to you."

He hesitated.

"Come on, Danny," she said. "We haven't even talked."

Patrick reached into his coat pocket and produced the keys to his Volkswagen van, which he had carpeted and outfitted with a stereo system. "Drop it off tomorrow morning. I'll get a ride home with Bobby Wise."

His smile seemed to say, 'After all, I didn't carpet this van for nothing.' Daniel knew Patrick understood something that he had yet to understand. Patrick had lost his virginity at the age of fifteen to a voluptuous senior who was now halfway through college and

who still went to bed with him from time to time. Patrick claimed
he was attracted only to older women. And it was as though his
experience allowed him to sense a climatic change in the coldness
of that darkened street. He tapped Daniel on the shoulder, whispering, "This is your chance, Danny," and a moment later returned to the bar. Meanwhile, the car keys already had gotten
wet and sweaty in Daniel's palm.

"Okay, Danny," Julietta said. "Now come over here and talk
to me."

He closed the distance between them. Soon they were standing
near each other, exhalations of air making nervous frosty billows
between their mouths. In a most natural manner Julietta leaned
forward, pressing her forehead against Danny's chest, and sighed.
"I'm glad you could get rid of him," she told his chest in a muffled
voice. She rotated her head to the side so that now she was peering
at Brenda. "Goodbye, Bren," she said. Glaring at them, Brenda
clucked her tongue, pushed off the car with the backs of her thighs
and strode back toward the wooden entrance of the Oaks.

"Do you want to go somewhere, Julietta?" Daniel blurted out.
He lingered on the pronunciation of the two *t*'s in the name as is
done in Italian. Julietta picked up her head and searched him with
caustic eyes. "You said my name just like my Aunt Maria says
it. You speak Italian or something?"

"A couple words."

"Really, how come? I thought you were a Jew?"

"Plenty of Jewish people live in Italy," Daniel explained.

"Oh?"

"And anyway, shut up about Jews," he told Julietta.

"Aaaa." Julietta pulled her head back for a moment and then
shook out her mane of hair. She peered at Daniel crosswise. "I
don't got anything against Jewish people, okay. I really don't."
Then she grinned. "I just kind of like saying the word Jew.
Sounds good to me. Aren't there words that sound good to you
to say?"

"I guess," Daniel said, growing impatient. "So where do you
want to go, Julietta?"

"That all depends. You got a car?"

"Yeah, I got the van," Daniel said, watching to see how Julietta
reacted to the idea of the word "van," which was equivalent to

saying, 'I got my own apartment' or 'My parents went away to the Caribbean and left me alone in the house.'

"Good going," Julietta said. "Where is it?"

He pointed across the street to the parking lot of the Oaks, filled primarily with souped-up American cars, where the VW was parked under a street lamp, glinting its faded paint job.

"Oh, you mean that Peacemobile?" Julietta said.

They were soon driving through the "ridges" where the Jewish people lived and where there were more places to go parking than on the Italian side of the railroad tracks where homes were in greater density. The homes in the ridges were primarily colonial and Georgian ones of five bedrooms or more set on half-acre and acre lots. It was now close to midnight and most of the neighborhood was dim. Unlike most other high school students, Daniel was not required to be home at any particular time. Having spent the first twelve years of his life in Italy jostled around in his parents' late night socializing, he had never been governed by a curfew on weekends.

He drove Julietta past his house, which was Georgian style. It was physically set apart from other homes in the neighborhood by the presence of wisteria that had been planted five years ago by Irene and had since scaled and strangled the brick walls. At first Daniel concealed the fact that he lived there. Almost every light was turned on. His parents no doubt were up in their bedroom; his father was probably snoring and his mother was probably devouring Elsa Morante, her Italian novelist of the moment.

"I wonder what's happening in that place?" Julietta remarked. "Looks weird with all that stuff growing up the sides," which prompted Daniel to tell her it was where he lived. Julietta's mouth gaped at the coincidence. How strange, Daniel thought to himself, that he was passing his mother up there in the bedroom on the way to having sex for the very first time. He imagined Irene wearing her delicate wire-frame reading glasses, fiddling with her loose strands of hair—not a worry in her head of where he might be. He almost wanted his mother to be concerned about him, to have set an arbitrary time limit for the night, so at least there would be a rule to obey or break, instead of having the whole night before him like an endless membrane pulsing with all sorts of possibilities.

"Pull over," Julietta finally said a few blocks down from the Fells' house. Daniel signaled and steered over to the lip of the road. He turned off the car, stretched his legs behind the driver's seat and heaved an elaborate sigh.

He turned to her. "So, how you doing, Julietta?" His voice gave away his anxiety.

"Don't call me Julietta," she said. "I hate that name. Call me sugar. Call me honey. Call me baby."

"Okay, baby, come closer to me." His whole body surged with the command.

"Cute," she said. There was that awful word again.

"Please don't call me that," Daniel said.

The expression on Julietta's face, at first obscured by darkness, was momentarily illuminated as the headlamps of a passing car infiltrated and wandered through the van. Daniel now saw that her outer hardness had softened; she actually looked sweet and vulnerable. That momentary glimpse of vulnerability reminded him of the disturbed face of Gianni Scaravento, whom she had spurned earlier. Then Julietta folded her arms behind her head and slid back in her seat, moistening her lips over and over again with her tongue. Hadn't Patrick told Daniel that men and women, once having lost their virginity, inadvertently began moistening their lips, allowing their tongues to lag out of their mouths during normal conversation: an involuntary quirk, which came from having known the deepest sexual pleasure? Daniel wet his lips, which signaled Julietta to raise hers. They exchanged stiff, open-mouthed kisses and then her head thudded against his chest.

"You haven't done it before, have you?" she challenged him.

"Yes I have," Daniel stammered his lie. "But I'm not very experienced."

"Good, cause I don't like virgin boys . . . pain in the ass," Julietta said in her older woman's voice.

The remark first made Daniel angry and then aggressive. A few moments later they were rolling all over the carpeted interior of the van. Julietta arranged it so Daniel didn't have to fumble around like a fool. She was out to enjoy herself and in order to do so took command. With a series of adept adjustments of her pelvis and hand, she guided him inside her. Once there, Daniel broke into exhilaration and sweat. As Julietta started moving against him, he quickly discovered how to participate in her rhythm. He felt her breath fluttering against his neck. After a few moments, however, he grew painfully aware of some sort of ball that kept getting batted around the carpeting by their moving legs. It would smack into the metal siding of the van and bounce back to their entanglement. He wanted to stop and put the ball aside but was afraid to come out of Julietta, for that would mean fumbling and worrying to get back in again, which in Daniel's inexperience seemed as difficult as striking a bull's-eye. So he put up with the rolling ball and every time it knocked against their legs Julietta giggled.

Finally she told him to pull out. Reluctant, he nevertheless obeyed. She quickly located the ball and put it on the front seat. Then she told him to lie on his back and climbed on top. Daniel placed his hands against Julietta's naked stomach, which was hard and beautiful like warm stone. The lights of a street lamp slashed her eyes when she rose to a certain height.

At some point it occurred to Daniel that Julietta was acting like the aggressive man, who enacted a pursuit and conquered him. She didn't seem to give a thought to contraception, shrugging it off—as a man would. And he told himself that if she wasn't concerned she must know what she's doing; after all, he had enough to worry about trying to act as though he wasn't a virgin. Of course, as soon as the act of love was over and Julietta and he were driving in postcoital, half-embarrassed silence back to the Oaks, Daniel began fretting. But stronger than his worry was a feeling of gratitude that Julietta was as experienced as she was and relief that he had finally shed his virginity, which had been like a thick skin encasing him in his childhood.

When Daniel arrived home he found Irene standing in the darkened kitchen, heating milk in a pan on the stove. He looked at the blue gas flames illuminating his mother's face. Her unkempt hair tumbled voluminously around the shoulders of her red bathrobe. "Hi, Daniel," she said. He purposely stood away from her, afraid that somehow he would give off the scent of his lovemaking. But soon he grew aware that Irene was upset about something.

She tilted her head to the side thoughtfully as she stirred the milk, which shimmered, opalescent in the darkness.

"Have a good time tonight?" she asked in a soft voice of distraction.

"Yeah," he said nonchalantly.

"You go to the Oaks?"

Taking a step toward her, Daniel found tears on his mother's cheeks. As result of what had just happened to him, he suddenly felt more mature than he did a few hours before. He felt capable of higher understanding, of consolation.

"What's wrong, Ma?"

Irene shrugged her shoulders and continued to stir. "Just argued with your Dad."

" 'Bout what?"

" 'Bout life," she said.

"Aw." Daniel struck a note of sympathy that released whatever Irene was holding back. The next moment she had crossed the room and was holding him and weeping. He couldn't help noticing that she was the approximate height of Julietta. Suddenly, Irene drew back in disgust, hurriedly wiping the tears from her eyes. She held Daniel at arm's length and glared.

"What have you been doing?" she demanded.

"I told you I was at the Oaks."

"And then what?"

Speechless and chagrined, Daniel offered no further explanation.

"You smell," his mother accused him.

Daniel looked at her without reacting.

Irene hurried through the thick shadows of the kitchen and opened a cupboard. She grabbed a glass tumbler, filled it with the warmed milk and fled the room. Some of the milk had spilled on the hot stove and he stood there listening to it sizzle.

4

"*Your mother refuses* to make love to me now," Harold told Daniel without warning. His lips tightened into a thin line. He was built a lot like his son, only heavier-set, and his flushed, smoothly shaven cheeks were beginning to get a little jowly. His fingers tightened around the steering wheel. "I know I shouldn't be saying it like this, but I . . . I don't have anybody else to talk to right now."

Daniel was shocked by his father's sudden revelation. Up until now his father had avoided subjects as intimate as sex. Sure, he could make lurid remarks about women's figures and their legs and the way they moved, but he had never spoken seriously of his feelings about Irene, not to mention their relationship. "It's okay, Daddy, you can talk about it," Daniel managed to say.

It was the following morning, a bright, cold Saturday, and the two male Fells were driving across the Tappan Zee Bridge. Every other Saturday morning they drove together over the Tappan Zee to check the ledgers of two condominiums Harold had invested in in Nyack. Now, as his father spoke, Daniel looked away up through the network of the bridge at towering metal girders with their dull rivet buttons, held aloft by twists of cables. He was thinking how much he loved the feeling of driving across bridges. He remembered summers when the family came back from Italy and how they drove from Westchester to Long Island across the Whitestone or the Throgs Neck Bridge on visits to his grandparents. Daniel remembered watching the metal girders graduating up until they were as tall as skyscrapers and then graduating down again.

"Is that why Mom was crying last night?"

Harold shrugged and changed lanes.

"She said you argued."

"We were trying to argue, but we weren't doing very well," Harold said. "We both kept getting silent. And then sulk to ourselves."

Daniel sucked in a fearful breath. He was unsure how to handle his father's sudden, adult-feeling confidence. "So how long has this been going on that she doesn't want to make love to you, Dad?" he asked tentatively.

Harold suddenly reconsidered his admission. He turned to Danny with dewy-blue, fearful eyes. "You mustn't tell her I confided in you. I feel so guilty about this," he added.

"Don't worry," Daniel reassured his father. "We can confide in each other. She doesn't have to know everything we say."

Harold reached over and patted him on the shoulder and then squeezed his shoulder blade until Daniel winced. His father seemed to fear something. They were on the last stretch of bridge, coasting its decline toward the west bank of the Hudson River. Daniel was afraid that if they didn't finish the conversation before hitting the opposite shore, the conversation would never be finished and would unravel until he did not know where it had begun or where it would end.

He plunged ahead. "Okay, so she won't make love to you anymore. But what does that mean?"

Harold grimaced. With one hand he let go of the steering wheel and began clawing through his bristly black hair. Daniel noticed that his fingers were chafed and their nails were bitten. "Lots of times love life sort of gauges what's going on in other places." He went on to say that for the last few months Daniel's mother had been avoiding being intimate with him. "But I don't know if you can really understand," Harold said. "Because in a way you depend on sex when you're married. It's an important thing. And I don't believe you've gotten to the point—"

"You're saying I have to have experience in sex?" Daniel interrupted.

His father managed to smile. "I was going to say you have to know what it's like making love repeatedly with the same person to really understand what it means when they stop wanting to make love with you."

They had reached the west bank of the Hudson; cars were backing up, feeding into the New York State Thruway. Daniel peered over to an adjacent car. He noticed a very suburban-looking family: a heavyset husband and wife in the front seat and three little girls bundled up in matching pink parkas in the back seat. Both parents were smoking long cigarettes. Daniel couldn't help wondering if parents' smoking in such a contained space could be in its own way as potentially harmful to the well-being of the children as his mother's refusing to make love to his father. Making love—he knew what that was now; the loss of his virginity still amazed him, still made him feel triumphant. But now he was also able to imagine what it must be like when that wonderful, exhilarating privilege was suddenly denied by the person who had once so willingly allowed it.

He turned back to his father and suddenly blurted out, "I already lost my virginity, Dad."

Harold clucked and coughed. A smile beamed across his dour face, and for a moment he seemed vicariously happy for Daniel. But then his mood changed, his face puckering up again. "I didn't even get to tell you the facts of life," he lamented.

"That's okay," Daniel said. "Mom told me a long time ago. She told me while we were still living in Italy."

"Great," Harold said. "Just what I want to hear right now. That your mother preempted me from telling you the facts of life."

"Hey, you should've taken me aside and told me yourself while you still had the chance," Daniel pointed out.

Harold smiled bitterly. "I should have, I suppose."

"I mean, here I am seventeen years old and this is one of the first times we've ever talked about sex," Daniel said. "Believe me, if you ever told me the facts of life after Mom did I would have acted like I had never heard them before."

"I guess you got a point," Harold said as he signaled to exit the Thruway. He shrugged and continued softly, "But by the time I realized I should be telling you about sex, I sensed that you already had learned most of what there was to know. So I never said anything. And here I am starting at Z and working backwards when I should've started at A and worked forwards."

That was a rotten excuse, but Daniel knew he needed to console his father. "It's all right, Dad, don't blame yourself," he said. "I'm not any worse for it, believe me."

There was profound silence after this. After a while, Harold said, "So, you lost your virginity, huh?"

"Yep," Daniel said. Although trying to remain serious, he ended up laughing.

Harold frowned at him. "What's so funny?"

"You're actually only a day late with the facts of life, Dad," Daniel said. "I lost my virginity last night."

Harold was hardly amused by this bit of information. He shook his head, dumbfounded at the irony of his own situation vis-à-vis Daniel's. "You're kidding me," he said flatly.

"I kid you not."

"Well, for Christ's sake," Harold said. He shook his head some more and then peered skeptically at Daniel. "You're not kidding me. You're really being honest?"

"Didn't I just tell you?"

"But last night?" Harold repeated, still disbelieving. "Really, last night?"

"No," Daniel said. "Tomorrow. The day after tomorrow."

As they drove through the town of Nyack, Harold kept talking. He explained at length that he had only recently stopped hoping that Irene's distance had to do with some sort of transition she was making. He now knew that her feelings for him had permanently changed. He had to accept that now, he said, as if he was trying to convince himself. As he talked to Daniel, Harold tried to sound calm and in control, but his voice was salted with pain. And the more he tried to conceal his distress the more the knowledge of his parents' sudden loss of love turned over and over inside Daniel. He thought of all the times during his life, especially in Italy, when his parents shucked off their clothes in the middle of an afternoon and locked their door; how they walked through the winding streets of Padua with arms slung around each other's waist and sat at the Caffè Pedrocchi holding hands over small cups of muddy espresso. Daniel asked his father what this change meant in terms of the future. Harold said he didn't know. Then Daniel thought of Alexis and how this knowledge might affect her. It would be too shocking for her to find out the way he had. She needed to be protected from it. But how could her protection be guaranteed? Here was his father blurting out something that was overwhelming and, Daniel had a sense, inappropriate for him to know. How could his father—or his mother, for that matter—be expected to use the right judgment when it came to explaining things to Alexis. He tried to think of what happened to the few families he knew who had gone through a divorce. It seemed to him that when a marriage failed and parents no longer lived together other things—like a sense of judgment, perhaps—began to disintegrate. Children were exposed to more; they were no longer as protected as they once were. As all this occurred to Daniel, he suddenly hoped that his mother could somehow get over refusing to make love to his father. He hoped that she *was* just going through a long, bad phase like the way she could get impossibly irritable with menstrual cramps.

They arrived at the condominium complex. They went to the office, where Harold checked the ledgers; the activity seemed to ground him. A smile broke over his face several times as he talked to the building manager in approval of the grounds keeping. Once or twice he grinned at Daniel as though to say, "I'm really okay, don't worry so much about me." And yet Daniel knew his father was not all right and saw the worry once again cast gloom over his face as they began to recross the Tappan Zee Bridge.

"I mean, I guess I have to start considering the alternatives," Harold said halfway over.

"Like what?"

"Like eventually finding an apartment. Somewhere."

"You don't have to start thinking about that," Daniel said quickly. "Things haven't gotten to that stage yet."

"The hell they haven't," Harold said.

Then the mood within the car changed precipitously. Daniel

felt something, some feeling pressing against his rib cage. It was almost as if he momentarily forgot who he was and that he could identify his thoughts and feelings. The act of sitting in that familiar car imbued with a faint scent of his mother's perfume combined with the rush of driving across the Tappan Zee Bridge suddenly evoked in him the most foreign and intangible sensations in the world. Daniel's breathing grew rapid and shallow. He rolled down the passenger window. Arctic air blasted him in the face. With his skin at first he could not detect the change in temperature, although he knew that a shock of cold was already reverberating throughout his body.

"What are you doing?" he discovered his father had been repeatedly asking.

"I can't talk about this anymore," Daniel blurted out. "Let's just stop talking about it. Okay? Okay?" In the midst of his turmoil he managed to glance sideways at his father, who was inadvertently slowing down and pulling over to the shoulder.

"Just keep driving," Daniel ordered him.

"But are you all right?" Harold asked. "You look like you swallowed . . . something bad."

"Just drive!" Daniel snapped.

Harold continued to drive, and slowly Daniel recovered his composure. "Now you okay?"

Daniel nodded.

"You sure?"

Daniel looked at his father's concerned face. "I'm fine . . . now," he said.

In silence they continued driving the rest of the way across the bridge. At one point Daniel peered down at the gray chop of the Hudson River that was rolling and glinting below them like the body of an enormous serpent. He closed his eyes and opened them again. He noticed that a tugboat had ventured away from its usual circuit down in Manhattan and was now on its way upstream to some undisclosed destination.

5

Daniel's evening with Julietta Polanno fed directly into the main-stream of high school gossip. A few of his soccer teammates came up and elbowed him enviously in the hallways. Patrick Riordan obviously had told the computer geeks, some of whom cast grotesque winks in Daniel's direction.

The first time Daniel spoke to Julietta after their night together they stood only inches apart in the main corridor of the high school. Her quickened breath was tickling his neck and he could feel the eyes of his classmates on them. Slightly giddy, he made the mistake of suggesting another romp in Patrick's van. Julietta's eyes narrowed as she made it clear that from here on in romantic overtures would be expected: dates to meet her at a certain coffee shop where lovers flocked to after school, drives through the autumnal landscapes, and most importantly, being seen together by other people. It struck Daniel to be a sort of backward courtship, beginning with a reward and following with his earning it.

Julietta often seemed to be traveling in the same direction down the hallways and would be sure to walk tightly with Daniel so that their shoulders kept brushing up intimately. She surrounded herself in varying effluvia of perfumes: Chanel 19, Charlie, L'Air du Temps. She'd ask him which scent he preferred, but he kept changing his mind. Whenever they would pass Gianni Scaravento,

Gianni would avert his eyes, hiding his wounded pride. Daniel could not understand why with all the fabulous-looking girls who were dying to go out with him that Gianni would still be interested in Julietta Polanno. That was when Patrick Riordan introduced him to the concept of forbidden fruit.

Vito and Mario Polanno suddenly seemed to recognize who Daniel was and began nodding to him. But the momentary favor of the alleged animal killers only made Daniel feel nervous, as if he were dating the relative of mad people who possessed a nuclear pebble that at whim could be dropped on his head and blow him out of existence.

On two occasions that first week of their romance, Daniel and Julietta sat holding hands in a prominent booth at the coffee shop, surrounded by four walls of bronze-foiled wallpaper, this amorous display setting off shivers of comment among students who were slurping chocolate malteds and egg creams. One afternoon after school he borrowed Irene's Chevy Nova. After sharing a powerful joint of Acapulco Gold, he and Julietta drove deep into the back roads of a neighboring township until they got hopelessly lost. They checked each other's eyes, decided they looked too stoned to ask anyone for directions and laughed hysterically at their paranoia. Finally Julietta leaned toward Daniel and kissed him open-mouthed. They necked passionately until he slipped his hand between her legs. She plucked his fingers away and mumbled something about "the weekend."

On Friday morning she was standing in a strategic position outside school with Brenda and their group of tough-girl friends. Easy to spot among the uniforms of tight jeans and sweaters and bomber jackets, Julietta wore a cerulean knitted dress with hose, heels and a burgundy raincoat that kept getting blown open by the brisk wind.

"Jeez Danny, she got herself all dolled up for you," Patrick said as they were walking up the cement steps from the parking lot. "Don't look at her. She's staring."

Patrick was bundled up in his father's Navy peacoat, a knitted scarf wound around his neck. His thinning pale hair was blowing back in the wind. His scalp was visible. It looked pink and babylike.

"Where should I take her tonight?" Daniel asked. "Or should I just borrow your van and drive her around?"

Patrick shook his head. "Uh uh. You have to take her some-where. There's always got to be a pretense for what comes later."

"But the first time she was so . . . aggressive about it."

Patrick threw up his hands. "What can I say? You caught her at the right moment. Now reason has set in. She wants to be wooed, Danny."

Daniel shrugged and bundled tighter into his ski parka. Some-thing about the requirements of dating unnerved him. He sud-denly got a tunnel glimpse of his relationship with Julietta: he'd begin to see her more and more until she'd become everything to him the way his mother had drawn the perimeters of his father's entire world; and just when life narrowed in such a way, Julietta would dump him for somebody else. It could happen. Plenty of students Daniel knew had been cut dead by a girlfriend's whimsy.

Patrick turned to him. "If you disappoint her at this stage it would seem like one of those 'find 'em, fuck 'em, forget 'em' situations. And that's certainly not what you want to happen with a Polanno."

"Except you know as well as I that Julietta was the one who found 'em and fucked 'em."

"Yeah, but she didn't forget 'em," Patrick pointed out. As they approached Julietta, Daniel's heart tolled faster and faster. He felt breathless by the time they reached her. Julietta smiled hesitantly. He had figured on saying hello to her and something like "How about ice skating tonight?" while walking up the steps. But when he noticed a red patch of skin on Julietta's forehead, his tongue thickened. Daniel couldn't help but stop short and ogle, which caused a pile-up of students who were scaling the steps close behind him. He inadvertently got knocked forward, Julietta's friends cackling at his awkwardness. He looked around wildly for Patrick, who had continued the climb and was now several steps ahead, peering back in bewilderment. Patrick had yet to notice that Ju-lietta had had her mole removed.

"Hi, Danny," she said sweetly.

Did she actually like him enough to have a dermatologist re-move her mole, in hopes that by improving her attractiveness she'd also be improving her chances to be his girlfriend? Or was it just pure coincidence? Maybe she had made the appointment a few months ago—how was he to know? "What about . . . what about the movies tonight, Julietta?" Daniel blurted out.

"Yeah?" Her whole face animated. "Good idea. Where should we meet?"

"How about . . . how about we meet at the Oaks first?" Daniel said. Julietta leaned forward and gave him a peck on the cheek.

Houghton's junior and senior high schools were located in the same building, although in separate wings. This meant that Alexis and Daniel would often bump into each other as they did at lunchtime on that Friday he asked Julietta Polanno to the movies instead of to the ice-skating rink.

In eighth grade, Alexis had already blossomed into a compact, curvy adolescent. She appeared to be a lot older and more sophisticated than most of her friends. She looked up to Daniel but was quite an independent thirteen-year-old and never imposed herself. For a brother and a sister the gap between thirteen and seventeen usually seems enormous, almost the span of another era, a feeling that slowly disintegrates until during the midtwenties it disappears. But Daniel was aware that in certain ways Alexis was better at communicating with her friends than he was. It occurred to him that most brothers going through what he was going through with Julietta Polanno would never discuss their private lives with their younger sisters. But he also realized that he could use her advice.

Alexis stood with a group of girlfriends on the grass embankment twenty yards up from the parking lot. They were holding sandwiches in gloved hands, munching and chattering in the cold. After a while a girl wearing yellow barrettes began what appeared to be a long-winded narration; Daniel noticed Alexis nodding her wind-touseled head. When he managed to catch her eye, she made a quick apology to her friends and trotted over.

"It's all over junior high" was the first thing out of her mouth.

"What's all over junior high, Alex?"

She frowned. "I told you not to call me Alex," she said. "Alex is a boy's name. I want to be called Alexis."

Daniel slipped his arm around her. "Even *entre nous?*"

"*Vada a castrare i porci,*" Alexis told him in Italian, which meant "Go castrate pigs," an expression they once learned from an alcoholic babysitter in Padua.

"Okay, *Alexis*," Daniel said emphatically and returned to the subject at hand. "So tell me why Julietta's likes and dislikes are so interesting to everyone else?"

"It's basic," Alexis said. "She's the first cousin of Polanno," lingering appropriately on the double-*n* pronunciation.

Daniel suddenly grew annoyed. "I hate all this gossip and pressure I'm getting from everybody about her."

Alexis glanced back at her friends, who were eagerly looking on. She turned to Daniel again. "Well, Danny, do you really feel the sparkles?"

"The sparkles?" Daniel mocked her. "Where did you get that one?" While living in Italy, Alexis and he used to trade slang they picked up from Americans.

"Just thought of it now." Alexis smiled and then she cocked an eye. "By the way, how many times have you gone out with Julietta Polanno? At night?"

Daniel shrugged. "Just once really."

"And what happened?" Alexis was beginning to look a little piqued.

He smiled tightly. "You're too young to understand," fumbling at what they both knew had ended up being a ludicrous statement.

"And you're irresponsible," Alexis piped up. "You obviously have no respect for this girl."

"Believe me, you don't understand anything."

"I don't want to understand. I don't want to hear about it anymore." Alexis left him dangling and walked back to her friends, who leaned toward her, their mufflers flapping like tentacles in the wind.

When Daniel got home from school that afternoon, Irene was in the kitchen, preparing to leave for Manhattan. Earlier that morning Harold had left for a meeting in Cincinnati and would be gone all weekend. Since his admission to Daniel of the previous Saturday, Daniel realized that lately his father had been making plans for weekend business trips to attend to various company accounts around the country. His mother talked of going into Manhattan more often. Irene always acted nervous before leaving for the city, as though needing to gear up for its more frenetic pace. She was wearing a new black cashmere suit Daniel had never seen before. The kitchen reeked of Norell perfume.

"God, do you stink," Daniel complained as he came in the back door.

Smiling, Irene came up to him and put a finger on the flushed part of his cheeks, pressing until she could see a white spot.

"I'm going to be out until pretty late," she informed him. "I'm going to the theater and then to dinner afterwards. So just stay home with your sister."

"But, Mom, I have a date tonight."

"I told you on Monday that I was going out tonight and you said you could be here."

"Well, rats, I forgot," Daniel said.

"Hum." Irene's eyes glinted with sarcastic light. "Is the date with this recent girl?"

His mother was smiling acridly. Her revulsion of last Friday night in the kitchen with the hot milk had since curdled into a sort of rancor.

"Yes, it is."

"What, may I ask, is her name?"

"Her name is Julietta."

"*Davvero?*" Irene said in Italian.

"Cut it out, Ma. This girl doesn't speak a word."

Irene rolled her eyes. "Who does in this town besides you . . . and the fruit sellers?" she said, expressing her disappointment that she had yet to meet anyone in their Italo-American town who spoke the sort of Italian to which she was accustomed—even though her own Italian was at best mediocre.

Daniel explained that Julietta was related to the Polannos and how the Polannos were notorious and that he had to be careful how he handled her for fear that these cousins would get sore. For that reason he hated to change his plans—couldn't Alexis sleep over at a friend's house? Unfortunately he was unable to communicate to his mother the true nature of the students' all-pervasive terror of the Polanno brothers. Irene frowned and said that if a gang of kids got out of hand or began bullying somebody, the police could always be relied upon.

Giving up on trying to persuade Irene, Daniel now asked with whom she was going to the theater.

"Marcella Auguri is in town. I'm taking her to see *Hair*. She sends her love, by the way."

Daniel was immediately suspicious. "How long has Marcella been here?"

"Three days," Irene said. As though in need of an activity, she opened her maroon leather handbag and began rooting for something. Daniel listened to the sound of pens clanking against little cosmetic bottles and nail files.

"I'm surprised she hasn't called me," he said. Whenever Marcella Auguri came to New York, she would always personally augment his reading list with one or two wonderful new Italian novels.

Irene looked up from her pocket book with a scowl. Even so, she looked remarkably attractive. Her eyes were artfully lined and shadowed, her cheeks subtly rouged. She took the most pains to make herself look lovely only when she would be away from the rest of the family. She put the purse down on the formica kitchen counter and then with two manicured fingers scissored a lock of layered hair and pulled it nervously toward the back of her head. During the past year, Daniel had begun noticing veins of gray in her otherwise auburn dishevelment of hair. The gray softened her handsomeness, brought her slate-blue eyes up to the color of lapis. "What has gotten into you the last few days?" she said crossly. "You've been acting so strange."

Of course Daniel wanted to say that he had been dwelling on that Tappan Zee Bridge conversation with his father. But it was far too difficult for him to just ask why his mother no longer made love to his father.

Irene glanced at the wafer-thin Swiss watch Harold recently had bought for her. "I've got forty-five minutes before my train leaves. Let's have a quick drink." She left the kitchen, her high heels clattering over the beige Mexican tiles. As she entered the dining room, where there was a wet bar, the sound of her heels changed to thudding as she stepped on the Persian area-rug.

Alone for a moment, Daniel reflected that there were actually lots of objects that Irene hankered for that Harold had ended up surprising her with long after she had stopped wishing for them. He again recalled what was said on the Tappan Zee Bridge. If his mother had ceased to feel love for his father, had that changed

her regard for things he had given her? The watch, for example
—was it now only functional, ornamental, no longer sentimental?
Were objects given in a fit of love tarnished by the light of indif-
ference?

Irene returned to the kitchen with a bottle of Tio Pepe and
two cut-crystal cocktail glasses. She set the glasses on the table;
poured herself a finger full and Daniel a half finger full.

"This is a good way to start the weekend," he said, slurping
his meager portion.

Irene smirked. "You and Alexis are not to go into the liquor
cabinet while I'm out. I'm going to check all the alcohol levels
before I leave."

"Don't bother. We've got our own stash."

"Don't be a smart ass."

Daniel watched his mother's face grow impressed by a thought.
"Wait a second," she said, "why don't you invite this girl over to
the house . . . what's her name again?"

"Julietta."

"Tell Julietta you've got to hang around here."

"I think Julietta expects to be taken out. If I invite her over
it'll seem like too much of a setup."

"Of course it won't. Alexis will be around."

"But it'll seem like all I'm interested in is . . . you know."

Irene chuckled. "Well, I'm glad this girl has at least a few
principles." Now she seemed relatively unfazed by the prospect
of Daniel's having a sexual life. Perhaps her virulent first reaction
had more to do with having to unwittingly smell the exudations
of his lovemaking; or maybe it was the irony of denying his father,
shrinking into celibacy while Daniel was emerging into pleasure.

"Did you have a lot of boyfriends when you were growing
up?" he asked.

She averted her eyes and shrugged. "We've talked about this
before."

"Just answer me."

"I told you I did."

"But Dad once told me that in college you had a boyfriend
for every semester." Both his parents had attended Boston College.

Irene smiled irregularly. "Pretty near."

Daniel took a breath. "So then what about Dad made you want
to stay with him . . . all this time?"

His mother had been staring out the bay window of the kitchen into the withered landscape of her dormant back garden; and this momentary repose was scrambled by his question. With a flick of her eyes her expression hardened. She was looking at him dead-on. "What exactly are you after, Daniel?"

"An answer."

"Let me ask *you* a question. What did you talk about with your father last Saturday when you drove to Nyack? He came back looking pretty shaken."

"That's because . . . I got dizzy in the car," he managed to say.

"I thought so," Irene whispered, and pressed no further. Perhaps she sensed that continuing such a conversation might lead them to an area she was unwilling to deal with just now before leaving for Manhattan. She peered out the window again. "You know your father is a wonderful man. He's just very different from me." So she chose to answer obliquely. "He's very inward whereas I'm more expansive. He likes to be at home and I like to get out. Sometimes it complements. And sometimes—" her voice hardened—"it wears thin."

Daniel shut his eyes and pondered the import of "wearing thin," while his mother continued chattily. "You know, I've been thinking about taking a life drawing class. How does that sound to you?" She held her nearly drained Tio Pepe up to the globe light that hung over the kitchen table. The remaining puddle of wine glimmered like back-lit stained glass. She lowered her glass and clicked it to Daniel's, making a one-sided toast of plans he felt she had not yet revealed to him. He impulsively reached for the bottle.

"Uh uh," she said. "A half finger to a junior customer." Her eyebrows knit in accusation. "And I am going to check the liquor levels. Not to mention take a blood sample."

By now a rosy flush had bloomed throughout Irene's face. Daniel suddenly wondered whether it was the effect of the sherry or perhaps her excitement about going off to do something shameful in New York City. Maybe she was lying to him about meeting Marcella.

After his mother left for the train station, he grew more and more plagued by his suspicions. Alexis came home. Daniel asked if she would consider spending at least part of the evening with a friend until Irene got back. After some intense grumbling, Alexis made a phone call. An avid chess player, she managed to book herself a match down the street against the father of one of her friends. As Daniel listened to her making the arrangements, he ardently wished he could share with her his feelings regarding their parents' strife but knew this was impossible. It would involve telling Alexis about the other things he had already learned, telling her about the night Irene was weeping in the kitchen and about his father's dark monologue on the Tappan Zee. There was only one thing left to do, he decided, and that was to learn whether or not his mother was lying about going to meet her friend Marcella Auguri.

His intent somewhat fortified by the sherry, Daniel went upstairs into his parents' bedroom. Although the room had been tidied earlier in the day by the Barbadian cleaning woman who came in twice a week, an air of turbulence prevailed, a stale smell of face powder blending in with the different perfumes that his mother kept on a plastic carousel. Her side of the room featured a tall gold-lamé shoe case with two dozen little drawers filled with her assortment of Italian shoes. Against a far wall was a bureau populated by silken scarves and blouses, various belts, embroidered zip bags filled with clusters of costume jewelry. To an outsider, the more flagrant display of her possessions gave a much better indication of Irene's existence than Harold's part of the room, his natural oak chest with nothing on it but a papier-mâché cuff-link box Daniel had made for his birthday in Italian day school, along with stacks of coffee-table books on sailing.

He went into Irene's desk drawer, got out her leather address book and looked under the A's for Marcella Auguri's telephone number in Padua. Impulsively picking up the receiver, Daniel suddenly hesitated. How would he be able to justify this phone call a month from now when the bill arrived? His mother certainly would know he had been checking up on her. And then the proper procedure occurred to Daniel. He'd make the call person-to-person for Marcella Auguri. If Marcella were at home, his mother would have been lying through her teeth and would be unable to blame him for catching her in such a lie. If Marcella Auguri was not at home, there would be no charge, although Daniel still would need to find out if she had gone to America.

His heart thudding against his ribs, Daniel called the operator and placed his person-to-person call. Recognizing the voice of Marcella's youngest daughter, Ornella, he managed to ask in Italian if her mother was in America. "Yes, Daniello," Ornella said, "but why?" "*Te lo scrivo*," he said ("I'll write you about it") before the operator cut them off. Listening to the last frantic sputters of the severed international connection, Daniel felt relieved that at least Irene had been telling the truth.

6

Daniel waffled around the house for the next few hours and at seven o'clock began taking a long shower. He was in the midst of an extended Julietta Polanno fantasy, a replay of her taking command and straddling him in Patrick's van, when he was startled by a bashing on the bathroom door. "What?" he shrieked above the drumming of the water. "How about *my* shower?" Alexis demanded. "You've been in there for a half-hour." Irene liked the master bathroom just so and discouraged both of them from using it.

Daniel killed the faucets, leaped from the shower and pulled open the bathroom door stark naked. Alexis louvered her hand in front of her eyes. "You're such a moron," she said. Without grabbing a towel, Daniel continued out of the bathroom and began marching around the hallway. "Would you please cover yourself," Alexis ordered him.

"Turns you on, doesn't it?" Daniel said.

"Oh, yeah, sure," Alexis said. "And look what you're doing." She pointed to the carpeting now saturated with water footprints. She reached into the steamy bathroom for a towel and threw it at him as she went in and slammed the door.

After fifteen minutes of scrabbling through his clothing, Daniel opted to wear a black cotton turtleneck, a pair of blue jeans and a white crew-neck sweater. When he looked in the mirror he thought that the dark turtleneck and the light sweater made a good contrast. The sweater made his face look flushed and healthy and the lighter tones in his blonde hair glistened.

While backing down the driveway in Irene's Chevy Nova, Daniel peered back at the darkened reaches of the upper windows of the house—by then Alexis already had left. If either of his parents were to arrive home within the next few hours—the Fells were known throughout the neighborhood as having a perpetually lighted home—they would probably think some sort of foul play had occurred. Daniel knew he should go back inside and put some lights on, but he was too anxious to arrive at the Oaks and meet Julietta.

He drove through the twisting lanes of the ridges en route to an overpass above the New England Thruway that led to the northern section of Houghton. There were heavy winds that night, the streets eddying with bone-dry leaves. That year the leaves had begun changing a few weeks earlier, and by the middle of November the town already had the barren cast of February. In the elaborate gardens of the houses Daniel drove past, he knew there were few traces of summer to be found: frostbitten zinnias and shriveled chrysanthemums.

At ten minutes past eight, Daniel finally walked into the Oaks. Although the place was packed with students, he could tell fairly quickly that Julietta Polanno had not yet arrived. Trying to remain inconspicuous, he forged his way toward the bar, nodding hello to acquaintances as he pushed ahead. By the time he found an empty vinyl stool, sat down and ordered a draft beer, it was twenty minutes past eight. Daniel began wondering if in all the confusion earlier that day Julietta and he had somehow crossed signals as far as where they were supposed to meet. Maybe he had told her to meet him at the ice-skating rink.

"She's not coming, Danny," a voice spoke softly from his left as a sinker of disappointment dropped into his bowels. Gianni Scaravento was sitting next to him on a bar stool, gripping a mug of draft beer. "She left a message with her girlfriend." Gianni tilted his head in the direction of Brenda, who was slowly wending her way toward them through the smoke-filled crowd.

Daniel looked skeptically at Gianni. "How do you know all about it?"

"I overheard some talk."

At this point Brenda reached them. She cocked her hands on her hips and looking dismally at Daniel said that Julietta could not make their date until eleven and that the abrupt change in plans had to do with family problems.

"Doesn't look like you're going to get to see your honey," Gianni said once Brenda had strutted away. His eyes had shifted to his mug of beer, which he shoved back and forth between his large palms. It was then that Daniel noticed how large and square Gianni's hands were, but hardly as rough as one might expect for a quarterback—soft-looking even. His fingernails were perfectly manicured.

Daniel resented Gianni's comments. He was aware that Gianni was conducting some sort of shrewd appraisal of him. "There's always later on, there's always tomorrow night," Daniel ended up saying as he swallowed some beer.

After a short silence, Gianni said, "Her Aunt Maria is going nuts."

Daniel took another swig of beer. "Who's Aunt Maria?"

"Julietta's Aunt Maria," Gianni said. "You know, the Polannos' mother."

Daniel was confused.

"Ever since the animals got flattened, Aunt Maria's been having nightmares," explained Gianni with a shrug of his dark, thick eyebrows. "She's ultra religious. Didn't take the news well when her friends started calling up and accusing."

"Pretty grim news, religion or no religion," Daniel said. "Anyway, how come you're so up on things?"

"My mother knows her. She was complaining to my mother a couple of weeks ago. My mother says Maria is sick over what happened. Maria secretly wishes they'd all get thrown in jail. Though that'll never happen." Gianni winked at Daniel.

And yet, as far as Daniel knew, nobody had learned definitively who actually had killed the animals.

Gianni glanced at the wall behind the bartender's serving area. The wall was covered with yellowed newspaper clippings, mostly published photographs of local fishermen displaying their over-sized bounties of stripers and bluefish and marlin. As Gianni fell deeper into the stare, his pupils dilated. Momentarily it seemed that he was considering something other than what they were discussing. But then he turned to Daniel and clapped him on the shoulder. "The truth is that the guys who are running this town would rather not find anyone local who's responsible."

And then Gianni rambled on how this sort of crime seemed to have more impact on people than any kind of gruesome double ax murder. It was such a merciless act. A zoo was a place where animals were supposed to be protected. But because they are unable to escape their confines, they are even more vulnerable than they would be in the wild. Killing them like that was a human betrayal. "And another thing," Gianni said. "When people hear the name Polanno they don't think Polack. You got to take that into consideration," referring to the fact that the Italians who ran the town feared adverse publicity for Italo-Americans if it became known that one of their own had been involved in slaughtering the animals.

Just then Debbie Lerner, the girl considered by all to be the most beautiful in high school, stepped between Gianni and Daniel, in order to talk to Gianni. In Houghton it was rare for a Jewish girl to be interested in an Italian boy. Debbie's hair was thick and tawny-colored, worn straight and long, her eyes a yellowish green. She stood there, her freckled hands resting on the small of her back. Her hip was cocked and her hair swayed like a pendulum as she talked to Gianni. It was as though she knew the movement of her hair would be alluring to Daniel, who was sitting right behind it. He listened to Gianni speaking. He noticed how when Gianni's voice went soft, there seemed to be lots of *s* sounds in his speech. He said "nice" several times, hanging on the *s*. "You look so nice, Debbie. We should get together and do something nice. Na, tonight I got to get home. My mom isn't feeling too nice," he told her. Gianni pecked Debbie on the cheek and then she pivoted around and walked back to a group of her Jewish girlfriends. Her mane of hair brushed against Daniel's denim jacket and the static left strands of it clinging to him. That night before going out, Debbie Lerner must have brushed her hair at least a hundred times.

"Nice girl, huh?" Gianni still spoke in the low voice he had switched on for Debbie Lerner.

Daniel looked at him carefully. Gianni Scaravento would really be great-looking if his skin were not so broken out. The problem seemed chronic; his cheeks were slightly pitted with acne scars. Somehow, in first knowing him, Daniel wanted his face to be perfect, to fit some image he had formed of Gianni as the handsome, intrepid quarterback. Then he thought of how Julietta had had her mole removed.

"I can't believe you just brushed Debbie off like that," he told Gianni.

Gianni grinned and continued jockeying the mug of beer between his palms. "Like you said before, there's always tomorrow night. If I show up here. Hey," he said. "You and I can double-date."

"You sound so nonchalant."

"Not really," Gianni said.

"I mean, I'd much prefer to go out with Debbie Lerner than Julietta Polanno," Daniel said.

Gianni chuckled, then made a fist and began to softly pound the mahogany deck of the bar. He shrugged. "Debbie's a lot of act. I mean, I'll go out with her. She's just the kind of girl my parents'd want me to settle down with. Nice girl, nice family. They probably wouldn't even care that she was Jewish. But Julietta, she's different." His eyes grew wide and slick. "I hear, Danny, Julietta's like an eel. She really wriggles, man. But with finesse, real finesse."

Daniel felt blood surging into his cheeks.

"So, did you get yours?" Gianni asked, immediately looking away. It was as though that perfunctory question asked among men their age was causing Gianni extraordinary discomfort. Daniel wondered then why did he ask it.

"None of your business!"

Gianni threw up his hands. "All right. Okay."

But now Daniel was angry. "So all this time you've been interested in Julietta just for a piece?"

Gianni screwed up his eyes. "No, man, you got it wrong. I never run after girls just to go to bed with them. I don't believe in that. But for a long time Julietta was coming on to me." He hesitated. "Until she saw you."

Scanning the smoke-filled bar and for a moment listening to the immense cacophony of a gleeful Friday night at the Oaks,

Daniel sighed and told Gianni, "Honestly, I can't help wondering why."

"You're blond. You got longer hair. You're cuter than I am," Gianni said. "And you blush easier. I guess that's what sends Julietta Polanno."

"I guess."

An awkward silence unfolded between them as they sat there nursing their beers. Several members of the football team lumbered in, wearing their Houghton varsity windbreakers. They all descended on Gianni, clapping him on the back. They, like everyone else in Houghton, Daniel included, pronounced his name "Johnny" and not "Geeahnnni," as was the proper Italian pronunciation. Daniel realized he had never seen Gianni Scaravento parading his varsity letters outside school. He observed Gianni's offhand manner with his teammates—his voice was higher-pitched than theirs, more of a baritone. He seemed detached from them and they, by comparison, were more respectful of who he was.

After the herd of football players moved on into the Oaks, Gianni softly asked Daniel, "You want to take a ride and smoke a little grass?"

"I thought you had to go home?"

Gianni smiled. "I don't have to go home," he said hoarsely, jiggling his head from side to side. "But I had to bullshit Debbie."

"So you mean your mother's not sick either?"

A nervous twitch suddenly afflicted Gianni's cheeks and the laughter in his eyes cooled. He looked at Daniel in momentary bewilderment. "No, no, she's sick," Gianni said. Somehow Daniel sensed that Mrs. Scaravento was more than just laid up with the flu.

Gianni dug a five-dollar bill out of the pocket of his blue jeans and slammed it down on the counter. He jerked up his chin, catching the eye of Ralph, the big-bellied bartender whose brother was Houghton's chief of police. "Ralphie, keep the rest, buddy," Gianni said, and then grabbed a thick wool maroon jacket from a coatrack and draped it over his shoulders.

"So when you play the big game?" Ralph called out as he dried glass mugs with a dishrag. "When do you play Rye?"

"A few weeks," Gianni said, faking a pass to him.

"Ooo. The big game," Ralph said, dropping his rag and catching the imaginary pass. "I got to go stop by Fishie and put a little down on you."

"You do that," Gianni said, striding toward the door.

"How much can I rely on you, Gianni?" Ralph called out hesitantly.

"A hundred bucks we win," Gianni said with a wave and. slipped through the door.

Outside it felt bitter cold, much colder than it really was. Daniel knew his profound chill was partly induced by the beer. How strange to be hanging around with Gianni Scaravento when he had expected to be romancing Julietta Polanno.

"You really think you're going to win the Rye game?" he asked.

Gianni still hadn't put on his jacket and was standing there in only his flannel shirt. "No idea."

"So why did you tell Ralph to bet a hundred?"

"What is he going to do, bet on Rye?"

"Maybe," Daniel said.

Gianni cocked both arms behind his head and stretched, continuing to refrain from putting on his jacket.

"Aren't you cold?"

Gianni rubbed his wide, rough-hewn face. "Na," he said. "I feel good."

Gianni Scaravento drove a hunter green Triumph. It was one of the classiest cars owned by a high school student. His father ran several landscape businesses in Westchester County and could well afford to buy him a sports car. As they got in the car, the seats cracked beneath them from the cold and the inner face of the windshield quickly steamed up from their breathing. Gianni put in the earlobe-shaped key, pulled out the choke, pumped the gas pedal a few times and with a flick of his wrist the car was revving. The foreign purring sound of the motor was hypnotic, preferable to the drone of Irene's Chevy Nova.

They quickly drove through the downtown section of Houghton and headed toward the ridges. A train from New York was just letting off commuters in the fluorescently lit station. Even though he knew his mother was not due home until much later, Daniel found himself scanning the Stamford-bound side to see if

Irene were descending onto the platform. He saw a woman of
similar build with wild hair staring at the billboard advertisement
for *A Chorus Line*. But the silver fox coat she wore looked unfamiliar. Besides, if Irene *were* standing in the cold waiting for a
Houghton taxi, there would not be any room in the Triumph for
her, unless one of them sat over the stick shift. When they were
finally cruising through the ridges, Gianni pulled out a bent, badly
rolled joint and pushed in the cigarette lighter. He placed the joint
between his lips while waiting for the lighter to pop. Daniel asked
him what kind of marijuana it was and he said, "Colombo." Was
he certain it was Colombian? Gianni got momentarily annoyed
and said he had heard Daniel was a connoisseur.

"You got that from Bobby Wise, didn't you?" Danny asked.

"Yeah. How did you know?"

"He's a dope fiend. And because I don't match him joint for
joint like everybody else, he thinks I'm picky. The point is,"
Daniel explained, "a lot of grass gives me a headache. And a lot
more makes me feel uncomfortable."

The lighter popped, Gianni reached for it and soon the small
contained space of the Triumph was choked in sweet, resinous
smoke. "What about it makes you feel uncomfortable?" he asked
mildly.

For a moment Daniel felt reluctant to elaborate; people were
loath to admit an inability to handle marijuana. He also could tell
by Gianni's eager approach to smoking it and particularly by the
clumsy way in which he had rolled his joint that he had been
smoking marijuana for maybe only six months.

Getting stoned on grass instead of getting drunk had just recently become popular among the Italians in Houghton. Unfortunately, they had no other source for it than the Jewish kids who,
for several years, had been procuring grass from reliable contacts
in New York City. It was as though a harmony were beginning
to be struck between the two groups; they now had a common
nexus: getting good product.

"Sometimes it gets me thinking about things I'd rather not
think about," Daniel tried to explain. "And then I don't seem to
have any control over changing the course of my thoughts. I get
in this rut of thinking and I just can't get out of it."

Gianni slowed down; Daniel could see his eyes were droopy

and that his thoughts seemed adrift. "Believe me, I know what you mean," Gianni whispered. "In fact, let's not talk about that part of it anymore."

Daniel suspected that Gianni was trying to impress him with his seriousness. He dragged a long hit of the grass, took it inside his lungs and kept it there. They drove on for a while, each meditating on inner landscapes.

"So what else do you want to talk about?" Daniel finally said. The effects of the marijuana had come on and his head was feeling light and euphoric. "By the way, this stuff is pretty tolerable."

The car suddenly sped up. Daniel couldn't tell if being stoned made it seem as though they were going a lot faster, or if, indeed, Gianni was goosing the gas pedal. "Hey, take it easy."

"Believe me, buddy," Gianni bragged as he shifted into third gear, "I know how to drive. I won't wrap you around a tree. I'm not planning on racking up this car." They were approaching a sharp curve at what Daniel felt was a dangerously rapid pace. Gianni down-shifted and the car hugged around it, the tires squealing from the strain. A stop sign stood just ahead, which forced him to brake.

As they came to a jarring halt, Gianni turned to Daniel with mockery in his large brown eyes. "Believe me, Danny, this car is built not to roll."

"I'm sure you can drive it. You just don't have to prove it me."

Gianni flared up. "Look, buddy, I'm not proving anything. Okay. I'm enjoying myself. Don't be such a wet blanket. I mean, I could have been driving around with Debbie Lerner."

Daniel looked out the window at a darkened English Vicarage type of mansion that rose behind cut-stone pillars with pineapple finials. "I didn't ask you to take me driving," he said.

"I know you didn't." Oddly, Gianni's voice now betrayed a sort of ache. "I wanted to talk to you a little. Because they say you're such a snob. I figured it'd be a challenge trying to have a conversation with a snob."

"I don't know where you get this snob stuff. I'm not a snob."

Gianni put the car in first and they started off again. As he pummeled the gearshift into second he started laughing. Daniel asked what was so funny and Gianni said that he had not yet made up his mind whether or not Daniel was a snob, but when he did he'd let him know.

"There's just one thing I don't understand," Gianni said after a few reflective moments.

"What's that?"

"Why you hide the fact that you speak Italian."

"I don't hide it," Daniel objected in a fluster. "I . . . just don't tell people."

Gianni turned to him. "But why? It's something you should be proud of. I mean, I wish I spoke it."

"You could study it if you wanted to."

Gianni turned to him. "Some people aren't good with language. Probably never occurred to you."

Daniel shrugged and then looked at Gianni shrewdly. "Who told you I spoke Italian?"

Gianni laughed. "Danny, we all know you speak Italian. People like my mother knew pretty soon after you and your family moved to town. I mean, here's this blond Jewish kid rattling off Italian in a little greasy grocery store."

"But how did *they* know I was Jewish?"

"Come on, Danny, your mother's a dead giveaway."

"I beg your pardon."

"Anybody who looks that dressed up in this town is a dead giveaway—"

"What, to being Jewish?"

"Yeah."

"I don't agree," Daniel said.

"Nevertheless," Gianni said. "They knew and they talked about it and pretty soon everybody found out."

"What do they want? Do they expect me to go around school singing arias?"

"Look." Gianni was now driving away from the ridges. As he did so Daniel began to feel more insecure about his safety. "Isn't it true that you hide it?"

Daniel hesitated. "I don't know. I suppose I do."

"Enough said." Gianni looked at his watch. "Heh. It's a little after eleven. Your date."

"I guess you better drive me there."

"Okay," Gianni said, hesitating a moment before adding, "but I can almost guarantee you she's not going to show."

"What makes you say that?" Daniel snapped.

"Just got a feeling she's tied up with her Aunt Maria. Unless she's deliberately doing a number on you. Playing difficult."

"You're just saying that because—"

"Hey, buddy, I'm only a little bit jealous of you. Look, I'll drive you by. See for yourself if she's there."

Gianni put the Triumph through a few quick maneuvers and in no time they had quit the ridges and were barreling toward the Oaks. He double-parked in front of the bar and waited while Daniel went inside. This late at night, most people had curfews and the earlier crowd had winnowed down to a few intoxicated stragglers, none of whom was Julietta Polanno. Daniel quickly surmised that she had stood him up on purpose. He went back outside and got into the Triumph, staring straight ahead. Gianni grunted an "uh huh" and took off.

Neither spoke for a good while. Daniel could feel Gianni stealing inquisitive glances at him in between steering the car. They were driving along a cold, slick road that led out of town. The Triumph was doing only fifty although it seemed that it was going a lot faster.

"I just don't understand what could have happened," Daniel complained. "Why she stood me up without even calling."

"It's got to be Aunt Maria," Gianni assured him. "She gets really nutso over the brothers and then Julietta's got to go running over there to calm her down."

"Aunt Maria should see a psychiatrist."

"Italian Catholics don't believe in psychiatrists."

"Speak for yourself," Daniel said.

Gianni dipped his head and made snorts of suppressed laughter.

"So where are we going now?" Daniel asked.

"Since you don't have to go back to the Oaks I thought we'd head up 684 and blow out a little carbon."

Six-eighty-four was a recently built superhighway that had lots of straightaways where cars could open up their throttles. "Just be careful," Daniel said. "You got somebody else in here with you."

There were few cars driving in either direction on the parkway that fed into 684 and it seemed much later than midnight. They passed a public golf course which gathered the moonlight's gleam and whose sand traps resembled snowy welters. As soon as they

entered the wider, smoother superhighway, Gianni engaged fifth
gear. Daniel watched the illuminated needle of the speedometer
nose past eighty-five and hover just below ninety. At that speed
the car developed a slight shimmying. "Tires need to be rotated,"
Gianni noted. "Look at this rack-and-pinion steering." He moved
the steering wheel maybe a half inch to the right and the car
sharply changed lanes. "Got to be careful," he said. "Or else you
can overcompensate."

Daniel turned to him. "You trying to worry me?"

Gianni frowned. "No, Danny. Why, you worried?"

"Well, I'm not driving. I'm not in control."

"You like to be in control, heh?" Gianni said. The drone of
the engine rose in pitch. The car was going ninety-five. They
were just passing Armonk.

"How far are we going?"

Gianni shrugged. "I figured we take it up to Bedford and back.
There's a nice diner up in Bedford where we can stop and have
coffee."

"I don't want coffee. It'll keep me up. Actually I'd like to go
home and get to bed."

"Well, I'd like a cup of coffee. I got to stay up," Gianni said.

Daniel got distracted by a whining at the window seals. He
tried rolling up the window a little higher to eliminate the sound.
Then he realized his heart was racing. "Why do you have to stay
up?" he continued uneasily.

Gianni's eyes began blinking, his hands tightening on the steering wheel until his arms shook. Then, shutting his eyes, he let
go of the steering wheel. He tilted back his dark curly head and
gripped the steering wheel with his knees.

"What the hell are you doing?" Daniel cried. "Would you look
where you're going!"

Gianni slowly turned to Daniel with a look of pain and bewilderment in his eyes. And then at one hundred miles per hour,
he switched off the headlights. The highway suddenly vanished
into complete and utter darkness orchestrated by the roar of the
engine that now seemed to be hurling them toward certain disaster.

Gasping, Daniel managed to cry out, and Gianni Scaravento
purposely waited a few more seconds before turning the headlights
back on.

7

This was nearly the very last ride Daniel ever took with Gianni Scaravento. He had been all prepared to call for a taxi as soon as they arrived in the town of Bedford. But after putting the headlamps back on again and continuing to drive at the speed limit, Gianni began apologizing profusely for losing his composure and for having driven like a fool. Then he explained why he had lost control.

He had been thinking about his mother and his thoughts had overwhelmed him to the point that he lost his judgment.

"At my expense," Daniel pointed out angrily.

Gianni was silent as they took the exit to Bedford and when they finally were off 684, he said, "She's really sick, man. She's got an illness." He went on to explain that his mother was hopelessly afflicted with Hodgkin's disease. He was the older of two boys; and not only was her condition difficult for him to accept, he had his brother, Tony, to contend with. Tony just didn't understand what was happening, that their mother would soon die.

Daniel calmed down and a while later they were sitting having coffee and butter crunch ice cream at the Bedford diner. They were now strangers among high school students who played football under a different banner, whose team colors were a foreign-looking blue and white instead of black and gold.

As Daniel stirred the yellow dollops of ice cream into figure eights, he remembered seeing Angela Scaravento at the football games; Gianni had inherited his mother's large, ironic eyes. Wrapped in a long beaver coat, she usually stood away from the crowd of fans rooting for the varsity and jeering the opponents. Hands jammed in her fur pockets, Angela would peer straight ahead without hollering, almost without moving. Now that Gianni mentioned her illness Daniel recalled that Mrs. Scaravento had always looked extremely pale.

While they talked, Daniel noticed that Gianni's eyes were following the movements of the upper-class Bedford girls who were carrying on innocuous conversations among the clusters of students situated in vinyl booths, conversations that seemed rich with intrigue and provocation because Daniel and Gianni knew they would never be part of them. "On the whole girls up here are nicer-looking than in Houghton, don't you think?" Gianni grinned. He appeared to take for granted that Daniel had already forgiven his unforgivable driving behavior. Daniel bristled at Gianni's assumption that he could so easily regain favor.

"Yeah, they're okay," Daniel said. He looked at his watch. It was nearly one o'clock in the morning. "Maybe we should go soon. It's getting late."

Gianni shrugged and seemed reluctant to leave.

"Don't you have to go home and stay up with your mother?"

Gianni, who had just made eye contact with one of the prettier Bedford girls, abruptly abandoned his silent flirtation. "I do every night until at least three." He swallowed. "She's insomniac."

"Insomniac because she doesn't feel well?" Daniel asked.

Gianni shrugged. "Yeah, but mainly because she worries."

According to Gianni, Angela Scaravento worried about what her family would do when she was gone more than she worried about dying. Her husband, Frank, was one of those fathers who felt that the hours he put into his daily work exempted him from any household responsibility. Thus far, his efforts to raise his children were actually made under Angela's supervision.

Angela came from a northern Italian family, who were scandalized by the fact that she had married a meridional man—an old story, Daniel told himself. Gianni's father was extremely handsome—Daniel had seen him at the same football games. Olive skin, dark wavy hair, light-gray eyes. He was taller than Gianni, more slimly built, and wore expensive designer clothing. Although he owned and managed several nurseries, spent his days reordering fertilizer and bulbs, tubers and shrubs, Frank Scaravento always dressed as though he were going to a board meeting.

Gianni spoke of the specialists his mother had seen as well as their prognosis, which was grim. She already had had the illness for three years, although it hadn't been properly diagnosed until the last two. She had gone into the hospital several times for various chemotherapies and each time her hair fell out. She'd feel better for a while but after a few months would once again grow weak and tired. The color of her skin was more pallid than someone who had never taken the sun.

Gianni finished the last bit of his ice cream, drained his mug of lukewarm coffee. Daniel found it curious that broaching his mother's illness had not dimmed Gianni's appetite. In some sense it seemed mechanical.

Daniel remembered his grandfather's funeral and how the mourners came directly to his parents' house from the cemetery. The caterers had heaped stainless steel platters with all sorts of hot steaming food, cold cuts and sliced bread. These so-called mourners—even the rabbi who had spoken the eulogy—grabbed plates, piled them with food and ate with barely subdued pleasure. Still arrested by the strong images of the coffin being winched down into the ground, dirt and flowers spilling over it, Daniel was repelled by all those chomping mouths full of roast beef and turkey and kasha varnishkas. He wondered how many animals went to the slaughter to provide nourishment for the lot of people who came to pay their respects.

He asked Gianni why at some point fatigue didn't overcome worry and allow his mother some sleep at night.

"She sleeps a lot during the day when nobody is home," Gianni said. "She doesn't feel so ill during the day. At night it comes on. And when it comes on she gets broody."

In the beginning of his mother's illness, Gianni would sometimes wake up from his own nightmares of her dying and hear faint whimpering sounds coming from the TV room. He would creep down the hallway and first see the television as a glowing blue cube, the station long ago having ceased to transmit. Sitting in his father's armchair in a pink bathrobe wrapped in a crocheted shawl would be Angela, her round shoulders shaking violently as she wept.

Gianni glanced at his watch. "I guess we should get going. So how you feeling?" he asked Daniel.

"Wide awake," Daniel said. "Must be the coffee." But he was thinking that it was really all the intimate talk. So many feelings within him were stirring. He knew the inner turbulence was in part due to his growing admiration for Gianni Scaravento, and yet he also felt awash with childhood memories of Italy. In this garishly lit diner he found himself steeped in the past. His mind's eye wandered to the beaches on the Adriatic; he could almost smell the exotic fragrances wafting out of the rich people's cabanas; he could feel the rough texture of the striped umbrellas rubbing against his calves. He remembered being a small child and walking into the Scrovegni Chapel with his mother, gripping her hand and looking agape at Giotto's emotional depictions: the dark confusion of *The Last Judgment*, mothers desperately pleading for the lives of their children in *The Massacre of the Innocents*, Mary supplicating at the feet of the dying Christ in *The Crucifixion*. Daniel now looked over at Gianni Scaravento, who had dipped his head and was staring into the empty boat where his ice cream had floated, now scraped clean. At this angle, you couldn't see the flaws in his skin; Gianni's face for a brief moment looked nearly perfect.

Gianni raised his head. "Well, if you don't feel tired, why don't you come over to my house?"

Daniel was startled by the suggestion. "But it's already so late."

Gianni frowned. "I told you she doesn't sleep at night."

"But maybe she'd rather meet me during the day."

"Believe me, at this time of night Angela loves company." Gianni stood up abruptly, plunking down a ten-dollar bill on the table. When Daniel dug into the pocket of his blue jeans, Gianni waved him off. "No, I want to pay. It's on me. My apologies."

Still sitting down, Daniel craned his neck and looked up at Gianni Scaravento as the unpleasant incident in the Triumph flooded back. "Oh," he said. "In that case, okay."

Then came the drive back to Houghton along the deserted 684, which had been plowed and paved through virgin forest. A black wall of trees loomed on either side of the superhighway and gave off a feeling of desolate imprisonment. No cars passed in the opposite direction; Daniel felt uncomfortable being alone with Gianni. Gianni, in turn, kept the speedometer needle riveted to sixty-five, as though to make a point of his present emotional sobriety.

Unlike most Italians in Houghton, the Scaraventos did not share their home with any relatives. Theirs was a small two-level house of neocolonial architecture. When Gianni pulled into the driveway, Daniel looked through the front windows and saw blue light flickering throughout the downstairs. He figured Mrs. Scaravento was looking at television. Gianni led him around to the kitchen door at the back of the house. When they went inside, Gianni did not put on the light. In the darkness, he ran his hand along the formica counter until Daniel heard the clanging of crockery. "Let's see what we got in the cookie jar." Moments passed, Daniel listening to Gianni paw through the cookies. "Ah, shit," he complained. "She forgot to order more Stella D'oros."

"Don't you think you've had enough food for one evening?"

"What do you want from me? I'm still hungry."

"Gianni," a raspy voice called from another room, pronouncing his name the way it should've been pronounced. "Who's with you, Gianni?" An odd sensation of recognition washed over Daniel.

Gianni left him in the kitchen and walked down the dimmed hallway. "Just a friend of mine, Ma," he said in a docile voice. "He wasn't tired so I invited him over."

"Bring him in to see me, Gianni. And turn on that light."

Daniel heard a flicking sound, and the room and hallway were suddenly brimming with warm light. He shut his eyes until they adjusted. Upon opening his eyes, he glanced around. The Scaraventos' house had darkly stained parquet floors, braided rugs and heavy maple furniture, some of it covered with mustard-colored fabric, noticeable on seat cushions at the breakfast table and picked up in the sofa coverings in the television room, where Angela now sat. The breakfast table was as large as a dining room table. Daniel's house had a more modern decor—and, he supposed was probably more tastefully done—a less-lived-in look overall. Their breakfast table was smaller and flimsier than the Scaraventos', which looked as though it were made to support heavy casseroles and bowls of steaming ravioli and huge slabs of roast beef. Although Irene had taken pains to coordinate the artwork and fur-

niture, to aesthetically pull together the Fells' according to a single
mood, Daniel found himself preferring the simple, heavy, mismatched comfort of the Scaraventos', even the Catholic watch-
words mounted on scalloped wood that were hung on the walls.

"Come on in the den," Gianni said.

Daniel followed him down the carpeted hallway and stopped
at the threshold of the room where the television was blaring. He
smiled cordially at Mrs. Scaravento, who just stared at him for a
moment without saying anything. As she looked at him, her head
tilted slowly to one side and he found something odd about her
gaze. "This is Daniel Fell," Gianni said.

"Angela Scaravento." She extended a frail hand, which Daniel
shook and which felt cool and dry. "Sit down." Angela indicated
the ottoman her feet were resting upon. When Daniel sat down,
Mrs. Scaravento did not move her legs aside to accommodate him.

She appraised Daniel for a moment longer and then turned to
Gianni. "You reeled in a long-hair."

"All the Heebs got long hair these days," Gianni said with a
smirk.

Daniel clucked his tongue and scowled at him.

"Don't be so sensitive, Danny," Gianni said. "I only meant it
jokingly. I brought you to meet my ma, didn't I?"

Mrs. Scaravento turned to Gianni. "So what does he care?"
Then she turned to Daniel, one of her eyes scrutinizing him, the
other dull and glossy, a lazy eye. "I know who you are," she said.

Daniel frowned "You do?"

"*Ma è il ragazzo che viveva in Padova,*" she said. "*Non è vero?*"

Suddenly, without warning, Daniel's Italian came out of its
five-year hibernation. Perhaps Mrs. Scaravento's beautiful pronunciation was the inspiration; perhaps it was a guilty reaction to
Gianni's accusation that Daniel concealed his knowledge of the
language.

"How is it that you speak almost without an accent?" he asked
Mrs. Scaravento in Italian.

"I spent each summer there until I was eighteen," she said.
"We rented the same house every summer in Vicenza. And I
studied in school."

"Vicenza?" Daniel cried out. "But so close to Padova. We used
to go to Vicenza for dinner."

Mrs. Scaravento giggled. "*You* lived in Padua?"

They talked of the seven domes and the balustrades of Il Santo, the Donatello reliefs, of strolling past the Gattamelata and Il Bò, the main building of Padua University. Many times Angela had been to the grand Caffè Pedrocchi, where the whole city drank cappuccino. At some point Daniel realized that Angela Scaravento was the very first American he had spoken to in Italian. It also occurred to him that in a way he expressed himself more colorfully in his adopted language. Soon, his hands were embellishing his words. He raised his eyebrows. His voice rose and fell with a different emphasis.

"Have you gone back to Italy?" Mrs. Scaravento asked.

"No, not since we left."

"Don't you miss it?"

"Yes, I do miss it."

Mrs. Scaravento raised her eyes to the ceiling. "I think it must be five years ago that I was there."

"It still amazes me that you don't have more of an accent," Daniel told Mrs. Scaravento.

"I guess the language came easier to me than to most people," she said, smiling. "I guess in that way I'm like you."

Daniel looked closely at her pale face and her troubled eyes. Her face was round and dimpled and although she was in her late forties, Mrs. Scaravento had few lines that told of her age. In certain places, though, her capillaries ran close to the skin and Daniel could see their blue cross-hatching. He remembered now that she was afflicted by a fatal illness, that her body was in revolt against itself.

"I wish my children would be interested in the language," Mrs. Scaravento said wistfully, still speaking in Italian. "I tried to get both of them to study it. But they refuse. They aren't even curious enough to go to Italy and see the country of their ancestors. They don't want to travel anywhere if it isn't to Florida. Or California."

"I guess it's just a question of getting them there," Daniel said. "Then I'm sure they'd love it."

Mrs. Scaravento frowned. She made a dismissive gesture with her hand. "I can't even get them to go see the Renaissance paintings at the Metropolitan Museum."

"Do you often go there?"

Mrs. Scaravento's pale face grew strained. "I used to go all the time. I took the train. It was easy. I used to have a girlfriend who lived only a few blocks from the Frick Collection. I used to love to go and look at the Turners and the Bronzinis. Or to the Metropolitan. We'd have coffee on Madison Avenue afterwards. But now . . ." She hesitated and then continued delicately. "Of course I can't." Was she assuming he knew the extent of the incapacity of which she now hinted? "It's too tiring for me to take the train. I'm trapped here in this house," she said. Then she looked at Daniel inquiringly. "But I'm sure your mother must take advantage of New York City."

"She's a member of all the museums, if that's what you mean."

"Do you ever go with her to the museums?"

"I used to. But she likes to go through them so quickly and is always hurrying me up. Somebody somewhere along the line told my mom that an hour is the maximum time to spend in a museum. According to her, after that you're saturated with all the impressions."

"I don't believe that for a minute," Mrs. Scaravento said. "It's just a question of opening yourself up. There are some paintings in this world that can hold my attention for a good half-hour. I could stand in front of them and forget where I am." Daniel glanced at Gianni, who was watching them with obvious pleasure. But when he turned back to Mrs. Scaravento, who was eagerly waiting to continue their conversation, the whole situation suddenly struck him in a different way. He grew nervous. He reached up to his head with his right hand and began twisting strands of hair with his index finger.

"That's a bad habit you have," Mrs. Scaravento told him.

"What is?" Daniel said.

"The way you play with your hair. Maybe you should have it cut short so you won't be able to do that."

Daniel laughed and put his hands in his lap.

"I've been curious about you," Mrs. Scaravento said. "I've wanted to meet you. I've asked Gianni several times if he knew you; he said he didn't."

Unable to decipher their Italian, Gianni had grown distracted and was now fiddling with some tools in a cabinet next to the bar.

Had he still been looking on, he might have caught the displeasure that crossed Daniel's face and wondered whether Daniel had just realized that this meeting was not as impromptu as it had seemed. But Gianni did not turn around and Daniel focused once again on Mrs. Scaravento, continuing their talk. After a while he asked himself why should he care about motivations. He certainly was enjoying his conversation, which was the more important thing.

"I've met your mother," Mrs. Scaravento said in English.

Daniel looked at her. "Oh?"

Mrs. Scaravento fluttered her hands. "She wouldn't remember me or anything, but we did meet at this luncheon. It was maybe two years ago when they had a fund raiser for the children's zoo." And then her face changed. "*Quegli assassini*," she murmured in Italian. Those murderers.

Daniel shuddered. The television was casting dappled processed light on the walls of the den and for a moment he could feel a swell of bleakness and futility. He was just then beginning to realize that every new thing in his life that autumn always seemed to home back to the Polannos and the crime against the helpless animals. Then he thought wistfully of Julietta and wondered why she had stood him up.

"Have you ever studied Hebrew?" Mrs. Scaravento broke through this musing.

Startled from his thoughts, he peered blankly at her for a few moments before saying anything. "No, I never did."

"But why not . . . if you're Jewish?"

"There were so few Jewish people in Padua. And my mother wanted me to study French before Hebrew."

This seemed to disturb Mrs. Scaravento. "I don't understand people sometimes. Aren't you curious about the language of your forefathers?"

"I know some prayers."

"I mean to express yourself. To know the phrases and words that stood for everything they went through."

"I've wondered about it," Daniel said mildly.

"And what about your bar mitzvah."

"I never had one."

Mrs. Scaravento clucked her tongue. "For shame. And it's such a beautiful ceremony." She paused and smiled. "I was to one once right here in Houghton."

Both were silent for a while after this. Daniel was imagining Mrs. Scaravento as a proud spectator of Jewish worship. Finally she said, "Well, I'm sure you must be tired. Does Gianni need to give you a ride home?"

"He's just got to give me a ride back to my car."

Mrs. Scaravento shifted around in her chair. "Gianni," she said in English, "your friend looks exhausted. I think you should get him back to his car."

Having never dreamed he'd incur criticism of his noncommitment to Judaism from a Catholic, Daniel looked up at Angela. And when she smiled back at him, her lazy eye rotated inward, almost as though it were more shy than the other eye.

8

It was five in the morning when Daniel pulled the Chevy Nova into his driveway. The night had worn to a paleness at its fringe and light was breeding just beyond the perimeters of the yard. He was vastly overtired and overstimulated from his bizarre evening with Gianni and from speaking so much Italian with Mrs. Scaravento. Strange places on Daniel's body ached; he felt as though he had just braved a two-hour soccer practice. If he hadn't been so weary and in such a hurry to get to bed he might have looked more carefully at the bristly conglomeration of objects lying on the front porch.

Around noon, when the mailman rang the doorbell with a package, Irene's distinct voice penetrated through Daniel's sleep and woke him. "I don't know what this is," he heard her exclaiming. "How long has it been there?"

"You're asking me?" the mailman said.

Daniel heard the front door slam; and then in her awful Italian, Irene spoke about dried flowers. "*Ma che strano*," someone answered her, which caused Daniel to bolt upright in bed. Marcella Auguri had accompanied his mother back from New York City.

Daniel put on his Viyella bathrobe, threw open the bedroom door and started down the stairs. Then everything turned a little

feverish and incongruous: Irene was standing just inside the door
holding at arm's length an ugly bouquet of wilted flowers that
looked as though they had been collected from various fallow
gardens in the neighborhood, wound with a piece of green twine
and deposited on their doorstep. When her bemused expression
lifted to take him in, it turned cold and resentful. "Worm," she
muttered, tossing the flowers on the floor and stalking back towards the kitchen. "What's wrong?" Daniel yelped. His view of
his mother was now replaced by that of willowy Marcella Auguri,
who wore a silk dressing gown and high-heeled sandals.

"*Caro*," Marcella said, "*vieni qua*," casting Daniel a worried
smile as she stretched her bony arms toward him. Hesitant now,
he continued down the stairs. Marcella gave him two quick pecks
on the cheek, continuing in a soft, rapid Italian, "How foolish of
you to call Italy. You got everybody so upset. They thought
something happened here."

Daniel summarized his transatlantic call while casting a sideways glance at the dirty bouquet of flowers on the marble tile of
the entryway. Who had left them?

"Darling, how disrespectful to your mother," Marcella continued to chide him.

Daniel remembered the plight of his father, purposely in ab-
sentia for the weekend, and then began to get angry himself. "You
don't understand," he told Marcella.

Marcella tossed her head, simultaneously rolling her eyes.
"What's to understand about somebody who is nosey? *Caro*, you
only should have seen her last night at the hotel when Paolo called
me. She grabbed the phone out of my hands to speak to him and
then he got furious with her . . . oh, so much confusion.

"Then she tried to call here at the house and when no one
answered? And then she got frightened thinking something really
happened, which was why you called Italy to find out where I
was staying. To get a hold of me. Oh, God, in ten minutes she
and I got twisted up into such knots. I had to call back Paolo and
find out exactly what you had said to Ornella." Marcella raised
her shoulders with a great deal of exaggeration. Her elbows were
covered with large pockets of loose skin, as though for years she
had kept up a nervous affliction of pulling at her elbows. Daniel
supposed Marcella pulled at her elbows the way he cracked his

knuckles. Irene always scolded him for it, warning that he'd develop arthritis later on in life.

Meanwhile, Marcella had chattered on, and Daniel missed some of her monologue. When he managed to tune in again she was saying, "When your mother finally figured out you called to check up on her she wanted to drive home and break your little balls. I had quite a job trying to calm her down. I finally told her when young men fall in love they completely lose their sense of judgment about other people's lives."

"I haven't fallen in love with anybody," Daniel said.

Marcella ignored his protest. "By the way, your Italian sounds pretty good to me. In fact, better than last time."

Daniel began to explain how he had spoken Italian the night before with Mrs. Scaravento. Marcella, however, was not really interested in hearing about the Scaraventos. She began ushering Daniel toward the kitchen, urging him to apologize to Irene for his stupidity.

Daniel's eyes once again alighted on the twisted bouquet of dried flowers. He turned to Marcella. "In Italy when they leave flowers like this on a doorstep—"

"*They* don't leave flowers on doorsteps, Daniel. The Mafia leave flowers on doorsteps. Does it mean the same thing here?"

Daniel shrugged. "It may."

"But have you done anything? Do you owe somebody money?"

"No."

"Well then, it's something else, probably. Probably a dog left it."

Daniel blinked at Marcella's odd assumption. "I guess I better go apologize to my mother," he said, now heading toward the kitchen.

As he walked down the hallway, the morning smells of freshly brewed coffee and toasted bread grew more pungent. Knowing he was about to take the venting of Irene's anger, Daniel warned himself not to get caught in a flare-up but to be relentlessly apologetic; it was the best way to extricate himself from his uncomfortable position. Irene was hiding behind the Saturday edition of the *New York Times*. All Daniel could see was her disheveled hair protruding from either side of the newspaper.

"Ma, put down the paper for a minute," he said.

"Screw you," she said, angrily turning the page.

"Look, I'm sorry," he said. "Okay. You're right. I acted . . . like a worm."

"You ruined my evening," Irene said tartly. "I couldn't even concentrate on the play." She crinkled up the paper on her lap and glared at Daniel, her lips curling with rage. "Did you go into my drawer?" she accused him.

"No I didn't," Daniel lied. "I called directory assistance in Padua."

Daniel watched his mother's face grow shocked and pucker up. Then, despite her will, she broke into wild laughter. She threw back her head and shrieked and howled until Marcella came scurrying into the room.

"What is going on in here?" Marcella said in English. She looked accusingly at Daniel and then raised her eyes to the ceiling. "Why is she laughing? Everybody is losing their mind."

Irene continued to laugh. She'd stop, look at Daniel for a moment, mutter "directory assistance" and then burst into uncontrolled giggles.

"Directory, what?" Marcella asked.

Daniel explained in Italian.

"Of course, such a thing exists nowadays."

Irene suddenly grew solemn. That Daniel possibly could be telling the truth irked her even more. "You're a louse for checking up on me," she said through clenched teeth. She pushed back abruptly from the table, stood up and soon Daniel and Marcella were left alone in the kitchen.

"She'll get over it," Marcella remarked after watching Irene's flight from the room. She turned to Daniel and said in a haughty voice, "But stop acting like a child. For the love of God!" and went to find Irene.

Daniel helped himself to the last cup of coffee from the pot that had been kept warm on the stove. He extracted a bagel from the freezer, defrosted it in the toaster and lathered it with raspberry jam. Still hungry, he took out another bagel and defrosted that. He had eaten half of the second bagel when he suddenly remembered there were matters to sort out with Julietta. It was time to call her and to see what had happened last night. The challenge of this dimmed his appetite, quickened his breath, made his fingers sweaty. He dumped the remnants of the bagel in the garbage, dropped his plate in the sink and wandered out of the kitchen.

It was then that he noticed the bouquet of dead flowers still lying in the hallway. Bending down in order to scrutinize it, he noticed a few dead crickets wound among the shriveled vines. Shrugging, he went upstairs to his room, where he dug through his wallet for Julietta's telephone number.

A raspy-sounding man answered the phone. After introducing himself, Daniel asked to speak to Julietta. The phone was muffled by a hand, which then rubbed the receiver to create a further sound buffer. The man eventually came back on, "Sorry, I thought she was here, but she ain't. Want to leave a message?"

"Sure. Can you tell her I called?"

"You could try her at her Aunt Maria's."

"That's okay, I'll just leave this message."

"God dammit!" Daniel exploded once he was off the phone. "What the hell is with her?" He couldn't tell whether or not Julietta was actually home and had refused to take his phone call. "This is getting out of control," he fumed.

"What is?" Alexis yelled from within her bedroom.

"Nothing, okay?"

The bedroom door cracked opened and his sister, looking tousled and sleepy, poked her head out. She was still wearing her nightgown. "What's wrong, Danny?"

"Julietta," he groaned.

"What about Julietta?"

"She stood me up last night. And now she suddenly seems to be avoiding me."

"But you got in so late. I figured—"

"That's because I ended up hanging around with Gianni Scaravento."

"Gianni Scaravento?" Alexis asked, her eyes lighting up. "You were out with Gianni Scaravento?"

"Yeah, what's the matter?"

"The heartthrob of the century, that's the matter."

Daniel frowned, suddenly jealous of Alexis's admiration for Gianni Scaravento.

"Don't worry, he's not as cute as you are," Alexis said, grinning. "You're the heartthrob of the bicentennial. . . . She stood you up, huh?"

"I can't figure out why."

"Nothing you said or did?"

Daniel shook his head. He explained about the messages from Brenda and Gianni's explanation about Aunt Maria's neurosis. "Do you think she suddenly got interested in somebody else?" he said, revealing the weakest link in his general worry.

Alexis shook her head resolutely. "I don't think so," she said. "I think Gianni Scaravento is right. Julietta probably just got pulled away by family problems."

This allowed Daniel to stop fretting, at least for the time being.

Alexis peered in both directions down the hallway. They heard murmuring from Irene's bedroom but nothing intelligible as actual words. Then she whispered, "I won fifty dollars off Liza's father."

"You played for money?"

Alexis eagerly nodded her head. She loved to gamble. "It was easy, too. He had a couple of drinks before I got there. Smelled to high heaven. Liza was so embarrassed. She fell asleep around eleven. And we played until one-thirty."

"Has he paid you yet?"

"Oh yeah. Took out a big old roll of bills and peeled off a couple of twenties and a ten. And then he made me swear never to tell her."

Daniel considered this for a moment. "I don't like the way this sounds. I don't think you should play chess with him anymore. Sounds like a dirty old man to me."

"Oh crap," Alexis said. "I can take care of myself."

"And what would you do if he got fresh with you?" Daniel asked.

"I'd kick him where it hurts," Alexis said. "That's what Mom told me to do if anything like that ever happened."

Daniel laughed. "There's just one thing you have to remember when you try to kick a man in the balls."

"What's that?" Alexis said.

"You can never miss."

Alexis stuck both her thumbs inside her mouth and made a grotesque face at him before retreating inside her bedroom.

Daniel had just punched in the digits of Patrick Riordan's phone number when the hushed tones behind his parents' bedroom door suddenly grew audible. He quietly replaced the receiver and tip-toed closer.

"It doesn't make any difference now." His mother was sounding extremely upset. "It's half shot through."

"But darling, you are not being sensible," Marcella said loudly in English. "Think about your . . . choices."

"You should have told me all this earlier. You shouldn't have said it was just a visit."

"But I wanted to talk to you about it all sensibly . . . the way we used to talk."

"But you have no idea of what my life is like here. Or the isolation."

"I-so-la-tion!" Marcella's voice warbled in a singsong emphasis of the word's syllables. "You have family all around you."

Irene made an attempt to lower her voice. "Marcella, the children are practically raised. They have their own schedules. They don't spend that much time at home. That's one of the reasons why I like to go to Manhattan. This place is always empty. Except when the cleaning lady comes. And even she's suspicious of me."

"What?" Marcella said.

"Oh, sometimes I try to get her to talk about herself. And she thinks I'm being patronizing when I'm only just interested." Then Irene added wistfully, "You know, when I see Alexis go off to a friend's house I envy her. I wish I could take the same sort of pleasure in seeing a friend. Everyone around here is so different. They're exhilarated by giving charity luncheons and playing tennis. They're not interested in seeing plays unless they're on Broadway." She paused. "Whenever I have a lunch date nobody wants to talk to me about anything like art or music. They brag about their children mainly. In a sort of endless gush. They talk about their kids with such rapture they almost make me think I never had any myself. Or that there's something wrong with me because I don't want to talk about Danny and Alexis all the time."

"You were never one to brag about your children," Marcella said.

Irene continued. "And when I'm sitting in the midst of all those ladies I often think I'd be better off spending my free time alone."

"Why don't you talk to Harold about maybe moving to Manhattan. Then maybe you wouldn't feel so isolated."

"He doesn't want to. He likes it here. He's got all his golfing and tennis chums. And besides it wouldn't make any difference now. It's not just the place we live anymore . . . I still can't believe he called you."

"But Harold my friend is too," Marcella defended herself, using improper syntax.

Oh God, thought Daniel. What a stupid inversion. Marcella will get absolutely nowhere speaking in English. For goodness' sake, why didn't she just speak in Italian. His mother understood Italian perfectly well.

Irene continued balefully, "He never suggests we meet in the city after work during the week so we can go out alone. He just comes home and then he's always sapped by the commute. And on the few occasions he does agree to do something he thinks dinner at a local family restaurant and then a movie will work wonders to please me. For a couple of years I got a subscription to the Metropolitan Opera. Harold went with me once. I couldn't get anyone else I know around here to go in with me. Oh, they might consider it for five seconds if it's *Tosca* or *La Bohème*, something they know is vaguely famous. And I love how they all give the same excuses: too busy with children, too exhausted from playing tennis." There was a pause. "Remember the way we used to get drunk on the train to La Scala?"

"Every week like clockwork," Marcella murmured in Italian.

"I mean when you mention going to the opera to someone they act like it's having to sit in a straightjacket for three hours in a skirt made of thorns. I felt so pathetic turning in my extra ticket every time I went. I finally stopped taking the subscription."

"Well, you know Harold never liked to do very much in Italy. You just need a friend like me to spend time with here."

"I don't agree with you. Life stimulated him a lot more in Italy. At least he'd be up for driving to Florence or Siena or just taking off and driving to out-of-the way churches."

"But to some people in Italy that's as unambitious as going to a movie here. Just a cultural difference in what people do to relax."

Irene continued on the heels of Marcella's comment, as though not having heard it at all. "He's become so sedentary and needy. He leaves me feeling so desperate and lonely and unhappy. And then he expects me to make love to him."

Outside his mother's bedroom door, Daniel gulped back a

groan that had reared up in his throat, an unwelcome recognition of something that had eluded him up until now. His mother's denial of his father had been like a shade purposely drawn against the bright promise of the family's continuing to be a family. But now he felt pitched up and plummeting into another realm. The shade had been lifted and the darkness was still visible.

"I've been feeling so old lately," Irene continued softly.

"Oh, don't be ridiculous," Marcella cried out in Italian. "Now you've fallen on absolute foolishness. Women only become more distinguished as they get older if they take good care of themselves."

"This has nothing to do with trying to age gracefully, Marcella. This has to do with being forty-five and having done absolutely nothing."

"So get yourself a job."

Oh God, thought Daniel, from a woman who had never worked a day in her life.

"That'd only solve part of this problem. I'd still have all this to contend with."

"You know, Irene, I think you're romanticizing your life in Italy. I'll remind you you weren't in bliss there, either."

"I was much happier."

There was another pause and Daniel heard a distinct rustling, as though perhaps Marcella were helping his mother into a dress. "Perhaps this is all just a stage," Marcella said finally in a muted voice. "Perhaps eventually it'll snap back to the way it was."

"You're just against divorce in principle," Irene muttered.

There was the word Daniel was hoping never to hear. It cut into him like a spill of acid. Weren't there supposed to be symptoms? Raging fights in the middle of the night. Affairs with other people. Mismanagement of money. Could just plain complacency and no sex really be so insidious? The idea was staggering.

"You only made things worse by coming," Irene was now telling Marcella. "You've only made me more impatient and anxious about everything."

"Oh, that's not true," Marcella said in a hurt voice. Daniel pictured her tugging nervously on the raddled skin of her elbow.

"Because you came here with a mission. As though you expected to talk me out of feeling the way I do. And I don't like that. You make it seem like I've made impulsive decisions. That I could change my mind as easily as I make it up."

"*Sei impulsiva, Irene,*" Marcella disagreed boldly. Daniel's heart pounded in the curt silence that followed the remark. He suddenly remembered his sister's proximity to the conversation. Had she heard any of it? He retreated down the hallway and listened outside her bedroom. The radio was on. He hoped to God she hadn't heard anything. When he returned to his previous position outside his parents' bedroom door, he heard Marcella saying, "It's just that I really want you to think about what you're doing."

"I haven't made any definitive move."

"Maybe if you hold on for a while things will come around."

"Marcella," Irene said softly, and Daniel felt her pause enveloping the entire house, "you shouldn't have come."

9

Daniel decided that the best place to run into Julietta Polanno on a Saturday evening would be at the Oaks and arranged to grab a ride there from Patrick Riordan. As they were driving along in the VW van, Daniel filled Patrick in on how he had met Mrs. Scaravento and spoken Italian to her and how the flowers had been placed on his doorstep. After commenting that Daniel had been keeping himself extraordinarily busy, Patrick grew quiet. Any further attempts at conversation only died like a lighted match in a strong wind. At one point as they were nearing the Oaks, Daniel swung around and surveyed the back portion of the van, thinking it might be resonant with some sort of nostalgia or purpose of that first time he had made love. Strangely, it had no such effect on him. In fact, the baseball was still there, rolling around as the van turned corners.

"Why don't you get rid of that ball?" he asked Patrick, who shrugged and kept on driving. Daniel studied the features of his friend's face, which were set and did not reveal any emotion. "What's wrong with you, anyway?"

"Nothing."

Unfortunately, Daniel had little time to reflect on Patrick's mood. They had just found a parking space a block away from the Oaks. They walked to the bar in sturdy silence and as soon as they stepped inside the crowded bar, Daniel felt a large, warm hand on his shoulder. It was Gianni Scaravento, looking per-turbed.

"Can't stay here, Danny," Gianni said in a confidential voice, his eyes scanning the activity in the bar.

Daniel frowned at him. "Why, what's going on?"

Gianni looked at him, appraising. "What did you do to rile Julietta?"

"What do you mean?" An undulation of dread broke over Daniel, who now ventured to glance around the Oaks. The place was noisy and crowded and yet he felt that he was the object of abnormal scrutiny.

"I mean Brenda said Julietta was going to show up here at eleven. But you showed up and she didn't—I have that right, don't I?"

"Exactly, Gianni. You drove me back here. You saw the whole thing go down."

Gianni rubbed his curly head. "Then I don't understand. Just a little while ago Julietta came in here like a demon. When I said hello to her, she took a swing at me. Then she beelined out." He smiled. "She must be jealous of me."

Daniel looked away. He couldn't understand why Julietta was behaving like this. Everything had been so perfect yesterday and now it had turned upside down. Without warning. The unpre-dictability of it all infuriated him.

"No, seriously, Danny, we got ourselves a problem here."

Daniel watched Gianni's face and waited.

"I think the Polannos are after you."

Just as Gianni announced this, they heard the ear-rending sound of shattering glass. A computer geek had tripped over his own shoelace and dropped a full pitcher of beer. Gianni and Daniel got spattered by froth; Daniel felt the wet coldness of the beer on his neck and shivered. Ralphie, the bartender, bellowed at the geek, calling him a klutz. Amid all this distraction, Daniel thought perhaps he had misheard and should ask Gianni to repeat what he said. But then he could clearly read the effect of the news on Gianni's face.

"Why are they after me?"

"That's what I wanted to ask you."

"I don't believe this!" Daniel exclaimed. He then told Gianni about the flowers that had been left on his doorstep.

"Asshole punks," Gianni commented with disdain. "Trying to act like big Mafia. All I can say is Vito comes to me, right? He says that I should tell you that they're going to get you and that I shouldn't hang around with you anymore."

"So what did you say?"

"I was cordial, but I didn't say I wasn't going to hang around with you. Come on, let's get out before they see you. Let's take a drive. It's not cool for you to stay here." Gianni grabbed his maroon jacket. "You think your friend will mind you're leaving him behind?"

Daniel searched the crowd for Patrick and then saw him sitting alone at the bar. "I'll go tell him."

Patrick had already drunk one mug of beer and was in the midst of ordering another. Daniel approached him slowly and clapped him on the back. "I'm going to take a ride with Gianni," he said. "He'll probably drop me home."

Patrick nodded and looked away.

"What's bugging you?" Daniel said.

Patrick turned to him. The beer seemed to be taking some effect and his face was no longer able to belie his feelings. He had a droopy look to him now, his eyes had taken on an injured glare. "I thought you were my best friend."

"I am, Pat."

Patrick slumped over a bit and stared into the amber depths of his beer. "Just thought you were," he said softly.

Daniel stood there for a moment searching for words of encouragement. "Look, I'll call you tomorrow," he said finally.

"Yeah." Patrick looked away again.

As Daniel worked his way back toward Gianni he felt guilty. Patrick Riordan must already detect that his loyalties were shifting; it was as if he could already sense the pull of Gianni Scaravento. In high school Daniel had watched many friendships vacillate and change; it was the sort of thing that seemed to happen. Perhaps people—himself included—were fickle by nature. Perhaps Julietta's sudden disloyalty to him was part of some romantic norm he didn't yet understand.

He finally reached Gianni, who had put on his maroon jacket and now encircled Daniel with his arm and escorted him out of the bar. Gianni was demonstrative the way his friends had been in Italy. Still, Daniel found himself cringing.

As they were walking through the cold street toward the Triumph, Daniel noticed a stocky hood wearing a black leather jacket. "Heh Fell, did they get you yet?" he asked.

"Fuck you," Gianni said to the kid.

"Heh, fuck you, Scaravento," the hood told him.

And then they were driving in Gianni's car; the memories of the previous evening surged back in full force: gliding along the smooth black roads of Houghton's ridges, passing the train station, the scare on 684. Daniel watched Gianni's dextrous hands pulling out the choke, putting it in and pummeling the gearshift between first and second and third gears. Daniel looked around the car and smelled the rugged odor of its leather seats. The Triumph seemed like an extension of Gianni. Soon, however, the anxiety came on like a cold stone dropping to the bottom of a well. Could the Polannos be after him solely because he had been to bed with their cousin?

When Daniel advanced this theory, Gianni shook his head and said that several high school guys had made love to Julietta Polanno; in fact, the Polanno brothers were not particularly fond of their cousin. Apparently they had had to dispel a number of rumors of her ill repute before the rumors reached their mother's ears. Without a daughter of her own, Maria Polanno felt especially close to Julietta.

"How do you know all this?"

"I told you Maria and my mother are close friends. They get together over *biscottis* and yack."

Gianni dug into the front pocket of his flannel shirt and pulled out another terribly rolled joint; this one looked as though it had gone through the washer and dryer, which it probably had. He lit the joint and sucked in a third of it on one hit.

"Bogart," Daniel commented.

Gasping, Gianni offered him some. Daniel declined for the time being. He waited until Gianni blew out several smoke rings before saying, "I can't understand something about Italian Americans."

"What's that?" Gianni said, blowing out the rest of the smoke that hadn't seeped into his lungs.

"They exaggerate everything. Like Mamma mia and Stella D'oros and all this hyping of the Mafia."

"You're right," Gianni said, laughing. As he laughed he inadvertently braked the car too hard and Daniel got thrown forward.

"Listen, if you can't drive right maybe you shouldn't smoke while you drive."

"Shut up, you precious little Heeb," Gianni said sweetly, continuing to steer with one hand.

Daniel was unsure whether or not to resent Gianni's slur, hoping it was said out of affection. "Please don't use that word around me, Gianni," he ended up saying.

They both fell silent as the question of the Polannos reasserted itself in their thoughts. Daniel saw himself cornered in some remote outpost at the high school, his head getting bashed into a locker, or lying brained in an alleyway. He asked Gianni what he should do about the situation. Gianni said he needed a chance to consider the different angles. He suggested they drive up 684 again to that diner in Bedford, hoping to see the same girls they had seen the previous evening.

But Daniel was reluctant to hazard another drive up 684. "There must be plenty of other places we can go where you can drool over the girls," he said.

"Hey buddy," Gianni said. "Don't you like looking at women?"

"I do, but Jesus Christ, right now I got things on my mind. I mean you just dropped a bomb on me."

Gianni turned to him. "Don't worry, the Polannos probably aren't going to get you right away. You may as well have a good time."

"That doesn't make me feel any better. I'd prefer they not get me altogether."

"You got to first find out what they're after you for," Gianni said. His eyes had tightened up and he looked very stoned. "They always let you know what they're after you for before they actually get you. They always have one of their friends tell you. And you haven't reached that stage yet."

"I'm surprised you're not offering to protect me," Daniel said.

"Part of being a big boy, Danny, is learning how to take care of yourself."

Daniel turned to him. "Maybe I should remind you how many Jewish kids ended up leaving Houghton for private school. On account of the Polannos. These guys must have cost the Jewish community a half a million dollars in private school fees."

Gianni frowned. "In your case, private school isn't an option. You're a senior."

For the time being they left off discussing the Polannos, although Daniel was still perturbed as to why Gianni hadn't offered to mediate on his behalf. Plenty of other Italian kids mediated when the Polannos were after one of their friends. And if there was anyone in high school who had influence it was Gianni Scaravento.

They decided to hit Hamburger Warehouse in the neighboring town of Larchmont. Hamburger Warehouse attracted high school students from all over Westchester County, particularly from the towns closest to New York City, and could be depended upon to showcase suburban "pieces." It was an immense establishment that had been used to store parts for transport planes during World War II. Owing to poor insulation, Hamburger Warehouse was equipped with huge furnacelike heaters, which had ducts for air conditioning during the summer. The battleship-gray walls were hand-stenciled with purple and pink polka dots, a sixties impression that yearned to be redesigned to suit the more streamlined seventies.

No sooner did Gianni and Daniel walk in the door than they saw Debbie Lerner and her friend, Rhonda Summers, sitting by a window in a vinyl booth. Exuding a "holier than thou" attitude, they were smoking Balkan Sobranie cigarettes. Debbie kept fingering her famous hair, tilting her head back to blow smoke up above her head. Daniel admired her beautiful throat.

"Let's just stand here for a minute and look at the wall menu and act like we don't see them," Gianni said.

"Why do we have to play games?"

"Because that's what getting dates is all about."

"Not for me," Daniel said. "I'm going to find a place to sit down."

"Oh shit, buddy, come on. If we play our cards right we'll be sitting with them."

Gianni was suddenly distracted by a group of well-built jocks wearing New Rochelle varsity jackets, who were barreling in the door, heralded by a blast of cold. Recognizing them from past scrimmages, he shook his head and drew in a low whistle. "Some immense guys on that team," he remarked to Daniel. "Thinking about the New Rochelle game can actually give me butterflies."

"I thought you already played New Rochelle?"

"No," Gianni said, irritated. "We played Eastchester."

"Eastchester. New Rochelle. It's all the same to me," Daniel said.

"Maybe you should go sit down," Gianni said.

"I will. In fact, I'm going right over to Debbie Lerner and Rhonda Summers and sit down with them."

"Go ahead," Gianni said. "I hope they tell you to go hide yourself."

But Debbie Lerner and Rhonda Summers invited Daniel to join them. When Gianni saw this he ordered two triple hamburgers, two quart-sized coffee shakes and a barrel of french fries, arriving at the table as though it had been his intention all along.

"So since when have you two become friends?" Rhonda Summers asked Daniel. She had olive skin, dark eyes and a sarcastic smile.

"Since a while," Gianni said.

"Interesting combination," Debbie said.

"Why?" Daniel asked.

"The cutest senior and the sexiest senior fast friends," Rhonda Summers said, correcting her posture so that her back arched and her breasts surged against her tight ecru-colored sweater. This stretching gesture, suggestive, feline, resembled reactions Daniel had witnessed in other women when they came under the spell of Gianni Scaravento—even before he and Gianni got to know each other. Gianni's very presence seemed to set them on edge, something he exuded—almost like an animal scent—ensnared them unwittingly in a powerful attraction.

"Which is which?" Daniel asked, despite his knowledge. "Who's cutest? Who's sexiest?"

"You figure it out," Rhonda told him.

Gianni put his strong arm around Daniel's shoulder. "We're actually queer together."

"Come on," Debbie Lerner said, lighting up another cigarette.

"I'd believe it," Rhonda Summers said in a thrilled tone of voice.

Gianni glanced at Daniel and then grabbed a handful of french fries from the french fry barrel and jammed them into his mouth. "Your friend is a little hard to take," he told Debbie with a mouth full of food.

Nervous, Debbie Lerner put both index fingers on either edge of her mane of tawny hair and flicked it behind her shoulders. Then she threw Rhonda Summers a cautionary look.

Rhonda, in the meantime, came to her own defense. "I'm not hard to take," she said, "I'm just honest. You're just a little sensitive, Gianni. I mean don't joke about being queer if you're so sensitive about being perceived like that."

Gianni frowned at Rhonda. "What are you, honors English or something?" He turned to Debbie Lerner. "Guys can't be friends anymore without people suspecting they're queer," he complained. "I mean nobody suspects girls of being queer." He leered at the two of them and took a monstrous bite of his triple hamburger. Daniel had thus far eaten absolutely nothing.

"You're taking this way too seriously," Rhonda remarked, taking advantage of Gianni's mouthful of food.

Gianni glared at her as he chewed. He swallowed prematurely and had to slug on his coffee shake to get everything down. "I'm a serious kind of guy," he grumbled finally. "I got lots of things on my mind. And I'll tell you something, Miss Judgment, I'd rather spend my time alone than be made uncomfortable by people."

"Okay, Gianni," Debbie Lerner said. "Okay." She looked helplessly at Daniel, as though expecting him to commiserate with her that indeed Gianni was being overly sensitive. But Daniel gazed back blankly at Debbie Lerner. He was on Gianni's side.

Suddenly, one of the New Rochelle varsity members, a lumbering, freckled fellow, approached the table.

Gianni grinned at him. "How ya doin', linebacker?"

"Name's Vincent Stakowsky." The kid cocked his hands on his hips and leaned toward Gianni. "You ready to get made into mincemeat this year, Scaravento?"

Bemused, Gianni looked up at him. "I wasn't really thinking about it. I don't like to think about football when I'm not on the playing field. You see, Dumbrowski—"

"Stakowsky."

"You see, Mr. Polack. I know I got a good arm, but my life doesn't revolve around football."

Stakowsky took a step back. His pimple-covered chin bunched up and his lips worked over themselves. "Hey, don't call me a Polack. Okay? And I won't call you guinea."

"Call me guinea." Gianni looked at Daniel, who felt himself surprisingly composed for suddenly being on the brink of hostilities. "Everybody is so sensitive about their heritage. My friend here, if you joke around and call him a Heeb, he gets bent out of shape. Now me, call me a wop . . . I could give a shit."

Debbie Lerner and Rhonda Summers burst into uproarious laughter. Daniel joined in and finally even Gianni chuckled. The next time Daniel looked up, Stakowsky's face was wrenching with humiliation. "Okay," he said, "you fucking wop."

It was over almost as soon as it started. And somehow in the midst of it, Daniel remembered the previous evening when Gianni had assured him of his quick reflexes. First Gianni rose from his seat. And even though Stakowsky was more massively built and taller, Gianni somehow towered over him. When the two flung themselves at each other, Debbie Lerner gave a shriek and squashed herself against Rhonda Summers, who swayed toward the window. Daniel remained stock-still, observing the entanglement with fascination. With his elbow Gianni broke free of this battle knot and then landed a lightning punch at Stakowsky's neck. Stakowsky fell to the floor, clutching the tomato-sized welt that immediately sprang up.

"Let's get out of here," Rhonda Summers cried. "Come on, Debbie, move!" They quickly gathered together their coats and handbags and fled the table without saying goodbye. Gianni stood there, wistfully watching their departure. He had broken into a sweat. Then he sat down heavily. Glancing at the writhing Stakowsky, he looked dolefully at Daniel. "Jesus Christ," he complained, "why can't anybody just leave me alone?"

"I don't know, Gianni," Daniel said as he noticed the other members of the New Rochelle varsity on their way over to their table. "I really don't know."

10

"*For goodness' sake*, will you quit moving?" Mrs. Scaravento scolded Gianni. With an antiseptic-soaked cotton ball, she dabbed at the gash that began at his temple and disappeared behind his ear lobe.

"It hurts. What do you want from me?" Gianni complained.

"It can't hurt as much as it did when the guy smacked you," she said.

"It hurts more."

"You're just lucky you got the hell out of there," Frank Scaravento said from the bar, where he was mixing himself a Scotch and soda. "Those guys probably would have loved to put you on the bench for the rest of the season."

Gianni had decided to take on the four New Rochelle varsity members who came over to avenge the fate of their linebacker, Stakowsky. But the manager of Hamburger Warehouse, a large and glowering man wielding a baseball bat, had immediately stepped into the melee and had thrown everybody—Daniel included—outside.

Mr. Scaravento turned away from the bar, swirling his Scotch and soda. The ice in his glass clinked and cracked. He kept his eyes riveted on Daniel as though he were an intruder. He plopped down in the easy chair Mrs. Scaravento had been occupying the previous evening and touched his scalp with an index finger. "Are we safe from bugs with you in here?" he asked Daniel, referring to his longer-than-usual hair.

Gianni, who was still being administered to by his mother, stiffened. "Shut up, heh, Dad. He's my friend."

"I was just pulling his leg," Frank Scaravento said, staring into his drink. "And remember who you're talking to," he told Gianni coolly.

"Well, don't be such an aaa—."

"Watch your mouth, kid," Frank Scaravento warned Gianni.

Mrs. Scaravento paused from dressing Gianni's wound. "Can the two of you save the I'm-the-big-guy stuff? We got a guest here. He doesn't have to see the two of you go at it."

"He's Gianni's friend, not a guest," Frank protested, patting his perfectly groomed hair.

Angela Scaravento glanced menacingly at her husband. "Look, he's my guest, too, okay. I want him here."

Frank Scaravento made a placating gesture with his hands. "All right, Angie, all right. I'm sorry. I didn't realize." He smiled graciously at Daniel and slugged his drink.

"So where were you when all this fighting was going on?" Frank asked Daniel.

Gianni blew air through his lips. "He was sitting there, legs crossed, taking it all in like he was some kind of cub reporter."

"You mean you didn't even try to protect Gianni's throwing arm from those animals?" Frank Scaravento said.

"It happened too fast." Daniel made an excuse. "He was mauling them anyway."

"Danny's better off." Gianni winced at his mother's ministrations. "Might have gotten flattened by one of those bruisers."

"I got a mind to call a friend of mine over in New Rochelle and give them a piece of my mind," Frank Scaravento said, taking another gulp of his drink.

"Just drop it, Dad," Gianni said. "It's over. I'll get them back when we win the game."

At that moment, Tony slunk into the room. With his dark, curly hair and strong, wide face, he resembled Gianni and Mrs. Scaravento. But his eyes were replicas of Frank's: an aqueous gray. Twelve years old, Tony actually resembled a little cupid. Digging his toe into the carpeting, he kept glancing up at Angela and pouting.

"Now, what's wrong with you?" she said.

"I cut myself, too."

"Where?" Angela said. "Come here, let me see."

Tony reluctantly moved toward where his mother was fussing over Gianni. He revealed a sliver on his finger that looked as though it had been sustained at least a week ago, the blood long since coagulated and dried. Gianni and Angela started smiling. "When did this happen?" she asked.

"Just now," Tony whined.

Gianni and his mother exchanged a knowing glance and refrained from teasing Tony any further. "Come here, sweetie. I'll fix it," Mrs. Scaravento said, selecting a small Band-Aid from the metal box of gauzes, adhesives and antiseptics that she was using to dress Gianni's cut.

Once Tony was outfitted with his Band-Aid he began to beam. Turning to Daniel, he said, "How ya doin'?" shaking hands. "Tony Scaravento." He stalked off towards his bedroom in an athlete's walk, which Daniel knew was his way of emulating his older brother.

Once he had left the room, Mrs. Scaravento said, "Now, Tony will be a real lover boy. He's a sweet kid. Does everything I ask him. He'll make a woman happy one day."

"What about me?" Gianni said.

Mrs. Scaravento looked skeptically at her older son. "You," she said, "must be kidding me?"

Gianni gingerly touched the slim piece of gauze and strips of adhesive that were covering his wound.

"Keep your hands off it!" Angela warned him. "You'll never make a woman happy," she told Gianni after a pause. "You'll just break hearts." The room fell silent after this remark.

"Take after your father," Frank Scaravento said almost proudly. "In the old days," he qualified when Angela threw him a condemning look. He continued to nurse his drink while watching a Peter Lawford movie on the color television.

"That's nothing to be proud of," Angela said.

When she finally closed her first-aid box, Gianni motioned Daniel to follow him into the kitchen. He absent-mindedly opened the enormous refrigerator, which was overstuffed with all sorts of food: several dozen eggs, loaves of Wonder bread, large bottles of ketchup, and relishes, mustards, cellophane-wrapped packets of chicken parts, ground hamburger meat, half wheels of Jarlsberg and white cheddar cheese. Gianni stood there staring at the vast array of food. Although the choices for a snack were limitless, he took nothing to eat. Daniel thought of his family refrigerator, which was half the size of the Scaraventos' although there were the same number of people in his household. Not only that, it was normally scant with food. Irene often forgot to do the marketing herself; and when she ordered by phone, she tended to forget staples she might have remembered had she wandered through the supermarket aisles. Irene was not the sort of person who made a grocery list. She was an impulsive shopper who always came home with strange new seven-grain breads and jarred foods like hearts of palm and Jalapeno peppers, varieties of low-fat margarine or butter. Cholesterol-conscious, she weaned the family off eggs and eschewed white bread.

"I just can't figure out what I want," Gianni murmured as he shut the refrigerator door. It was as though he had been talking about more than just food.

Silent for a while, the two listened to the freon whirring through refrigerator tubes, which obviously had to work overtime to keep all the provisions chilled. "Listen, buddy," Gianni said finally. "I'm going to bed. I feel kind of weird after that fight."

"I don't blame you," Daniel said, reaching for his suede coat, which lay over a chair at the breakfast table. "Why don't you stop by my house tomorrow. I'll introduce you to *my* mother."

"That'd be nice," Gianni said. "But there's just one thing."

"What's that?" Daniel said.

Gianni glanced down the hallway to the den, where his parents were sitting. His face twitched, full of feeling. "She's going to be up all night alone," he murmured.

"Your father never stays up?"

Gianni's shoulders and forearms tensed with momentary anger. "You see him in there getting looped. In a half-hour he'll be dead to the world. He can't take the fact that she's gotten sick on him. He doesn't know what to do with himself."

Gianni took a step towards Daniel and they were standing very close to each other in the Scaraventos' kitchen. Anyone who came might find something objectionable, even unsettling, about how close the two of them were standing. Daniel reflected that in Italy two friends would often stand just a few inches from each other, just like this, talking intimately. But here in America a much greater physical distance between people was required.

"She really likes you," Gianni said with soft urgency. "Oh, you don't know. You can't believe how much she talked about you this morning. What a nice kid you are, she said. How smart she thought you were. And she says your Italian is really nice." He hung on the *s* sound. "She said you spoke the language like you really had respect for it. She said she wishes some of your manners would rub off on me. She said she wishes you'd get me to do better in school."

"So what are we leading up to?" Daniel said as if by now he didn't know.

Gianni let his hand rest on Daniel's shoulder and then squeezed him affectionately. "Stay a couple hours with her and talk. It's hard for her, you know. Stay with her awhile. I'll help *you* out," he said.

"Sure, okay," Daniel said.

"Good night, buddy," Gianni said. On his way out of the kitchen, he scooped out the contents of the cookie jar and shook his head unhappily at the meager results.

Daniel watched Gianni, cookies in hand, file down another hallway, which led to his bedroom. He wondered why Gianni had not yet invited him to see his room. Perhaps Gianni's room was a pigsty. Then again, perhaps it was spotless.

He realized he should have asked Gianni to clarify what he had meant by "I'll help you out." Was the remark geared toward the threat of the Polanno brothers? At face value their conversation seemed to read, "You do me a favor and I'll do you one." He doubted that Gianni had been keeping the offer in the back of his mind all night long, waiting to extract a promise from him to keep his mother company. Daniel knew that Gianni did not operate in this manner. His offer to help was probably tendered not long after it occurred to him.

Frank Scaravento was snoring in his armchair by the time Daniel returned to the television room. Angela peered at him. "You going to stay for a while?"

"Sure," Daniel said. "But what time is it?"

Angela glanced at a carved German clock that was mounted

in a wall niche formed by two structural beams. "It's only eleven-thirty," she said.

Daniel chuckled at this.

"I guess by now Gianni told you I stay up most every night," Angela said.

"Yeah, he did."

Mrs. Scaravento leaned towards her husband and clapped her hands. "Frank," she growled. "Frank!"

Frank Scaravento jolted awake and looked around wildly as though he hadn't a clue to where he was. "Wha, wha?" he said in a hoarse voice.

"You snore too much when you sleep like that. Besides, it's not good for your back. Go into bed."

Frank Scaravento picked himself up, fiddled with his sprayed hair and then lumbered out of the room. Once he had left the room, Mrs. Scaravento let loose an elaborate sigh.

"*Cos'è*," Daniel began in soft Italian.

Mrs. Scaravento answered. "Na. Nothing. I was just thinking how I haven't fallen asleep in my own bed at night for almost a year and a half."

Daniel inwardly winced, unable to help reflecting that his own parents no longer made love. "But not by choice," he told her.

Mrs. Scaravento fixed her odd stare on Daniel. "What makes you say that?"

Daniel fumbled. "Just that I'm sure if you were feeling better you might be sleeping in your own bed at night."

One of Angela Scaravento's eyes narrowed; the other remained open in a sort of dull scrutiny. What was it about her eyes? Daniel wondered again.

The answer came when Mrs. Scaravento grabbed the local paper and began reading. She put the column of printed matter below one eye, which she trained from left to right. The other eye, the lazy eye, she did not use at all for reading. After a while, she caught Daniel staring at her.

"What's wrong?" she said.

Daniel shrugged and glanced away. "Nothing," he said nervously. There followed an awkward silence. He bunched his lips together inside his mouth and bit them.

"Gianni didn't tell you?" Angela said. "About my eye."

Daniel shook his head. "No, he didn't tell me."

"I lost it when I was a child," Mrs. Scaravento said. "I've had a glass eye since the age of nine."

"How did that happen?"

Mrs. Scaravento smiled sardonically. "That's a little bold of you to ask, don't you think?"

"Sorry," Daniel said quickly.

Mrs. Scaravento glanced away, her expression sobered by the distant memory. "It's all right. I don't mind telling you."

"Are you sure?" Daniel asked. He suddenly worried that Gianni would disapprove of his asking such intimate questions.

Mrs. Scaravento waved him off.

Her family had gone to Italy for their yearly summer sojourn in Vicenza. Their eighteenth-century house was surrounded by hundreds of acres of wheat fields where she and her sisters would play. The very fringe of the fields was edged by a train track. They were forbidden to play anywhere near the tracks, although they were allowed to consult train schedules and watch the locomotives wind up through the misty valleys and speed past. They shared this pastime with some of the farm children who lived in the area. Except that the farm children were unruly and often threw stones at the flatcars. One afternoon they were clustered closer to the tracks than they were normally allowed. The train was steaming up the ridge towards them, jetting up a plume of charcoal smoke. To herald its passing a group of girls began singing and dancing to a folksong. Angela remembered the soft feeling of her sister's hand on one side of her, the rough calluses of a farm girl on the other side. As they reeled in a circle, she threw back her head and saw twirls of clouds that resembled dabs of whipped cream on the pale sky. Suddenly she heard shattering sounds close by and then the train lurching with a squeal of its brakes. Flakes of something cold rained on her, flakes which first felt like snow. She wondered if the engine had sprayed out coolant or perhaps even cold steam. But then needles of pain erupted in her eye and she realized that her face was covered with shards. A boy had thrown a stone that broke a train window and slivers of glass had flown back at them.

Had her family been in a city they probably would have been able to save Angela's eye, but as they were out in the provinces,

the first doctor who treated her prescribed the wrong medicine
and didn't recommend that she immediately see an eye specialist.
By the time they took Angela to a proper hospital in Venice, the
eye was terribly infected and eventually had to be removed.

As Daniel sat there, listening to Mrs. Scaravento's voice crac-
kling under the weight of her story, he remembered stories his
parents had told him about people they knew who had been mis-
diagnosed by Italian country doctors. It saddened him to think
that Mrs. Scaravento had been dealt such a massive serving of
bad luck.

"I can see why Gianni never told me," Daniel said. "About
your eye."

Mrs. Scaravento smiled wearily. "Gianni has difficulty with
a lot of this anyway. But then again, you two haven't known each
other that long."

"In fact we've only known each other a few days," Daniel said.
To him, their acquaintanceship felt as though it already had been
going on for months.

"You mean, as long as you and I have known each other?"
Mrs. Scaravento asked incredulously.

"Exactly the same amount of time."

"Have you found"—Daniel hesitated for fear of posing the
question too indelicately—"that having just one eye limits you?"

"Well, I don't drive," Angela said. "But beyond the things I
can't do like driving, I found that in a way my sight has improved.
At least in quality. Remember I told you before about having the
patience to stand for a long time in front of a painting? I guess
when I recovered from the injury and finally got over the fact that
I had lost my eye, I actually felt thankful that I had an eye left.
I grew to love visual spectacles, even though I could only see them
in two dimensions. Even as a girl I used to go into the Scrovegni
Chapel and wander among the frescos. I love Giotto." Her voice
dipped into a low, lusty rumble; and Daniel knew that she really
did love Giotto and wasn't just saying it to please or impress him,
something his mother might have done. "I guess it's because his
work has so little dimension, and yet in a way it has even more
dimension than the painters who came after, who used perspective. There's so much emotion on the‾walls of that chapel.
Like"—she paused, scrubbing her fingers through her thinning

hair, her pale face shiny with rapture—"like the expressions of
the faces of those Roman soldiers in *The Resurrection* . . . do you
remember that one?"

Daniel's sudden lack of memory bewildered him.

"Of course you do. Christ has risen and they've seen the mir-
acle and are cowering with shame? There's so much you can
perceive from their faces and yet their faces are just barely scratched
on the plaster. Their eyes are like bent lines. But so much about
them is revealed. . . . I also became more aware of colors. Wait
until spring and you'll see my garden. God's grace." She invoked
the potential blessing of the beyond by glancing quickly up at the
low ceiling.

Daniel fell into reverent silence. He was moved by this woman's willingness to be intimate with him while hardly knowing
him. By now the glimmer of purpose had gone out of her face
and a look of weariness had replaced it. He asked if there were
nights she felt like sleeping and didn't constantly stay awake.

"Sure, I get one or two of those a week," Angela said, folding
her bony, almost skeletal hands carefully on a lap that was filled
with some embroidery she hadn't touched since Daniel had sat
down with her.

"So then where do you sleep?"

"I still sleep out here."

"But it must not be very comfortable."

Mrs. Scaravento looked at Daniel warily. "What are you getting at?"

"Why wouldn't you take that opportunity to sleep with your
husband?"

"It's not that I wouldn't take the opportunity. It's that I don't
want to disturb him, going in and out of the bedroom. He gets
agitated enough over my condition." Mrs. Scaravento explained
that after all these years she didn't need to display marital solidarity
by sleeping with her husband every night. The important thing
was that she and her husband loved and took care of each other.

Mrs. Scaravento's one healthy eye narrowed as she asked what
fascinated Daniel so about sleeping arrangements. And without
thinking it might be indiscreet he haltingly confessed to what he
knew was going on between his parents. He explained they had
been close for so many years, how to him their marriage had

always seemed more solid than the marriages of their friends. Angela began fidgeting halfway through his explanation and finally gathered up her embroidery. She was sewing a blue border on a white linen handkerchief, which presumably belonged to her husband. "It may be a stage," she finally suggested.

"I hope so," Daniel said.

"Has your mother talked to you about it?"

"No, just my father and I talked."

"You've got to hear your mother's side of the story," Angela said. "There're always two sides of a story."

"Well, I have an idea of how she feels," Daniel said, and explained about the conversation he had overheard between his mother and Marcella.

Angela thoughtfully considered Daniel's interpretation of his mother's point of view, and then looked at him disapprovingly. "That was nosey of you," she said. "And I'll warn you now. When you hear things that aren't meant for your ears they're always more upsetting than hearing them directly. You'd be much better off getting it from her firsthand."

"She hasn't approached me about it yet."

"So you bring it up."

Daniel shrugged. "I don't . . . feel ready to hear her side of the story. I'm afraid she'll tell me something I don't want to know. She's always like that. Saying things I'm not prepared for." He hesitated. "I . . . I don't want my parents to split up."

Mrs. Scaravento smiled crookedly at Daniel. Her expression was one of grim acceptance and it made Daniel feel that part of her could foresee the future as far as he and his parents were concerned. "But what happens if your mother and father no longer are happy?" she asked.

"I don't care. Let them stick it out until Alexis, my sister, goes to college. It's only four more years."

"That's a long time to 'stick it out,' " Mrs. Scaravento pointed out.

Daniel turned to her, somewhat annoyed. "Why are you saying that? Why are you trying to suggest they shouldn't stick it out?"

Mrs. Scaravento suddenly turned paler and her lips, blue in the dimness, began trembling. "Because, Daniel, I don't have much more time. I'm aware of that every single moment I'm awake. Maybe that's why I don't sleep," she posited. "If I'm to live another three years and continue to stay up at night it'll be like living six years. If I stay awake for five years it'll be like living for ten." Angela suddenly laughed. "When your time is limited you think about how you could have really enjoyed yourself. So . . ." She broke off, as if reconsidering what she had just said. "If people aren't content they shouldn't be together. They should do whatever they can to be content; they could wake up tomorrow with something wrong and then not have enough time to do anything."

And then falling silent, Mrs. Scaravento recommenced embroidering her husband's handkerchief. The room filled with the dialogue of the late movie that had replaced the one Frank Scaravento had begun watching before falling asleep. Daniel was drawn into a dance sequence circa 1950: men in black tie waltzing effortlessly with women in long gowns that skimmed the ballroom floor and revealed lovely, gleaming ankles and calves. Everything back at that time struck him to be so much simpler; the choices in life far fewer or maybe just a lack of choice to begin with. But then again he had witnessed the 1950s only through the lenses of feature films. Perhaps then things were just as difficult in their own way. He looked at Angela, whose nimble hands worked steadily with her needle and thread. He knew she had a point about personal happiness; he just wanted his parents to stay together despite their difficulties, the way she was staying with her husband.

11

Since Daniel had begun the evening in Patrick Riordan's van, he was forced to walk home from the Scaraventos'. It was a fairly direct route that skirted the well-cared-for Italian neighborhood, crossed the main artery that led out of Houghton and finally began winding up into the wealthier ridges where the Jewish people lived. Throughout the evening his attention had been disrupted by the nagging concern of Julietta's sudden withdrawal and the Polannos' threat of vengeance. But with Gianni getting into his fight and then the distraction of Angela's brooding, Daniel had less time to dwell on them.

Now it was different. It was quite cold outside though the night air had taken on the sedentary stillness characteristic of another season, a warmer season. And walking home on this roadway that was like a fissure between the houses set back deeply on their properties, houses so completely dark they seemed abandoned, Daniel felt as though he were treading between two worlds. He was leaving the comfort of Angela and her Italian memories, en route to his own house with all its ambivalence. He was leaving a conversation in which he had revealed himself to someone he hardly knew but somehow trusted—in a way more than he trusted his own parents—and was returning to those parents whom he knew so well and who made him feel so terribly constrained.

And what could really have happened to put Julietta off? Whatever it was undoubtedly had to do with why her cousins had suddenly sworn their vengeance. These two concerns had quickly linked together in a single pinwheel of anxiety. Somebody must have committed some sort of gaffe, for which Daniel was being blamed.

He grew more and more uneasy as he walked. There were several times during the journey when Daniel saw a pair of headlights approaching from far down the road. He'd watch them carefully, his concern growing more and more feverish as they grew nearer. On two occasions he felt certain that the cars slowed down when they reached him; he even thought he could detect accusing faces pressed against the windows. He saw glowing tips of cigarettes and gesturing silhouettes, but no one called out. No one bothered him.

When he reached the overpass of the New England Thruway, Daniel meshed his fingers in the cold concertina wire fence and flattened his forehead against the metal diamonds until he could feel an intaglio impressed upon his skin. He stared down on the barreling traffic, surprised at such a steady stream of cars at four o'clock in the morning. A whole segment of society coexisted at night, insomniacs like Mrs. Scaravento, marauders like the Polannos.

His house looked dim except for a spotlight that burned down into his eyes from the rooftop. Glad to be safely home, Daniel started whistling as he walked around to the back door. When he passed the bay window, he stopped. Someone was sitting in the darkness, slumped at the kitchen table. He moved closer to the window and barely distinguished Harold.

When Daniel came in the door, he flicked on the globe light above the kitchen table. His father was dressed in a rumpled suit and tie and was clearly unshaven. He blinked and squinted at the harsh intrusion.

Harold glanced at his watch. "It's after four o'clock in the morning," he said. "Where have you been all this time?"

"Come on," Daniel said. "Don't tell me you've been waiting up for me?"

Harold shook his head and straightened up in his chair. "Do me a favor. Turn off that light."

Daniel reached for the switch. The light vanished, and his vision was overwhelmed by throbbing blackness. He groped his way to the kitchen table, located a chair with his fingers and sat down. He waited until his eyes had somewhat adjusted to the darkness.

"I thought you were supposed to be in Cincinnati."

Harold shook his head. "I've been in Manhattan since Friday."

"But what have you been doing all weekend?" Daniel said.

Harold shrugged. "Staying at the Waldorf."

"The Waldorf?" Daniel exclaimed. The Waldorf-Astoria was a tourist hotel—not the sort of place where a native New Yorker like his father would stay even if he was forced to spend the night in Manhattan.

"There was lots going on to be distracted by," Harold said with the trace of a sad smile. "In fact, there was this big affair, maybe five hundred people, for a sixty-five-year-old newly wed couple. Neither had been married before. Imagine going for sixty years alone and then getting married. Shit, no matter how happy those two are they probably won't have more than fifteen or twenty years together." He paused for a moment, biting his lip. "Your mother and I have been married twenty years."

"Dad, I still don't understand why you spent the weekend in a hotel."

Harold now turned to look at Daniel straight on and Daniel was shocked. His father's face was puffy, his eyes bloodshot. The air in the room was fouled by sour-sweet vapors of alcohol. A chill gradually spread over Daniel.

"I wanted to know what it was like being alone," Harold said.

"But Dad, you and Mom have been separated before. When you first went to Italy. And the trips you made back to the States."

"But this is different," Harold said. "I wanted to see what it was like to be alone when your mother was nearby. I knew that on Friday she'd be in the city. I wanted to experiment how I'd feel spending the night close by but apart from her."

Daniel was alarmed by his father's rash behavior, something he had never before witnessed. "But why, Dad, why would you want to do that to yourself? It wasn't necessary."

Harold looked at Daniel as though his question, while being rhetorical, was also ludicrous. "Because she doesn't care for me anymore," he said. "Because all of this . . ." he made turbulent motions with his hands . . . "this life is coming to an end. And I just forced myself to take a preview of the future before it actually happened."

As Daniel reflected on the revelatory conversation he had overheard between his mother and Marcella the previous day, he could understand all too well now why his father feared the worst. It was as though his father were riding a tidal wave of depression that had been jarred into motion by a series of decisive rejections.

Harold, meanwhile, had been staring hopelessly at the kitchen table, absent-mindedly picking at the imperfect whorls in the wood. He pushed back his chair, which scraped along the linoleum with a hair-raising sound. Then he sighed. "I suppose I could continue to live with it like this. I know other people do it. But it's become too painful for me to come up against that coldness in her. I just can't subject myself to it any longer."

"Dad," Daniel agonized. "You've just got to find some way to work it through. What if she *is* just going through something right now, something that has more to do with her than with you? If you could just understand—" He broke off. His mother's conversation with Marcella had shown the problem to be far-reaching and vast. He felt himself diminishing the effect of her words for his father's—and, ultimately, he supposed, his own—benefit, trying to drum up hope that his mother would home back to a state of loving his father when he sensed she already was soaring irrevocably towards a life apart from him.

"It's impossible to overlook anything so basic when you're close to somebody," Harold said. "One day you'll see what I mean."

"But . . . think of Alexis," Daniel sputtered on despite this aching realization. "She's going to be so upset. Can't you wait at least until she goes to college?"

"Daniel, you don't seem to understand. I want to be married. I love your mother. This is her decision. I don't have any choice but to try and get on with my life."

Furious, Daniel rose from the table and began pacing through the shadows that interwove the kitchen as daylight was spun over Westchester County. Stopping for a moment, he heard tentative chirps of winter sparrows. The morning was pressing upon them. "I feel like going upstairs and waking her up."

"You can't do that, Danny. Marcella's here. Besides, your mother's not going anywhere. You'll have plenty of time to talk to her."

"Marcella," Daniel said with disgust. "I don't know why she had to come."

"No Danny, I wanted her to come. She came to try and talk to your mother."

According to his father, Marcella had received a long letter from Irene, whose contents, disturbing as they must have been, prompted her to call Harold at his office and then book a flight to New York. Harold welcomed the good intentions of her visit, even though he felt that once Irene had made up her mind, nobody—not even Marcella—could sway her.

Daniel kept from mentioning that he had overheard anything and how ineffectual Marcella really was. Instead he stood at the bay window and looked out over the wintry yard. By now his eyes had somewhat adjusted to the fleeing darkness and he could make out the denuded maple trees, the barren garden filled with iced stalks and half-rotted leaves. "Dad, do you think Mom's seeing somebody?" he asked in a trebled voice. "I mean, could she have fallen in love and be keeping it secret?"

His earnest question at first provoked a groan from his father. "That's not the case," Harold managed to say.

Daniel turned to him. "But how can you be sure?"

"Well, I can't be completely sure. But she swears up and down it isn't so."

"Maybe she's afraid of hurting you," Daniel said.

"Your mother could never spend very much energy on denying something that was true."

Daniel nodded glumly. Irene had always been too open about everything: her various dissatisfactions with the rest of the family, her own disappointments and even her own anxieties, which Daniel had felt she should at least try to conceal from them. And in a way her honesty made the situation even more difficult. Her lack of love for his father must really be definite enough for him to want to be alone. Daniel wondered whether if she had fallen in love with another man, her withdrawal perhaps would not seem so perplexing and inscrutable to his father.

And yet, he could sense that in the midst of all his pain, his father still respected his mother's decision. Harold's fear was all too visible, but there seemed to be no trace of rage or resentment in it—at least for now. There in the kitchen at that strange time between morning and night, despite his own anger, Daniel also found himself momentarily respecting his mother. He realized why the incident of his calling Italy infuriated her; his actions proved he distrusted her, proved that he was afraid of being deceived. No, if Irene had been carrying on with another man, she would never deny it.

"I've wondered something." He finally spoke aloud.

"What's that Danny?"

"When did things really start changing? I mean, did it all start coming apart once we came back from Italy?"

Harold pondered this for a moment. And then he said he was unsure whether it had been a natural progression in the course of the marriage or if it did have something to do with moving back. "Don't think I haven't considered it," he said.

"Mom's had trouble adjusting. It's been especially hard for her to meet people."

"But she's met people," Harold pointed out. "I don't think that's it, really."

His father went on to say that in Italy, the very element of foreignness, which the family had to deal with day in and day out, had been a constant challenge that perhaps kept them all in a state of exhilaration. It was so easy to focus on just being Americans in Italy. Trying to fit in, trying to belong, made their home a familiar zone where they all could relax and regroup from the constant trial of being strangers. But once they came home to America, to a familiar world, certain things suddenly began to seem hollow.

"Well, you and Mom may have felt like foreigners," Daniel said. "But I never did. I was born there."

"I could only speak for your mother and me," Harold said. "I could never speak for you. For all I know, Padua feels more familiar to you than Houghton."

"I bet," Daniel said, "that if you had any idea of this ever happening you might never have agreed to leave Italy at all."

"Are you kidding?" Harold said. "I would have signed on for twenty more years."

Daniel looked sorrowfully at his father. "Ask the company to send us back."

"Yeah sure," Harold said bitterly. "They'd send us back all right. And your mother would refuse to go."

Daniel clucked his tongue.

"Wait a minute," Harold said. "Forget your mother for a moment, Danny. What about you, would you go back?"

Daniel hesitated. He suddenly felt a welling up of feeling for Gianni and Angela Scaravento, a desire to know them better and even to become even more involved in their lives. "Sure I would," he said finally.

But Harold sensed his reluctance. "Even you," he said sadly.

Daniel thought that for now it was best to hide his new friendship with the Scaraventos; his father was feeling too vulnerable, too alone. "I guess you're right, Daddy," he said. "I guess things do change."

"Maybe you should get some sleep," Harold suggested gently. "You'll be exhausted tomorrow."

"What are you going to do?"

Harold shrugged and began peeling his fingernails. "Stay here a while and think. Marcella is sleeping in my bed."

"How silly!"

He smiled wistfully. "Your mother thought I was in Cincinnati. And Marcella's like the sister she never had. I don't mind." He looked at Daniel, his face suddenly overrun by fear. "It's going to be hard, the next few months," he whispered.

"Don't say that. Please!"

"But Danny, I can't lie to you."

Daniel looked away, shaking his head. He was bursting with divided sympathies, which just now seemed impossible to sort through. "Good night." He turned back to his father and kissed his whiskered cheek. Harold smelled of garlic and booze and musty train stations. Daniel quickly withdrew. He began walking out of the kitchen. When he reached the doorway that led into the depths of the downstairs, he turned around to see if his father was still looking at him. But Harold was turned away, hunched over, his cheek pressed to the breakfast table, and Daniel could tell that he was grieving.

12

The raspy-voiced man who answered the phone at Julietta's house grew less cordial each time Daniel called. The outcome was perpetually the same; Julietta was never there, which Daniel interpreted to mean that she was unwilling to communicate with him. This was confirmed in school early Monday morning; she absolutely refused to speak to him. Unfortunately, whenever he found her—between classes or at lunchtime—she was always reinforced by Brenda or some such other girlfriend who did the talking for her: "She don't want to look at you, man, so go fuck a duck." Daniel protested that a misunderstanding had obviously occurred and that he should be given a chance to find out what had caused Julietta's withdrawal. But Julietta cast her eyes down, clamping her hands over her ears and shook her head.

"No discussion, asshole," Brenda said, happy to be the spokeswoman for Julietta's scorn. And yet, whenever Daniel looked carefully at Julietta's face, he felt he spied the reverberations of conflict rather than actual anger. It was as though she was casting him off unwillingly. He would get a little thrill of hope, thinking that perhaps in some way he could get through to her. But then it began to dawn on him that this might be just the sort of thing that happened when you made love to someone you really didn't know. It was as though during sex your intimate needs grappled and once they were done grappling, a feeling of awkwardness was brought on, or regret or even repulsion.

By the middle of that week it grew obvious that Julietta had set her romantic sights on the middle linebacker of the football team, a horse-faced Italian boy whom Gianni Scaravento described as dim-witted. Whenever Daniel saw them walking, arms linked, through the hallways, he felt detonations of jealousy. He brooded that he had suddenly become unattractive to Julietta, felt scrawny and unsexy in comparison to the football player. He was seized by fits of depression and, strangely, elation. Normally he would have taken his troubles to Patrick Riordan. But ever since that night at the Oaks, Patrick had been avoiding Daniel and had begun spending time with some of the computer geeks whom he had previously ridiculed. Once, in fact, when Daniel approached Patrick at his book locker and tentatively asked for some advice, Patrick got flustered, muttering that he had to get to a class and didn't have time. "Ask Gianni," Patrick said mockingly. "He's Don Juan."

"I want to talk to *you* about it," Daniel said.

Patrick took out a paperback of French grammar and put it on top of a calculus textbook that he held under his arm. Then he looked at Daniel. "I really can't advise you, Danny. I've never been in your situation."

"What does that mean?"

Patrick slammed his locker. "It means that I've never been dumped by a girl before."

Daniel watched his friend hurry away to his French class. "Eat shit, Patrick," he said under his breath.

During that time when Daniel would go home in the afternoons and listen to the radio in his room, he found that he was unable to listen to popular or rock music. Most of the song lyrics had to do with the problems of love, their melodies purposely tugging on the frets of emotion. He would lament his few coffee shop dates with Julietta and the wild stoned-out drives. Classical music, however, left him with a much clearer picture of the future, and as the days went by he slowly grew inured to Julietta's sudden inexplicable change of heart.

Besides, he had his other problem to contend with.

As the next few weeks passed, on several occasions, he was

approached by friends of Vito, Mario and Mickey and reminded in toothy snarls coated with spittle that he was on the Polannos' hit list. These nameless friends kept saying that time was running out and that he'd soon be victimized—but for exactly what they would never say. Although Gianni had already assured Daniel that there was probably no connection between the Polannos' threat and Julietta's loss of interest, it did seem that one had something to do with the other. Gianni sent word to the Polannos through their intermediaries that he was Daniel's friend and that he would stand up for him if it came down to a fight. But the Polannos weren't completely intimidated; they probably felt they could take Gianni Scaravento, three against one. However, they must have realized that starting a fight with the star quarterback would create a lot of heat in the local underworld, especially among such people as the bookies who took bets for the high school game and perhaps even with the stragglers of Mafia families in New York City who had moved to the suburbs and who rooted faithfully for the home team. The Polanno brothers had certain tacit understandings with these people.

When Daniel and Gianni left school together, the Polanno brothers would often be leaning against their perpetually shiny Trans Am in the high school parking lot. No eye contact was made. Gianni gave Daniel a lift home from school and would then spend the rest of the afternoon in football practice. Sometimes before going off to play football, Gianni left Daniel with Angela, who brewed pots of coffee, spread doilies on the kitchen table and set out a plate of hard Quarismali bars and wedges of homemade carrot cake. She would always be wearing her pink quilted bathrobe that every so often showed pale flashes of her legs that were riddled with blue varicose veins. The two of them would whittle away the rest of the afternoon, speaking in Italian, and eventually established a regular pattern of meeting twice a week. Gianni would drive Daniel home when he came back from his football practice. It all seemed very comfortable.

For several visits Daniel and Angela pored over seed catalogs from Frank's nursery, discussing which vegetables and flowers Angela should plant in the spring. She drew a rough sketch of her garden area, plotting rectangles with marigolds, Transvaal daisies, delphiniums and plum tomatoes. She and Daniel haggled

over the color of an azalea bed (she wanted salmon; he was a purist
and preferred white). For years Angela had been nurturing Albertine roses. Daniel found this perplexing. He knew the Albertine rose from Europe, knew that although it was full-bodied and
had an intoxicating fragrance, it would bloom only once in a
warmer season.

"But the fact that it *only* blooms once is what makes it special,"
she explained to him. "It only gets that one chance. And when
you look at it you know that it won't flower again until next year.
That way it seems all the more precious. Besides," she said. "I
don't need to look at roses out my window all summer long."

"I'll help you with the garden when it gets warmer," Daniel
promised.

· Angela turned to him with a wry smile. "You'll have to. I can
only supervise. Otherwise I'll have to hire a gardener. Last summer was the first summer I wasn't able to garden myself," she
added. "And the guy I ended up using wasn't worth what he
charged."

When Mrs. Scaravento wasn't looking, Daniel would open up
the mammoth refrigerator and stare at all the wonderful staples,
fresh and dewy from daily grocery deliveries, and would feel
momentarily content. To him, the well-stocked refrigerator was
a telltale sign of how tightly knit the Scaraventos were as a family
and how they had grown even closer as a result of Angela's illness.
Indeed, as her illness progressed their refrigerator seemed to get
more and more crammed with food. Assuming that cooking wea-
ried Angela, neighbors arrived with lasagna, enormous pots of
spaghetti Bolognese, cauliflower with cheese, canolis and lemon
custard pies.

It seemed to Daniel, that despite their adversity, Frank and
Angela were in command of their household. This was in sharp
contrast to the feeling of disarray that had suffused his own home,
where Irene and Harold had fallen into a near-silent coexistence.
Harold continued to plead weekend business trips, which he actually did take in order, he explained to Daniel, to keep himself
distracted from the strife. Irene enrolled in an intensive Italian
class at the New School in New York and Daniel and Alexis were
often left to fend for themselves for days on end. And in the midst
of these mutations, Daniel noticed that the contents of the Fells'

refrigerator grew scantier and scantier. He reflected that under the strain of adversity, the Scaraventos fortified themselves with food and with the comfort of friends. But the Fells, already isolated from the suburban world, grew weaker and more anemic. No one in the ridges would think to bring them lasagna. Then again, no one in the ridges made lasagna.

Late one afternoon when Daniel was visiting Mrs. Scaravento, Gianni didn't arrive home from football practice at the usual time. He would punctually return at four-thirty, tired and ravenous, and dig into an early dinner of whole chickens or meat-filled ravioli or leg of lamb his mother had prepared for him. Eating at that time of day was as vital to Gianni's physical constitution as gas is to an automobile. Naturally, by the time five o'clock rolled around, Angela began fretting. Then the phone rang. Of late she had been having difficulty walking and shuffled her way to the phone, her bedroom slippers scuffing along the carpeting. Daniel always got nervous whenever the phone rang. Sometimes it would ring six or seven times before Angela could answer, and often the calling party gave up before she grabbed the receiver. Once Daniel had offered to answer for her, but she stubbornly shook her head. Perhaps by relying on his alacrity Angela would then be admitting to herself a certain incapacity. That day, however, she managed to pick up after five rings. Upon hearing the other party, she nodded her head at Daniel, indicating that it was Gianni.

"What happened?" she demanded. There was a pause and Daniel heard traces of Gianni's excitable baritone voice filtering out of the earpiece. "Ah, that stupid car," Angela scoffed. "I don't know why your father agreed to buy it for you. It's so unreliable. I don't see why you couldn't have gotten a Buick, something normal. All right. All right. You must be hungry. Don't faint now. It's warming in the oven. Yes, he's about to leave. I'll tell him."

Angela put down the phone. "The car won't start. Gianni's in the high school parking lot, waiting for a tow. You'll have to walk home unless you want to wait for Frank."

Daniel politely declined Angela's offer. He gathered together his school books, put on his ski parka, kissed her cold, dry cheek and headed out the door. To shorten the trip home, he cut through backyards. He was in the midst of crossing a street when a car bore down on him, careering madly all over the road, its headlights flashing. Daniel immediately recognized the black Trans Am screeching to a halt. Suddenly, from the opposite direction, streaked a red Corvette that swerved and skidded to a stop. Both cars were now boxing Daniel in. In the Corvette he recognized the hood who had told Gianni Scaravento to fuck off that night a few weeks ago when they were leaving the Oaks. The Corvette began inching toward Daniel, the hood jeering, "Polannos gonna get your ass now." With a thumb and forefinger, the hood flicked out a glowing cigarette butt. Daniel ducked. The cigarette butt bounced off the shoulder of his ski parka. Clusters of cinders caught the wind, a few of them stinging his cheek. Daniel swatted them away. Then the Corvette began backing up, its engine revving. It made a U-turn and thundered away.

The driver's door of the Trans Am opened. Tall, wiry Vito Polanno got out and began walking casually toward Daniel. Daniel was about to make a dash for it when Vito said, "Don't bother trying to run, Fell. It'll just be later than sooner." For the moment amazingly calm—he supposed part of him was relieved that the waiting was finally over—Daniel peered carefully at the narrow face and small, flinty eyes, which had large, shaded hollows beneath them. Vito appeared droopy and tired. Vito, in turn, was looking at Daniel as though surprised by something in his appearance. Suddenly, his hand shot out. Daniel flinched slightly, but then realized that an introduction was in the process of being made.

"Vito Polanno."

Shit, this must be his idea of a classy mugging, Daniel thought. "Hello, Vito," he said with as much sincerity as he could muster. Vito flicked his head in the direction of the Trans Am. "Like you to take a ride with us."

Daniel stiffened. "Look, you've got this all wrong."

Vito patiently shook his head. "No, you got it all wrong."

"I didn't do anything to Julietta. There has to be some kind of mistake. But nobody will listen to me; she won't—"

"Julietta?" Vito interrupted. "I could give a shit about Julietta."

Daniel was dumbfounded. His mouth gaped as he whimpered, "You don't?"

"If I wasted my time running down every guy who dicked Julietta I'd be busy for the next fifteen years. Now just get in the car."

"Well then, you must have made a mistake. You see I haven't done anything at all."

Vito smiled like a rodent. "How about being born a Jew?"

Daniel lost his composure. "Why don't you guys just get it over with? Beat me up or whatever you have to do. But don't bring my religion into it, for Christ's sake!"

"Fuck, man, you're pretty damn feisty. I was just kidding. Why don't you be quiet for a while and take a ride."

Daniel looked Vito up and down. "You know, Gianni Scaravento is a friend of mine."

"So, the Pope blesses my mother every Easter. What difference does that make?"

"Because if you guys do anything to me—"

"Who said we're doing anything to you, Fell. I just asked you to take a ride with us and you're acting like a priss pot."

Daniel was about to tell Vito rumor had it that people had been victimized in the Polannos' car and that he would rather do almost anything in the world than take a ride in their Trans Am, but he figured it would only blacken the situation. "All right," he said. "I'll get in the car."

"That's a good little Jew boy."

"Don't call me that!" The next thing Daniel knew he had taken a swing at Vito.

Sleeves of air rushed past him. Something shot out and receded, causing a buzzing in his nose. The street was yanked out from under Daniel like a carpet, the sky whirled over his head, and he heard the whomping sound of his head hitting the pavement. There was a splitting sensation at his temple, a salty film in his mouth. He looked up and saw a blurry image of towering Vito Polanno. "Ah shit," Vito was saying, his voice distant and tinny-sounding. "What did you make me do that for? I didn't want to hit you, for Christ's sake. God dammit, you're a wild one." He turned and stalked back to the Trans Am. Daniel heard him say, "Mickey, give me that box of Kleenex, will you." A moment later, Vito returned and threw something on the street. "You got blood all over your face," he told Daniel. "You better clean yourself up. I mean I try to talk to you sensible and you go ape shit."

"What do you mean sensible?" Daniel found his words through a muddle. "You called me a Jew boy."

"So, I called you a Jew boy. I could've called you a lot worse. I'm an Italian boy. What's the big deal?"

"It was the way you said it."

"All right. I'm sorry. I'll be careful how I talk to you. I'm sorry about the punch, too."

Daniel checked to see if all his teeth were still intact, which they were. His nose hurt a lot, but it wasn't numb or anything, which he knew was the telltale sign of fracture. His mouth was loaded with bloodied saliva that he spit out into a wad of tissue. "I guess I'm okay," he said.

Vito strode back to the Trans Am and leaned against it, waiting. After brushing himself off and standing up, Daniel got a gush of dizziness and for a moment had to clutch his head in his hands and take deep breaths. But finally everything cleared and he was able to walk over to where Vito was standing. At that precise moment, a line of cars began filtering through the ridges: commuters returning home from the train station. Tired eyes curiously sized up the parked car and the two teenagers standing outside it. To any bystander, however, nothing was visibly amiss.

The two brothers who waited in the car wore brown leather jackets with shiny pocket zippers and tight jeans—identical to what Vito wore. Their hair was plastered down with shiny gel and looked angry. Each languidly smoked a cigarette. Mario, the pudgier one, was sitting in the passenger side; Mickey manned the back. Mickey automatically scooted over and Daniel got in next to him. Besides reeking of cigarette smoke, the car was redolent of cheap men's cologne that reminded Daniel of the cloying disinfectant used in Greyhound bus terminals.

"How ya doin', Fell?" Mickey said, refusing to give Daniel the courtesy of regarding him.

Mario, however, turned around in the passenger seat and eyed him. Vito, meanwhile, got in the driver's side. Once the car had ignited and was charging off, Mario said, "Boy, you really don't look like a Jew. I didn't know Jews were blond."

"Cut the Jew stuff," Vito instructed his brother before Daniel could protest.

Mario glanced at his older brother with angry bewilderment. "What are you talking about, man?"

"He don't want to be dumped on."

"Did that ever stop me?" Mario said. "And what are you nuts, Vito? Since when did you start respecting Jews?" Vito slammed on the brakes. He reached over and with an index finger poked Mario in his soft stomach. "You gonna listen to me or you going to keep acting like stroonz?"

"Mario, just shut up, heh?" Mickey barked from the back seat.

Suddenly overwhelmed by his brother's will, Mario looked puzzled. "Well, fuck me," he said.

By this time Daniel had revived somewhat from the shock of being punched out. Noting that there was trouble among the ranks, he began racking his brain as to what could be the Polannos' purpose. And why was Vito suddenly acting so protectively?

They veered away from the ridges and traveled the main road that led out of town, the same road that had conveyed Gianni and Daniel to 684. Vito gunned the car, which climbed rapidly to sixty. Daniel had to admit that the Trans Am was much faster than the Triumph. Suddenly, it occurred to him that he was riding in the same car with the people who supposedly butchered the animals. He thought of the pairs of throttled doves and broke out into a sweat.

Mario pulled down the passenger side visor, which held a vanity mirror as well as a brown filter cigarette that fell into his lap. He kept looking in the mirror until he caught Daniel's eye. "*Parla l'italiano?*" he asked with a pretty decent accent.

Daniel looked at him and shrugged as though he didn't understand.

"Fell, do me a favor," Vito said. "Don't waste our time. We know you speak Italian. For Christ's sake, Angie told our mother, okay."

"Then why did he have to ask?" Daniel said.

Mario turned around to face Daniel and continued in Italian. "Your father worked in Padova, right?"

"We got a lengthy file on you," Mickey said, guffawing. He obviously was the joker of the three. He suddenly leaned forward,

scouring the legs of his blue jeans for dirt specks. He overtly
scratched his crotch and then looked condemningly at Daniel. His
eyes were green like bits of sea glass. "By the way," he said.
"Julietta's pregnant. Did you know that?"

A pain shot across Daniel's forehead as the three brothers burst
into laughter.

"He's just bullshitting you," Vito said.

"That dumb lying cousin of ours," Mario said. "She's the one
who caused this shit to begin with. That big mouth."

Daniel wanted to ask what exactly had Julietta caused but
sensed that this question might not go over too well.

"I guess we should explain why we got you in the car with us
today," Vito said. "So your gut can rest easier." He sniffled.
"We're not getting you. I mean, let's put it this way, we didn't
plan on getting you. That's not why you're here."

"Oh no," Daniel said. "A punch in the nose . . . piece of cake."

"Heh man," Mario said. "You swung first. I saw you!"

Vito slowed down the car. He pulled over to the side of the
road and turned around in the driver's seat, shaking his narrow
head. "Heh kid," he said to Daniel in a surprisingly apologetic
tone of voice, "I really didn't mean to whack you one. I'm sorry.
Okay?"

Daniel said nothing. Vito put on the directional signal and the
car slipped back into the flow of traffic.

"There's just one thing I want to say before we tell you what
we want," Mickey spoke up. "You're going to have to tell everybody, including your friend Gianni Scaravento, that we worked
you over for dumping Julietta."

"Mickey, you're such a dumbo," Vito said. "That's not the
way to approach him."

"Why not?" Mickey asked with annoyance.

Approach him? Daniel was surprised. Up until now it had not
been clear that the Polannos wanted something specific from him
that could not be extorted with violence. Indeed, since he began
riding in the Trans Am, Daniel had formed all sorts of imaginary
hypotheses as to what the Polannos were up to. These hypotheses
ranged anywhere from being forced to help them commit some
outrageous crime like setting fire to the Jewish Community Center
in White Plains to passing them the answers to an important
history exam.

Meanwhile, disgusted with his brother, Vito floored the car, which took off in a squeal of rubber. They were suddenly doing seventy in a forty-mile-per-hour zone. Daniel pressed his head against the back seat, hoping they wouldn't have an accident and praying that a police car would trail them. The Trans Am eventually slowed down to fifty, an indication that Vito's temper had cooled somewhat. "I'm gonna drop you guys home and talk to him myself," he warned his brothers.

"No way," Mario said. "We're in this together."

"Then let me handle it . . . Mickey." Vito caught his brother's eye in the rearview mirror.

"Aw right. Aw right," Mickey said.

By now Vito had driven far outside Houghton, even past the exit that led to 684. They were nearly to White Plains. He began, "When you were banging Julietta—"

"I wasn't banging Julietta," Daniel interrupted him.

" 'Scuse me," Vito said politely. "When you went out with Julietta, you must've said something to her in Italian."

"I may have."

"Well, she said something to our mother about this kid who speaks Italian. Then our mother happens to mention it to Angie when she goes to visit Angie and Angie says it's you and that she knows you and that you're a great kid and all that."

Mrs. Polanno had asked her sons about Daniel several times. She seemed curious to meet him herself. According to Vito, she spoke Italian better than Mrs. Scaravento. Native born, Maria Polanno had even done some translations when she was first married to their father.

"Where's your father now?" Daniel said.

There was a silence, during which the brothers shifted in their seats. "He got killed," Mario said uncomfortably. "Long time ago. We were just little kids."

"He was at a train station when an express train came by," Mickey said. "Some guys near him got into a fight and knocked into him and he got pushed onto the tracks."

"Killed instantly," Vito appended.

"That's too bad," Daniel said. "I'm sorry to hear that," while thinking, 'Never had a father to keep them in line.' He was almost feeling sympathetic. It amazed him that these Polanno brothers were actually real people; all along Daniel had only considered them under the classification of evil entities. It was nearly inconceivable to him that they could experience such things as grief and even torment.

"Get to the point, Vite," Mario said.

Daniel expected Vito to blast Mario for his impudence, but instead Vito nodded silently, as though Mario had recognized that it was difficult for him to arrive at the point. "The reason why we wanted to talk to you has to do with the animals," he said quietly.

A flush flared into Daniel's cheeks and his breath grew shallow. He began to see silvery specks before his eyes and was unable to blink them away. Then he grew aware of a nauseous feeling twirling around in his stomach. For a moment he could smell animal decomposition, remembering an occasion in Italy when he watched a hunter skinning a dead raccoon and had ended up vomiting from the stench. "I think I'm going to be sick."

"Crank down the window," Mickey cried. "I don't want it all over me."

The windows in the Trans Am were electric and needed to be operated from the front seat. Mario hit his control lever. Sheets of cold air forced their way in and soon revived Daniel from his queasiness. His hair blew wildly all over the place; the Polannos' slicked-down locks were hardly ruffled by the turbulence.

"Can I go on with this?" Vito asked, once the window was rolled up.

"Okay," Daniel said weakly.

"Look," Vito said. "We didn't do it. That's the whole problem. And the police know it. That's why they haven't arrested us."

Daniel remembered Gianni's opinion that the police didn't arrest the Polannos for fear that any indictment would give the Italian-Americans in Houghton a bad reputation in New York State.

"You see, we're not worried about the police," Mickey said.

"We're worried about our mother," said Mario.

In the past few months since the crime had been committed, Mary Polanno had been getting phone calls from her town friends confirming the rumor that her sons had slaughtered the animals. And since the very first phone call came in, the issue had flowered into an obsession with her. She ran to the priest and asked for guidance and the priest told her to tell her sons to confess. But when she confronted the brothers and they denied the accusations, she threw a tantrum. She took to bed and refused to eat for several days until Vito had to practically force feed her lima bean soup. Once an amply built woman, she quickly shed twenty pounds and now was as gaunt as a scrawny chicken.

"She prays all the time now and cries over it," Vito said sadly.

"She keeps making one novena after the next," Mario added.

"We tried to explain to her that it was a rumor, that it wasn't us," Vito said. Then his face congealed around a different thought. "Have you ever heard of the Barzinnis?" he asked Daniel impulsively.

"Can't say I have."

"Well, the Barzinnis are these brothers from White Plains. Who decided they were our rivals. We think they did the animals and then started a rumor to cause trouble and make it look like it was us."

Daniel meanwhile had been eyeing the rearview mirror, hoping to catch Vito's backward glance. He wanted to peer into Vito's eyes to see if he could detect the cold glint of a lie. But Vito refused to look his way, which only made Daniel all the more suspicious of the Polannos' story.

"But you're not even sure it was the Barzinnis," Daniel finally said.

"Nope, but we got a good idea," Mickey said.

"But why are you telling me all this?"

"I'm getting to it," Vito said.

"Wait a minute," Daniel broke in. "Before you get to it, why should I believe what you're telling me? I don't even know you. For all I know you could be—"

"Ahhgh!" Daniel cried out as Mickey jabbed a fist into his side. "We didn't fucking do it, kid, all right!"

"Get your hands off him or I drop you home!" Vito snapped.

Mickey protested. "Look, I'm tired of being nice to this bozo. He's too much of a smart ass."

"Get off him!"

Mickey lurched away from Daniel. The car had just reached the on ramp to the Cross Westchester Expressway. For lack of anywhere else to go, Vito took the exit and soon they were driving back toward Houghton. It seemed as though they were going at least eighty miles per hour. His heart still racing frantically from Mickey's ambush, Daniel tried to locate the speedometer, but Vito's tall, bony shoulders blocked his view of the instrument panel. The silence in the car was seething. "Shit," Mickey finally broke the mood, rolling down the window again. He tried to spit outside, but the air rushing in slapped most of his gob against the glass.

"That does it, you pig!" Vito cried when he noticed the mess. "I'm taking you home."

"No," Mickey protested, plaintively like a child.

"You're out of this now," Vito snarled.

"I don't want to go home. Then pull over and drop me off."

Vito slammed on the brakes and swerved the car over to the macadam shoulder of the concrete highway. He jumped out of the car and yanked the front seat forward, waiting for Mickey to climb out.

"Heh, I'm sorry," Mickey said in a meek voice.

"Get out!" Vito ordered.

"Please, I promise to keep my mouth shut."

Vito reached in and hauled Mickey out of the car. "Hitch home," he said. "But before you do, clean up your pig spit." He pointed to the splat on the window. "Hey Fell, give me that box of Kleenex."

Tears welled in Mickey's eyes as he dug out a handful of Kleenex and halfheartedly wiped off the window. He handed the box of tissues back to Vito, set his handsome jaw and started walking away. Vito waited until Mickey had traveled a hundred yards down the highway shoulder before starting up the car and following him. He drove up to within a few feet of his brother and then honked. Mickey whirled around. With a jerk of his head, Vito indicated for him to get back into the car. Without a word, Mickey climbed in the back seat and sat there, subdued and speechless for the rest of the ride.

Vito continued to voice his concern for their mother's loss of appetite and how she had suddenly grown susceptible to migraines and flus. She already had high blood pressure and was taking medication for her condition. He happened to answer the phone one day when her doctor called and was informed that his mother was in danger of bringing on a stroke.

"And then we came up with you," Vito said, turning around to peer at Daniel, even though he was doing eighty-five on the Cross Westchester Expressway. "I realized that there was a small chance you might be able to help us." He turned around and once again began driving into a long, sustained pause.

"Just go on, tell me what you want from me," Daniel prompted him. He couldn't quite believe that the Polanno brothers' lives would convolute in such a way to involve him.

Vito gripped the steering wheel tightly. "See, we know she wants to meet you. And that if we introduce you to her she'll like you. You two will speak Italian and after an hour you'll be as good friends with her as you are with Gianni's mother. We already tried to get our friends who know where we were that night to tell her we didn't do it, but she don't believe them. She thinks they're lying for us. But you, you'd be different. If you told her you were with us that night and that we were all somewhere else, she might believe you cause you're a Jewish boy from the other side of the tracks and can speak to her in her own language. She wouldn't think you were trying to help us out."

"But why *should* I help you out?"

Mickey flinched with the urge to say something but then quieted himself. "That's right, stay quiet, asshole," Vito told him.

"Cause we could make you a deal," he continued. "I mean like if she believes what you tell her and everything."

"A deal?" Daniel said. "What kind of deal could you make me?"

"We could protect you?" Mario offered.

"I don't need protection. Look, this is crazy," Daniel said. "I mean I could understand helping if we were all good friends but I don't even know you guys."

"Well then, you'll just have to get your ass kicked in," Mario said.

"Hey." With his thumb and middle finger Vito flicked Mario's temple. Mario took his punishment without flinching. "My brothers are a little dumb," Vito explained to Daniel and then turned to Mario. "If we beat him up where is that going to leave us?"

Vito now caught Daniel's eye on the rearview mirror. "See, you and me can obviously talk. I think we should take this further. Explore the possibilities, you know what I'm saying. I think we should have coffee or something tomorrow or the next day when these jack-offs aren't around. You see, Danny"—this was the first time Vito didn't call Daniel by his surname—"our ma, Maria, she's so sick over this whole thing. We gotta find some way to snap her out of it."

Newly aware of the power of his position, Daniel angrily retorted, "Well then, you shouldn't have had your friends tell me all these weeks that you were after me. You had me climbing the God-damned walls of my bedroom!"

"What could we do? We never had a choice," Vito said. "We can't have anyone know about this. We had to have *them* all think we were after you. So we go through the motions."

Daniel shrugged and fell silent, still dissatisfied. The Trans Am hugged the exit off the Cross Westchester Expressway that led to Houghton. They drove for a while in silence. Suddenly Daniel remembered Julietta's rejection and wondered if it were at all connected to the present circumstance. He asked Vito as much.

Vito nodded his head, as though he half-expected, half-dreaded that Daniel would ask such a question. "I'll tell you, Danny. Julietta is the one who caused this because she told our mother first."

"But your mother would have found out anyway."

"Maybe. But as soon as she heard it from Julietta, Maria started calling people to find out more. Only when it got around that she was asking for info did people start calling her.

"So Julietta's been on *our* shit list. When we decided we needed you to help us I realized that you going out with Julietta might make our ma suspicious and think because of Julietta you were on our side. We decided to tell her to keep away from you. Believe me, man, Julietta really likes you. And she's doing it against her will."

"But that's not fair to me!" Daniel protested.

"Lookit," Vito said. "We talked. So now you know what's happening. If you want to keep seeing her, wait a while so Maria doesn't find out right away."

"That's no longer possible. Julietta is already seeing someone else."

"What, that geek?" Mario said. "That meat head?"

"Maybe to you he's a meat head," Daniel said bitterly.

"She'd dump him for you," Vito said.

"What do you know?" Daniel said.

Vito shrugged. "Ask her."

But in the silence that followed Daniel realized that even if he were able to start seeing Julietta again, there would be a taint on their relationship. He was surprised at his sudden ambivalence. But if there were hope for the future there was also further risk that things might not work out, a possibility for more disappointment.

"So where are we dropping the kid off?" Mario asked.

"At his house," Vito said.

It was nearly six-thirty when the Trans Am cruised down Daniel's street. He didn't want the Polannos to know his exact address right away—not that it would be difficult for them to find out—and asked to be dropped five houses down. As Daniel was climbing out, Vito said, "You got access to a car, don't you?"

"That depends."

"Well, how about on the weekend?"

"More than likely. My father has been going away so I might be able to use his car. But why?"

"There's this diner up in Bedford. Nobody from around here goes to it."

"You mean the one near the Exxon station?" Daniel asked.

Vito looked crestfallen. "You know that place?"

Daniel explained he had recently been there with Gianni Scaravento.

With a little less conviction now, Vito asked if he could meet him at the diner at 12 P.M. on Saturday and Daniel said he would try. In school on Friday, Vito went on, Daniel would be approached by the driver of the red Corvette, who, totally ignorant of the real situation, would expect a yes or no answer that he would then pass on to Vito. Once the rendezvous had been semi-settled in this fashion, Daniel climbed out of the car and waited until the Polannos drove away. He shuddered, as though he had just shed a damp article of clothing. He watched the red taillights of the Trans Am taking distance until they resembled embers fizzling out into the welling of the night.

13

Daniel arrived home to a dark kitchen. There were no smells of dinner cooking, no foil-wrapped steaks or chicken breasts or fish fillets thawing on the counter. The house was poised in silence. Irene obviously was planning to order in Chinese from the takeout place next to the Shopwell.

For a while, Daniel stood among the pleats of shadows, collecting his thoughts. The movable butcher block had been rolled out to the middle of the linoleum floor. The butcher block always reminded him of an execution site. On a whim, he placed his head and neck on the cold wood that was carved up with knife blade crosshatches and stained a slightly darker color from meat blood. He shut his eyes and tried conjuring up an anxiety of death, such that plagued martyrs of the middle ages the moment before they took the axe. What must it be like to get severed from life at the very place where it made its most lively impression? Is the head able to convey a sense of itself tumbling without body to the ground; is there a last lingering glimpse of the sky or the executioner's face or the scaffold fizzling into nothing?

Daniel shuddered away his peculiar thoughts and went to open the refrigerator. He sighed. There was a new carton of eggs, fresh lettuce and tomatoes in the crisper, a shriveled salami, a package of lemon pound cake. He closed the refrigerator, left the kitchen and roamed through the downstairs to the bottom of the staircase.

He called for his mother and sister. No one answered. He quietly made his way up to the second floor. He called again. Still no response. He went first to Alexis's room, which was shut. Knocking briskly, he announced himself. After a moment's hesitation, Alexis snapped back, "Leave me alone!"

"What's wrong?" he asked. "What did I do?"

"Just bug off."

Daniel placed his ear against the door. He heard the creaking of a rocking chair as well as the soft tinkling of a music box Harold had bought for Alexis in Vienna which played Schumann's *Kinderszenen* on a tiny brass keyboard with a metal barrow of strategically placed spurs. Whenever Alexis brooded she would sit in her antique maple rocking chair, lulling herself rhythmically to and fro like a metronome set upon largo. The rocking chair was the only piece of furniture that had survived when her nursery was dismantled. He imagined her rocking there, clutching her velveteen trinket box, fingers worrying through tangles of necklaces and rings. She'd twirl the pearls on her antique choker and dangle her amethyst pendant from its chain and polish her sterling Victorian hair clips. She had collected jewelry from all over Europe but rarely wore it; she claimed to be saving it for some future occasion.

Daniel continued to his parents' room and knocked. "Come in," said Irene after a moment.

Irene was in a dressing gown and under the covers. Her hair was gathered up messily on top of her head and her daily makeup had already been erased. Daniel loved the way his mother looked without makeup. She was inclined to smudge kohl on her eyelids, which tended to make her look tired and manic. Ironically, Daniel's memories of Irene's excitable states always seemed to occur when she was heavily made up. Her twitching eyebrows would be accentuated by the already exaggerated marking of her pencil; her rouged cheeks flushed to a greater degree, her painted lips more convoluted. Her face minus the smoothing of base powder showed an early middle-aged roughness along its angled planes.

Daniel murmured, "What's going on? With Alexis. And why are you in bed? Are you sick?"

Irene slowly shook her head. "No, I'm not sick. Sit down with me here." She pointed to a place next to her on the bed.

Daniel's instinct told him to remain where he was. "No, that's okay, I'll stand," he said, crossing his arms over his chest. He noticed the Uris novel *Exodus* lying on the marble-top night table, his mother's place marked with a nail file. His heart began to toll faster and faster inside his chest.

Irene's face puckered in disappointment. "Come sit near me, Danny."

"Just tell me what's wrong," he insisted.

"It's not easy," she said with a grimace.

Her reticence now confirmed his fears. "I think I already know what's wrong," Daniel said, turning to leave the room.

"Stop right there!" Irene ordered. "Don't walk out when I ask you to be here."

Stiffening, Daniel whirled to face his mother. "Okay," he said, his voice shaking. "But I don't know if I can . . . hear it." With a gasp he forced his breath up into his face, hoping it would dam his feelings. In the meantime, he kept getting strobelike memory flashes of the Polannos, sitting in their car, and Mickey's gob on the windshield.

Irene said, "But if you'd sit next to me, it'll be easier for me to explain."

Daniel held his ground. "Why should it be any easier on you than it is on anybody else?"

"Boy!" Irene jerked up her knees and wrapped her arms around them. "It really sounds like you've been talking to your father."

"I'm sure he's told you we've talked."

"Yes, but he didn't detail any of the conversations."

"Oh, bullshit," Daniel said.

Irene shut her eyes and tilted her head back and rubbed her temples with her hands, seeking inward composure. She opened her eyes again and peered blankly at Daniel. "Okay, since you're being so resistant, maybe you should have this discussion with your father."

"There's no need for discussion. You know I know what you're going to say. That you and Dad are finished with marriage. That you're going to get divorced."

"Separated," Irene corrected.

"What's the difference?" The tears were in his eyes now and his knees were knocking. The tension in the room iced his blood; his hands still felt numb from the outdoors.

"Separation is just trial. Divorce is permanent. This would just be a trial."

A trial? But didn't she give Marcella the impression that things were irreconcilable? No matter, Daniel allowed himself to be tempted by the remote possibility that the marriage could be saved. It was as though the dimness of the bedroom was suddenly spangled by a luminary of hope. In a moment he had crossed the room and hurled himself onto his mother's bed. He gripped her shoulders; and she felt frail, as frail as Angela. And yet the decision she had made seemed to be stronger than all of them put together.

"Oh Ma," Daniel said, "don't do it. Please don't."

Irene began weeping in staccato; her sobs ebbed and cracked throughout the bedroom. His head on Irene's shoulder, Daniel glanced over at his father's chest of drawers. He noticed a cameo photograph of his parents on the beach at Forte dei Marmi. Looking tanned and wind-blown, they were perched precariously on the dark, pointed rocks of a jetty. The photograph, a recent addition to his father's sparse effects, seemed to be displayed at an ironic time.

Daniel drew back from his mother, who was now wiping her eyes and mumbling apologies for having lost her composure. "I know it's hard for you to understand," she said, blowing her nose. "I guess you shouldn't have to understand. I guess you should be thinking of yourself and how it'll be affecting you and your sister."

"Alexis already knows, doesn't she?"

"Yes, I told her earlier."

"What was her reaction?"

"Different from yours."

"How so?"

Irene shrugged and blew her nose again. "She clammed up. She said practically nothing."

"Well, what do you expect? She had no idea." Daniel said, looking away. He felt ill, a flu-like pressure in his head as he worried about his sister.

"She stormed out of the room before I finished," Irene explained wistfully.

"Maybe I should try to go and talk to her," Daniel said.

"You should probably wait. She's still a little stunned. I'm going to talk to her again tomorrow."

Daniel stood up off the bed, suddenly furious. "*You* should wait!" he said, stalking back and forth across the large bedroom. "You should wait until she goes to college before you get separated." As he stood there, his breath giving out from the strain of confrontation, he noticed objects in the room, such as his mother's shoe box and her wardrobe closet, pulsating with the urgency of her decision, all of which seemed like conspirators in the marriage's dissolution. In a half-open closet he could distinguish the bright sleeves of dresses and blazers that would soon make her look dazzling for somebody else.

"Daniel," Irene said sadly. "You're jumping way ahead of me now. There are so many things I need to explain. So much about this decision that you have to understand."

"If it's already decided," Daniel said, "then why does it have to be explained? I don't want details and explanations . . . about something like this."

Irene chuckled miserably. "But honey, it's necessary. There are reasons. Things have happened."

"But I don't want to be made any more upset by specific things."

"Okay, but don't think your father and I haven't discussed waiting . . . until Alexis was older. Unfortunately, then it would be waiting five years."

"Don't tell me anything about discussions with Dad. Because he'd wait the five years. It's you who won't wait. It's you who wants everything to change!"

"Now wait a minute," Irene said. "That's not true. Your father *doesn't* want to wait longer. He can't even wait another month. He's just as unhappy as I am."

"What do you expect, Mom? He's unhappy because you don't love him anymore."

"I *do* love him."

Daniel reeled back from the unexpected words, which now seemed like a monstrous lie concocted purely for the purpose of making it all easier for him to assimilate. "Okay, then you don't want to screw him anymore!" he snarled.

"Ssssh!" Irene exclaimed, horrified. "Alexis." This was her first reaction. Then she jumped off the bed and stood with bent knees and cocked elbows, glaring at Daniel. "Don't you refer to it like that!" she cried.

"But that's what it comes down to, Mom. You're tired of it."

"No, it doesn't come down to that," Irene objected. Her face was shining with the purpose of her resolution, which once adopted, must have certainly unburdened her. She bent forward, unruly hair cascading into her face and then through a tangle of bangs, she peered at Daniel with her lapis eyes. "It comes down to twenty years with someone and ending up in a different place than I began. It comes down to maturing. It comes down to having different needs."

"Mom, to me it all comes down to one thing. And that's sex. He still wants you but you don't want him."

"Oh, my God, listen to the child psychologist." Irene snorted. "You lose your virginity and suddenly you think you're Dr. Joyce Brothers."

This took Daniel by surprise. Perhaps it was true. Perhaps he didn't know enough about such things to judge his parents or to comprehend what can build up residually in a marriage after a long period of time. Suddenly purged by doubt, he turned meekly to his mother. He hated his lack of control over his parents' future, hated the inward swell of desperation. "But isn't there a way you can work it out? I mean, can't we all somehow wind this whole thing back?"

"What do you mean?"

Daniel took a deep breath. "Well, I know you were much happier in Italy." He paused. "Maybe Dad could get us sent back."

A semblance of panic struck Irene's face. Something embarrassed her so acutely that she had to glance away. "I *was* happier in Italy." She looked at Daniel again.

Daniel suddenly went giddy with the prospect of saving his parents' marriage, of recapturing the past in a future time frame. He clapped his hands together. "I know Dad would go back to Italy. I really think that's what we all should do. I'm sure Alexis would even agree. In fact, I'll go ask her now." He turned and began hurrying from the room.

"No!" Irene cried. "Don't talk about this to your sister. Stop for a second."

Daniel looked back at his mother, who was now sitting in a slumped position on the side of her bed. Her bathrobe was hiked up, revealing her bare, muscular legs. She had beautiful legs, much more beautiful legs than Mrs. Scaravento, who was approximately the same age as she. Daniel watched his mother's chest fluttering in and out with whatever sentiments that still needed to be revealed.

"I want to go back to Italy," she said.

"So then what's the problem?"

Irene leaned back her head, revealing chords of white muscle at her throat. She emitted a guttural sound from deep in her larynx. And then she gazed mournfully at her son. "I want to go back to Italy, Danny," she said. "But I want to go back alone."

14

"*I could give* a rat's ass about the Polannos now," Daniel said. "What difference does it make if I convince their mother they didn't do it? They say she's sick. Your mother says she's a nice lady. So I set her mind at ease. It's not as though I'm involving myself with what happened to the animals if those guys actually did kill them."

"Of course they killed them."

"We don't have proof. And I mean they're not even going to be arrested."

"You're just being easy on them 'cause you're upset. Otherwise you'd feel differently."

At first Daniel ignored Gianni's reference. "But your mother says the woman's miserable. . . ." He faltered, breaking off.

Gianni shook his curly head. "I feel bad for you, buddy." He reached over, squeezing Daniel's shoulder, and his touch felt momentarily reassuring. "I hope you can get through this."

Daniel wondered if he appeared so vulnerable as to shed doubt on his own ability to endure his parents' separation. "I think you should worry about yourself," he said defensively. "In fact, I think you're crazy to be driving me up here when you've got the biggest game of the season in three hours."

Gianni shrugged and switched lanes. "There's nothing I can

do. We went over all the plays a hundred times. I got a good sleep last night. If I just sat around I'd only get nervous."

"*You* get nervous?"

"Of course I get nervous."

"I didn't think you really cared enough about football to get nervous. That's why I always thought you were so good. Because it was just a game and you could be cool about what you were doing."

Gianni smiled and said that was the nicest compliment he had ever been paid and that Daniel was a good friend to him. There certainly was a warm feeling circulating between them on that morning drive up 684 to the diner where Daniel was due to meet Vito Polanno. It was a cold, flawless day, the superhighway was bone dry, with endless visibility on its straightaways. Way off in the distance rose humps of the Adirondacks. In comparison to that blind, dark drive they took a few weeks before, Daniel now enjoyed the fact that Gianni was speeding. As the seconds passed he was being spirited farther and farther away from Houghton, where a hole had been ripped into his life the night Irene announced that she wanted to return to Italy alone.

"Go faster," he now urged Gianni.

"Why?" Gianni asked.

"I don't know. Sometimes I like a switch in pace."

"Reckless," Gianni said.

"Yeah, I'm feeling reckless." Part of Daniel didn't even care whether or not they got in an accident.

"My mom was sick about it when I told her," Gianni said. "She says to come over and see her as much as you want to. She likes you so much now I'm getting a little envious." He smiled when he said this.

"You don't have to worry about that, Gianni," Daniel reassured him. "She dotes on you like no mother I've ever seen."

"What do you mean?" Gianni said. "I mean if my father didn't insist on it she wouldn't even go to football games and watch me play."

Daniel supposed that a dying mother was more of an ordeal than a mother rejecting a family. Death left grief and guilt and longing in its aftermath. Divorce, however, seemed to alternately promise the torment of rejection and a yearning for something lost which always left a possibility of being regained.

"I don't think her reluctance to go to the games has anything to do with you, Gianni," Daniel said. "I think it has to do with the fact that she hates the sport. All the contact and the tackling."

Gianni turned to Daniel with a skeptical look on his rough-hewn face. "Sounds like you know my own mother better than I do."

Daniel gazed out the window. They were passing a reservoir whose surface was as smooth as a membrane. He wondered when it would ice over for the winter and be good for skating, or if the depths of the water were too turbulent to freeze. "Ah jeez, I'm not suggesting I know her better than you. I just see her in a different way. I guess cause she's not my mother. Like things you'd see about my mother that I wouldn't see if you got to know her."

"But I would never get to know your mother," Gianni pointed out with a trace of bitterness.

"Why do you say that?"

"She's not interested in normal Italians. She likes the high-class kind. Like that woman you told me about. That Marcella."

"But Mom likes you. She's going to the game with me and Alexis today. And only because you're playing."

"It's just curiosity," Gianni said.

"I can never convince you of anything," Daniel said.

They drove for a while in silence. Daniel closed his eyes and lost himself in the roar of the Triumph's engine. Then Gianni asked him when his parents actually planned to separate.

"Right now my dad's looking for an apartment in the city. We'll probably have to sell the house and move after I graduate."

"How come?" Gianni asked. "Doesn't your mom want to keep living there?"

"They say they can't afford it. He's got to buy a place in the city; it's not worth renting cause rents are so high. He needs liquid cash for a down payment on a co-op. And we don't really have all that much. He's salaried, you know."

"But your family seems like they're well off."

"I thought we were, too. But apparently, according to my parents, we're not." Daniel grimaced. "Barely upper-middle class. But hanging by a thread."

Gianni laughed and changed lanes in order to pass a slow-moving Plymouth. "I wonder what we are?" he mused.

"Probably lower-upper-middle class," Daniel said. "Hanging by a garden hose."

"Shaaatup," Gianni said, taking a playful swipe at him. "Glad I don't live at your house. I wouldn't be able to take all the worry over being upper middle or lower upper. Which reminds me, how's your sister taking all this?"

Daniel shrugged. "She's very quiet. She won't discuss it with me. She just wants to be alone."

Whenever Alexis got upset or moody she became territorial and guarded her room and her possessions from the rest of the family and would spend long hours rocking back and forth in her antique chair. If she was using the bathroom—even washing her face or brushing her teeth—she would not allow Daniel to take anything out of the medicine cabinet or even grab a Kleenex until she was through. And yet, when she was feeling lighter about things, she could be sitting on the toilet and would let Daniel come into the bathroom. Unlike most girls her age, Alexis was not embarrassed about bodily processes and her budding figure and felt nonchalant about being seen without clothing.

"Women are so interesting," Gianni mused. "I'd love to have a sister."

"I don't know if it's any better than having a brother."

"Ah, come on, look at Tony. He's this little puppy dog. Follows me around. Everything I do is right. Never argues with me. Always gives in. I'd love to have a little feisty princess in the house. Somebody like . . . Debbie Lerner," he said, his face taking on a hypnotic glow.

Daniel chuckled to himself and then asked, "She why you weren't at the Oaks last night?"

Gianni nodded and turned to Daniel with a face full of rapture. "She's so beautiful, man. So fucking beautiful."

Daniel got a nasty thrill of jealousy, which began as a buzz of heat all over his body and ended up as a cold shriveling behind his ribs. "Did you make it with her or something?"

"We didn't make *it*, Danny, we made *love*."

"Excuse me. I guess I don't know the difference."

"No buddy, I don't think you do."

"That's not a very nice thing to say to me."

"Well, I'm serious about her, man. I don't want you talking about her in an unkind way."

"I wasn't demeaning her. I was just curious about her."

"Well, she's not curious about you," Gianni said. "She wants me, okay?"

"Don't worry about it. I would never ask her out." At least not while you're seeing her, thought Daniel.

Gianni shrugged. "But I see the way you charm people. I don't mean to say it's Jewish or anything, but I've seen it in other Jewish people. Something like . . ." He paused. "Something like you could get something quicker than other people because you could anticipate it. I mean you got seven angles on most people's angles. You're a manipulator."

"Fuck off," Daniel said.

Gianni burst into laughter. He pounded on the steering wheel and laughed and laughed. "I was just babbling," he said finally. "I didn't know what I was talking about. I love you, man," he said in a grave voice. "I really love ya, Danny," he said.

Vito was eating a large springy piece of angel food cake saturated in raspberry syrup. When he saw Gianni accompanying Daniel into the diner, a nauseated look leapt across his face; and Daniel could read his lips saying "shit" under his breath. However, Vito was able to recover his composure and continued to devour his dessert even after Daniel and Gianni were standing at his booth.

He finally looked up from eating and eyed Daniel venomously. "What the hell did you bring him for?"

"He brings me everywhere with him, Polanno," Gianni answered.

"What is he your boyfriend or something?"

"Sure."

Vito dropped his fork, which clattered on his plate and then he pushed away the piece of angel food cake. A waitress who happened to be passing by interpreted his gesture and swooped down on the plate to whisk it away. "I ain't done yet," Vito snarled at her.

" 'Scuse me, honey," the waitress said, simultaneously winking at Gianni.

"Scaravento, why don't you go"—Vito made a piston motion with his fist and whistled through his teeth—"with her in the

back and let me talk to the kid. This doesn't have anything to do
with you."

"I'm his interpreter," Gianni said lightly.

"He don't need an interpreter," Vito said. "Me and him communicate just fine. Right, Danny?" he asked with a sad smile.

"I just would rather Gianni sat in on this," Daniel said.

"All right, suit yourself," Vito said with annoyance. "But I'll
tell you," he warned Gianni. "I don't need a devil's advocate."

Daniel and Gianni sat down opposite Vito. Gianni flagged
down the waitress and said, "Bring us two just like our friend
here," pointing to Vito's angel food cake. "Only a little more
generous than you were with him."

The waitress laughed and said she'd try her darnedest. Vito,
meanwhile, was looking puzzled. "Heh, Scaravento," he said.
"Don't you got a game today?"

"Yeah. So."

"And you're eating this crap before you go out there?"

"Why, you're eating it?"

"Heh, come on, Scaravento. You know there's lots of grand
riding on you today. And when you should be warming up, you
are out of town eating junk food and butting in on other people's
business."

"I always eat carbohydrates before games," Gianni said. "And
I'm making this my business. So let's just get this discussion over
with."

Vito turned to Daniel. "I suppose now I have to explain everything to him?"

Daniel shook his head. "He knows already."

"Let me just interrupt for a second, Vite," Gianni said just as
the waitress arrived with two pieces of angel food cake; his piece
was twice the size of Daniel's. "Thanks, honey," Gianni told her
as he leaned forward. First his eyes narrowed and then Vito's eyes
narrowed. It was like Calabria about to take on Sicily.

"From my end of town the word is that you guys did the
animals."

"Look," Vito said. "I swore up and down on a stack of Bibles
before the priest that I didn't do it. We were out of the area that
night at another bar. With friends of ours who back us up."

"Which friends?" Gianni challenged.

Clucking his tongue, Vito angrily shook his head and looked down. His voice dropped. "Joey Capetta. Ralphie Giacomo. And Tommy Morabito."

"You mean you were out with your gang, Vito," Gianni said. "Would you spare me?"

Vito slammed his hand down on the table. "There's no more proof than that I can give."

"Then tell me how come it gets back to me and my uncle. How come it gets back to my mother?"

"Did you ever think that maybe she's influenced by my mother? The only way I can say that it gets back to you is through the Barzinnis. The Barzinnis are trying to do us in."

"The Barzinnis don't know my uncle. They don't know the bookies. Even the bookies think you guys did it. I saw the odds. They're taking bets for Christ's sake."

"You asshole," Vito said, and he and Gianni suddenly burst into laughter. Then Gianni clapped Vito on the back. Daniel was fascinated by the lightning transition between fury and mirth.

The conversation lulled while Gianni dug into his cake. Daniel began eating his, however, with more savor. Vito watched them. His face was serene.

"Look Vito—" Daniel said finally.

"You got whipped cream on your cheek," Vito told him. Daniel tried to wipe it away. Vito shook his head. "No man, the other cheek." Daniel pawed the other side of his face. "Now you got it."

Daniel continued. "I don't mind trying to help you out. I just don't want to learn at some point later on that I was helping you guys get away with something."

"I told you that won't happen. Because we're not suspects. And besides, it isn't the point," Vito whined. "I just don't want my mother to die on me!" he cried out in the restaurant. "If she croaks from worrying what difference will any of it make then?"

Gianni stopped shoveling the cake, his fork raised halfway to his mouth. He stared vacantly at Vito. It was as though he were hearing some high-pitched frequency that momentarily paralyzed his attention.

"You know what I'm trying to say, don't you, Scaravento?" Vito sounded arrogant.

Silent, Gianni continued staring at Vito and finally swallowed what was in his mouth. "I don't know," he grumbled.

Vito leaned forward. "This kid can put her mind to rest. That's all I'm asking of him."

Gianni shrugged and then fixed his eyes on his plate. "Hey, it's up to him."

"All right," Daniel said, looking to see if Gianni would object. But Gianni was now steeped in his own thoughts, seeming uninterested in what the decision would ultimately be. "I'll help you out."

"Holy God in heaven," Vito said, looking up. "Thank you."

"But then you gotta start going to church again, just like you used to," Daniel told him.

Both Vito and Gianni guffawed and then Vito called for the check. The angel food cakes were on him.

The parking area surrounding the diner was packed with gravel. Gianni and Daniel pulled out after Vito and waited behind him until there was a pause in the flow of traffic on the road that wound back to 684. When it came Vito's turn to take off, he floored the Trans Am, which sent up a barrage of pebbles that pelted the windshield of the Triumph. "Jesus Christ," Gianni remarked. "He must be happy."

The Triumph had just embarked on 684 when Daniel noticed something. "Gianni," he said. "Look at that spur."

"Where?"

"Right there on your side of the windshield. Was that there before?"

Gianni turned his head sideways and squinted at the blemish to his windshield, which was difficult to see while driving. Then his eyes widened in anger. "No, it wasn't there! Look what that stroonz did!"

"What are you talking about?"

"Vito. When he peeled out back at the diner. And the pebbles shot up . . . ah shit, that asshole is going to pay for this."

Daniel studied the spur, which made a neat gouge deep into the glass. "How do you fix something like that?" he asked.

"I don't think you can," Gianni said. "I think you have to get a new windshield!"

"Really, just because of a tiny little crack?"

Gianni once again tried looking at the windshield. "Depends on how deep it goes." He clucked his tongue. "I can't really tell right now. I'll take a better look later when we get back. That dumb, stupid greaser."

They were both silent for a moment and then Gianni heaved a deep, anxious sigh and began to drive faster. "Man, now I'm really beginning to get nervous about the game. This sugar rush doesn't help me any."

"You'll be all right," Daniel said. "It's good to be nervous." He was peering far ahead, watching the forest line curling gently to match the pathway of the pavement. Through his peripheral vision, however, he could make out the spur in the window glass, which bothered him. It was like a piece of sand embedded in the heart of a oyster.

15

That night, half-reclined in her husband's easy chair, Angela intermittently watched the opening scenes of *Casablanca* and talked with Daniel. It was her pattern to break off from their conversation, squint at the television and then gaze off into a shadowy corner of the den, as though a certain conversation or scene in the movie reminded her of a memorable unpleasantness. Then, at certain times Angela seemed visibly to brighten, her brooding countenance flickering with thoughts that momentarily buoyed her spirits. And while they were sitting there, their faces bathed in ghostly television light, Daniel asked what had stirred her. She said, "*Niente*," in Italian, which, to him, was more definitive than saying "nothing" in English. Angela's Italian tended to be oratorical and Daniel never questioned her as much about things as he did when they spoke English.

Tonight she seemed particularly dejected. Daniel knew her mood had little to do with the fact that Houghton had lost the Rye game 7 to 6 or that Gianni had taken the brunt of the loss on himself and locked himself in his bedroom for most of the night. After Daniel had driven his mother and sister home and returned to the Scaraventos', Angela told him secretly, while Gianni was in the shower and Frank was in the den knocking back a stiff Scotch, that she was glad that Houghton had lost. "Athletics come too easily to Gianni," she had said. "He thinks he's going to get a scholarship to some Ivy League school and play his way through an education. He needs to wake up a little bit."

"He may have a chance," Daniel had told her.

"Believe me, Frank and I have done some investigating. His chances aren't so wonderful. The scouts aren't that impressed with him. His grades are mediocre. And anyway I'd prefer that he get a better education in a small school than be a football jock at Harvard."

"But he could eventually turn pro," Daniel halfheartedly suggested.

Angela looked at him skeptically. "He doesn't love it enough, Danny. You know he doesn't." She went on to say that in Italy, university students managed to be as assiduous in their learning as they were in athletics. She disliked Gianni's very American attitude that proficiency at a sport would safeguard him throughout adult life, would guarantee him job offers and permanent respect.

At half time during the Rye game Angela had gone to sit in her friend Lucille's Toronado and drank coffee from a thermos. Before leaving the stands she extracted Daniel's promise not to tell Gianni that she had stopped watching. Angela threaded her way through the crowds toward the fringe of the playing field, her beaver coat rippling out behind her like the train of a primitive princess.

She now turned to him. "You've gotten quiet, Daniel."

"I was just wondering why you left the game at half time."

Angela appraised him with her good eye. "I was cold out there and aching."

"I thought part of the reason why you went and sat in the car was because you didn't want to meet my mother."

"That too," Angela said.

"But why?"

Angela smoothed her bony hands along the front panels of her bathrobe, jiggling her head and shoulders in an embarrassed shrug. "I didn't want her to see me like this," she said.

"But that's ridiculous. You look fine."

Angela turned to Daniel full front, her immobile eye casting a glassy, inorganic glare. "Don't tell me I look okay. I look like hell! You didn't see the way I used to look before I got sick." Her voice softened. "And your mother is so beautiful. She makes me feel ashamed."

Daniel reached out and smoothed out the wringing knot of Mrs. Scaravento's hands. "She's not *that* beautiful. And you have a beautiful soul. A more beautiful soul than hers," he added.

Tssking, Mrs. Scaravento fervently shook her head. "It warms me to hear you say it, but you still shouldn't talk like that about your mother. You're just angry with her."

"I'm not angry," Daniel protested.

"Daniel, you're entitled to be angry if you want to be angry."

"I can't really be angry. I guess I still hope they'll reconsider and change their minds."

"Honey, that doesn't sound very realistic," Mrs. Scaravento said gently.

Daniel bowed his head for a moment, then slowly began to explain how confusing and upsetting it was to watch his parents sitting at the breakfast table every day, passing each other the silver coffee pot, shaving slivers of butter from opposite ends of the butter stick. They'd munch their toasted bagels and talk about usual things like friends and income tax, while he and Alexis sat there, in baffled awe, stealing hopeless glances at each other. The family was supposed to be ending, but here they all were functioning as though it were to continue forever. It reminded him of a game of pretend they all used to play when they would take trains throughout Europe. Irene would portray the Duchess of Amalfi, Harold the Duke, and Daniel and Alexis the prince and princess respectively. They'd all concoct an incredibly lavish life of boring leisure, carrying the fantasy to its full extreme with fleets of cars and a dozen châteaux and mansions scattered throughout the world. And yet, as they played, Daniel would inwardly relish the fact that their real lives were ordinary.

Now Harold and Irene were playing a game that did not include their children. The rules seemed advanced and contradictory. If they could get along at breakfast, share bagels and coffee as well as the newspaper, it would seem they could certainly remain married.

"Honey," Mrs. Scaravento said. "I understand what you're saying. But I think it'll be easier for you to accept all this when your father finds a place to live."

"No," Daniel disagreed. "It'll be harder."

"Only because then you'll finally be facing it."

Daniel turned his frayed attention to the scene in *Casablanca* where a prominent Frenchman is prevented from entering Rick's. Soon after, Ilsa comes in with her Czechoslovakian husband and is seen by Sam, the piano player. "She's so luminous," Angela said of Ingrid Bergman. "It's like there's warm silver running beneath her skin. She looks like she'll be young forever."

"In this film she'll be anyway," Daniel said.

"I wish I had movies of myself as a young woman," Angela said wistfully. "Or just of the years in my life when I looked my best."

Daniel wondered if Angela referred to the years before she lost her eye. He wondered if she was aware of the disquieting effect induced by the odd mismatched setting of her eyes. His attention shifted back to the television screen. Humphrey Bogart is stalking across the room demanding why Sam is playing the strictly forbidden song "As Time Goes By." And as Sam glances toward Ingrid Bergman, his look reveals a great deal: fear of Rick, yet obedience to a lover's request, awareness that Ilsa is the only person in the world capable of undoing the damage that's been done to his boss.

Angela turned to Daniel suddenly, her face wadded up in dread. "There's something I want to tell you," she said. "I have to go into the hospital tomorrow."

"What for?"

"Some tests."

"How—"

" 'How come you're having tests?' is your next question?" Angela said. "Right?"

Daniel's mouth dropped open. "I'm sorry" was all he could think to say. "I won't ask about it."

"I'll tell you!"

"Don't worry, you don't have to tell me."

"I've started to black out," Angela said in a trilling voice that also sounded shocked. It was as though she, too, were hearing the truth about her latest complication for the very first time. "It'll be the middle of the afternoon and I'll wake up on the kitchen floor and not even know how I got there."

Angela burst into tears. Cautiously, Daniel approached the

armchair, unsure whether or not she wanted to be comforted. But when she felt his tentative grip on her shoulder Angela threw her arms around his chest and gripped him tightly, weeping even harder. Her sudden swing of mood in some way recalled his own father's futility. "It's okay," he murmured, "I understand," as he held her and patted her brittle, unbeautified hair. This close to Angela, Daniel could follow the thinning pattern of her hair, much of it fallen out as a result of her last radiation treatment. There were visible patches of white scalp. He suddenly realized that at some point, way before his parents or anyone else he knew, Angela Scaravento would cease to be and would only continue to exist in fixed memories such as photographs and anecdotes. He could smell an ailing odor that leached through the inane, flowery scent of her perfume. She smelled stale and toasty, the way his grandmother smelled in her apartment before she died one night in her sleep.

"Have you told Gianni?" he asked once Angela's weeping had abated.

She pulled herself away from him and wiped her eyes. Daniel now made the morbid discovery that her false eye also wept. The pocket of wrinkled skin below it shone with tears. This filled him with an even more intense feeling of pity.

"I haven't had the chance. I didn't think it would be good to tell him tonight. He's upset enough as it is."

"So you'll tell him tomorrow?"

She shook her head. "Frank's taking me at eight o'clock in the morning. Neither of the boys will be up. They'll find out after I'm there. I think it's easier that way."

Daniel shrugged. "Okay, if that's what you want."

"You know what?" Angela said, bitterness flavoring her voice. "I don't care if I'm doing the wrong thing by not telling them beforehand. I just don't have the strength for that kind of concern anymore. I've got to concentrate on coming back from the hospital. I just don't want anything to happen to me this time. I'm not prepared for it yet."

Daniel wondered if people could really prepare themselves for *it*. He was unable to say anything in response to Angela's remark; the only alternative was to watch the movie. He felt very strongly for Angela and wanted to do something more to help besides keeping her company, but he couldn't think of anything. He felt powerless. And as though sensing his distress, his need to do something, Angela asked him to go put on the tea kettle.

When he entered the kitchen he found Gianni rummaging through the cupboards in the darkness. "You still here, huh?" Gianni said flatly.

"You mind?"

"Course I don't mind," Gianni said in an unconvincing manner. He jumped up to reach a top shelf, yanked out a box of soda crackers and landed lightly on his feet, cradling the box in his arms. It was as though by catching the box of crackers Gianni were reversing the outcome of the pass that had spiraled just beyond the thirsty fingers of the tight end, and thus cost Houghton the Rye game. Gianni tore into a packet of crackers and stuffed three of them into his mouth. Daniel took the tea kettle off the stove, filled it with cold water and put it on a gas flame.

As soon as Gianni swallowed his first mouthful, he whispered, "Why was she crying just now?"

Daniel knew he had no right to withhold information. And yet he also knew that Angela and her husband had planned how to break the news of her impending hospital visit to Gianni and Tony, and he didn't want to get in the way of their decision.

"Oh, you know," he whispered back. "She's depressed again. I think maybe she's a little upset that you took losing the game so hard."

"Why shouldn't I take it badly?"

"I guess maybe she thinks other things are more important. But look, I don't know why I'm interpreting. Go ask yourself, why you heard her crying."

By now Daniel's eyes had somewhat adjusted to the kitchen gloom. As Gianni's features grew clearer, Daniel could detect a scowl and began to lament his last statement. "Would you like me to go home now, Gianni?" he asked softly.

"No." Gianni snarled in a low voice. "I want you to stay," his tone obviously contradicting his words. As Daniel wondered what Gianni's feelings really were, he heard the water in the tea kettle beginning to stir.

"Maybe I've been spending too much time over here," Daniel said. "Maybe it's beginning to get on your nerves."

Gianni shrugged. "If I discouraged you from coming over I'd be going against what my mother wants."

"But that doesn't matter" was all Daniel could think of to say. He certainly felt rotten.

"Let me ask you something," Gianni said. "Why are you always so eager to come over here? What is it about my family? What is it about my house, heh?"

Dread pulsed through Daniel. He didn't quite know how to explain it, but he was petrified of losing something. What was he afraid of losing? He felt Gianni growing impatient with his silence. Still, Daniel was unable to summon up a clear answer to the question. Oh, he supposed he loved that solid feeling of life at the Scaraventos', life that flourished in spite of Angela's illness. Being at the Scaraventos' fortified him for the return to his house of divided loyalties, where people were confused and where the future was completely up in the air. But it was really much more than this.

"I enjoy it here," he said. "I didn't think I was making myself a nuisance."

"Come on, Danny," Gianni said, drawing close to him the way he drew close the first night Daniel had visited the Scaraventos. "You know you're not a nuisance to anybody. I just want to understand why you always like to be here."

"Maybe because I envy your family life," Daniel said, hesitating. "Maybe because I envy you."

"What are you nuts or something?" Gianni whispered fiercely. "Here my mom is dying and nobody can deal with it and you tell me you envy my family life. You're fucking blind if you can see something here to envy. As blind as my mother's eye."

Daniel looked at Gianni in horror. It was Gianni's first mention of Angela's eye.

"Don't look so surprised," Gianni told him. "And you have nothing in me to envy either. You got it way over me. You're smart and you'll go to a good school. You'll get out of this town for good and never come back."

"But you'll do well, too. Won't you?" Daniel asked in a small voice.

Gianni put the box of crackers down on the counter and slipped his hands into the pocket of his bathrobe. He looked down at his large, hairy feet that today had run forward and backward, turned and pivoted, but had not performed well enough to win the Rye game. "Can I tell you something?" he said. "Have you ever seen some of those fat Italian guys who work for the town highway department?"

"Yeah."

"Well, let me tell you, in their day, they used to be the football team stars."

"But you don't have to end up like them," Daniel said.

"Maybe not," Gianni said. "Maybe not. It just occurred to me after the game was over today that here I am a senior in high school and just played the big game of the season and lost the big game of the season. What's next is what I'm asking. And what if today was the high point of my life?"

Locked in Gianni's dilemma, Daniel fell speechless. The kettle began to shriek and he mechanically went to the cupboard for Angela's favorite box of Darjeeling tea and some cups and saucers. He opened a utility drawer and fished out the tea strainer; Angela preferred loose tea. Gianni watched his preparations.

"But then I don't know what the hell I'm objecting to," Gianni suddenly blurted out. "After all, you're so nice to her. You're so nice to Ma."

Daniel stood there holding a tray weighed down with china and the tin of tea and the full kettle, which was still spitting out steam although it was no longer on the stove. His hands shook from the weight of what he was carrying. The clatter of crockery and stainless steel eventually drowned out their murmured conversation and carried into the den.

"What's going on, Danny?" Mrs. Scaravento called out.

Gianni quickly whispered, "Don't tell her I'm in here, okay? Good night, Danny," he said. "Good night, my friend." He quickly left the room.

Although Angela had dabbed her eyes, their brightness revealed that she had been recently weeping. Her peculiar gaze penetrated Daniel as he entered the room with the tray. As he set down the tea things, he glanced at the television: one of those disquieting scenes in which people are swarming pell-mell through the narrow streets of Casablanca.

"Was that just Gianni in the kitchen?" she asked flatly.

Daniel nodded.

"Came out of isolation enough to fill his stomach."

"Ah, give him a break," Daniel said.

Angela cast her eyes down and shrugged. Then she looked at Daniel meaningfully. "They care so about me, right? They're so concerned. But do you think one of my boys has ever brought me a cup of tea? Not once. You wait and see. I'll be on my deathbed and they'll still expect to be waited on."

Daniel giggled. Then he looked at Angela, who suddenly burst out laughing. The two of them howled until they could hear Frank Scaravento call out from the master bedroom, "Shad up, you hens!"

Daniel resented being called a hen. His abrupt silence smoldered with resentment.

Angela started pouring the tea. "Don't listen to Frank, honey," she said. "He's not very broad-minded. And anyway he's wary of you."

Daniel frowned at her. "How come?"

Angela shrugged as she put two lumps of sugar in a cup and poured her tea. She asked Daniel how he liked his: plain. After handing him a steaming cup, she stirred her own tea until the sugar cubes melted. The sound of the spoon tinkling against her china cup sent a shiver down Daniel's spine. Finally, Angela looked at him fixedly and said in a very low voice, "One night I told Frank you brought me a lot of comfort. And he didn't like hearing that. I nearly told him that I wish we had a son like you."

16

The vacant feeling of the apartment was more overwhelming than any sense of its apparent small size. It was a quiet two-bedroom place with a bank of triptych windows in the living room that beckoned in a steely light, which, Daniel knew, made it premium goods in the New York City apartment-hunting inventory. He turned to catch Alexis's reaction. She was tilting her head sideways; her hair looked freakish and discolored as though part of it had caught on fire. That, however, was due to her strange haircut. One night recently she had taken some scissors and begun hacking away indiscriminately. Afterwards she had gone down to the cellar freezer, got out foiled packets of brownies Irene had made for a United Jewish Appeal luncheon and ate them, frozen, until she got sick. In a last-ditch effort to reverse what Alexis had done to her hair, Irene took her to Vidal Sassoon in Manhattan. But the effects of her hack job were so severe, the salon could do little more then style it into this messy, burnt-looking mop.

Harold, Alexis and Daniel had been standing close together with their coats on in the middle of the living room. Alexis finally went to the window and Daniel followed her there. "Nice view of the river," she coolly remarked as he slipped his arm around her. She stiffened at first to his touch, but then collapsed warmly against him, allowing her head to fall against his neck. Daniel loved her more than both his parents, of that he was completely sure.

Harold patiently awaited their verdict. He had put off signing the lease pending his children's approval of the place where they'd be spending a certain number of their weekends. But before Daniel turned around to tell his father what he thought, he carefully surveyed the view. The river was twirling around itself like a liquid rope, the surface strongly manipulated by bottom currents. His father had stressed the East River vista as the apartment's strongest feature, which gave it a high resale value in perpetuity. Nothing would ever block this panorama; there was no land left east of them in Manhattan on which an obstruction could be built. But all Daniel could think of was the Hudson River flowing beneath the Tappan Zee Bridge on the Saturday morning earlier that autumn when he had first learned about his parents' estrangement. And he knew that he would always associate endings and changes with moving bodies of water, knew that one day maybe forty years from now he'd be standing at this very window of an apartment his father had never sold because of its resounding resale value. He'd be more appreciative, certainly, of the view of Roosevelt Island, of the bustling slip of Queens and of silver flecks of airplanes in their near motionless hovering patterns over Kennedy airport. But he would be feeling a similar pressing melancholy because by then his father would have passed away.

Alexis turned from the windows and gave her opinion first. "It's nice, Daddy. Her eyes darted over the freshly painted walls. "It just seems so small and so empty."

Harold, who was allowing his sideburns to grow a little lower these days and who had lately begun to look rather dapper in an updated wardrobe of pinstripes and custom-made shirts in pastel cottons and V-neck cashmere sweaters, who seemed to have eradicated all polyester traces from his dress (the complacent influence of the suburbs), was wounded by Alexis's candor. "But honey, it's not just this room. We've got those two nice bedrooms."

"I guess it's just so much smaller than our house in Houghton."

"But our house is three thousand square feet. I'll never find an apartment in Manhattan that big. Unless I moved into a loft."

"Why don't you look at lofts," Daniel suggested. "I like lofts." Harold took off his full-length coat with its fur collar and dropped it in a heap on the dusty parquet floor. Alexis and Daniel were befuddled by their father's needless, dramatic gesture. "Danny," he began again.

"Dad, don't be so predictable!" Daniel snapped. His father looked at him as though he was a moving flame in a fireplace. Then his face drooped with hurt. And then Daniel apologized.

"Danny," Harold began again. "But a man like me doesn't belong in a loft."

"What does that mean?" Daniel said. He looked around the empty apartment, wishing for a chair to sit in so he could at least put his elbow on his knee. Furniture certainly liberated conversations like these, provided opportunities for physical lulls in which people could sit forward or cross their legs. "Who are you that you can't live in a loft?"

Angry now, Harold blurted out, "I'm an unmarried, Jewish man who's not very imaginative."

Alexis clucked her tongue.

"I'm an unmarried, Jewish man from the suburbs who spent ten years of his life in Italy and who doesn't . . . know how to cook, for Christ's sake. You have to know how to cook if you want to live in a loft. You know how large the kitchens are in lofts and how people who live there cook all these ten-course meals and give dinner parties and are always entertaining. A loft isn't for a person who has to eat out by necessity."

"Dad, there's simple solution," Daniel said.

"What's that."

"Taking a cooking class."

"Where do I take a cooking class?"

"At the New School."

"How do you know about cooking classes at the New School?"

"Mom was going to take one," Alexis said and then giggled nervously.

Daniel approached his father. They were nearly the same height now. "Take the place, Dad." He looked around the apartment once more and sighed. It's a nice pad. I'm sure you'll make it look wonderful."

"I found this great decorator who says that I should do it in an Oriental motif."

Daniel couldn't care less about his father's choice of decor.

"It's just hard for me to like it," Alexis spoke up.

"Why?" Harold said, approaching her and stroking her mangled hair.

As Alexis struggled for appropriate words, her face crimsoned and soon tears filled her eyes. "I don't want you to move, Dad," she blurted out. "I don't think I'd like anyplace you'd move to."

"Ditto," Daniel said.

Buoyed by their regrets, Harold picked up his overcoat, gathered his children on either side of himself and ushered them towards the door. "I'll sweeten my departure with a visit to the best delicatessen in New York," he said as he opened the door. Soon they were standing in the hallway and he was fumbling at the triple locks with an unfamiliar set of keys.

Finally, he turned to face them. "Shall we go?" he asked.

"I suppose," Daniel said.

Alexis was smiling crookedly, only dimly consoled by the prospect of going to a delicatessen. Daniel, in turn, wondered why eating was supposed to make people feel better about irrevocable things that in themselves were difficult to swallow.

PART TWO

17

Mrs. Scaravento was to remain in the hospital until the middle of January. Her blackouts had been diagnosed: a small cancerous mass was pinching clusters of nerves at the base of her spine. She was dosed with high radiation and given a drug whose name was so long and complicated it was referred to by its initials. As a result of her sessions with radiations she once again lost nearly all her hair.

Then, as soon as the tumor shrunk away, she caught pleurisy and had to be given intravenous transfusions of antibiotics as well as have her lungs drained. While hospitalized, Angela tried to discourage Gianni and Tony from visiting her too often. She reasoned that these visits to her hospital bed would needlessly disturb her sons. In her opinion, it seemed, death would be easier for Gianni and Tony to accept than day-to-day suffering.

"They reclassified her," Gianni told Daniel Christmas Eve as they were driving around in the Triumph. There had been a snow storm the day before and the ground was blanketed with three inches of glittering fluff that absorbed and refracted the light of buzzing street lamps. The sleepy town of Houghton, smoothed out beneath drifts, resembled the plane of a desert.

"You mean they think she has a different disease?"

"No, her stage," Gianni said. "She was IIA before and now she's IVB. It's gotten more advanced."

"Sounds like she's gone into the army," Daniel said, huddling into his ski parka away from those cold, cryptic numbers. Although the heater was blowing air from its ducts, nothing could warm the sympathetic chill circulating within him.

"That's not funny," Gianni said.

"I'm sorry, Gianni. It was just my first reaction."

However, Daniel's mind kept running with that image of numerical classification. He pictured legions of patients with Hodgkin's disease in its various phases: men and women in hospitals all over the world this Christmas Eve; in Philadelphia, where there was no snow; in Atlanta, where the news had reported a record of eighty-five degrees; even in places like Holland and Ethiopia. Those with lower classification such as 1A were more able to fight back, and those with higher numbers more powerless.

"We went to see her yesterday," Gianni said. "Me and Tony. We had to ask the doctor when she would be asleep . . . otherwise she'd have made us go home."

"How is she doing?"

Gianni ignored the question. "I felt so stupid," he went on. "I brought her this box of Christmas candy. I picked it out special—she loves pecan log bits—and had it gift-wrapped. I figured she would wake up or something and I could give it to her and say Merry Christmas because she wouldn't be home with us tomorrow."

He paused and as Daniel waited for him to continue, they arrived at a red traffic light. Another car drew up alongside them. It was packed with raucous high school students. Somebody waved to Gianni; however, he refused to acknowledge them. Daniel realized that Mrs. Scaravento's condition, although of utmost importance to him and Gianni, in reality had a small radius.

Gianni continued. "When we got there, I felt so stupid for bringing the candy. In fact when I saw her I forgot I was holding it. I mean, I just couldn't believe it was her. Danny, they forgot to put her cap on before we arrived so we saw her scalp. She almost has no hair now, and what she has is sort of downy and gray. She looks like she's from another planet. I mean, how could her hair turn gray so quickly?"

"She could have been coloring her hair for a long time now," Daniel suggested.

"She hasn't been. I'd know it. And then her face looks all sunken and wrinkled. It's like she's aged ten years since she went in.

"When Tony first looked at her he got sick to his stomach. He threw up on his way to the john and then he couldn't stop crying. She had this tube up her nose. I think that must've scared him. He thought she had already died or something. Thank God she didn't wake up and see him so upset."

"I'd like to go visit her with you sometime, if I may," Daniel said.

Gianni whirled on him. "You stay out of that hospital! She doesn't want you there. She said specifically to my father, 'Don't let Gianni bring Daniel Fell.' Ask him if you don't believe me."

Daniel recoiled from Gianni's harsh switch in mood. He felt a sharp pain in his jaw. "Why would she say something like that?" he managed to ask, wondering if Angela had been embarrassed when he had witnessed her breaking down as they were watching *Casablanca*.

"She doesn't want anybody to see her like this," Gianni snorted. "She doesn't want people coming in and ogling to satisfy their curiosity. She's dying on us!" he cried, his voice deafening within the confined space of the car. Daniel could smell the nervous foulness of Gianni's breath.

Daniel shut his eyes and allowed the stinging rejection to suffuse him. He had never felt so close to a friend as he did to Gianni Scaravento, never felt so injured by a friend's words. This must be what adult life was like, the bitter dividend of loving someone. And if that was the case maybe he didn't want to grow up anymore. It would be better to remain in childhood on the brink of maturity. It was difficult for him to imagine how his father was able to endure the torment of his mother's rejection. How could he go on living with that day after day?

"Take me home, Gianni, okay," Daniel said in small voice.

Gianni threw the car into a higher gear and began speeding through winding roadways of the ridges in the direction of Daniel's house. The roaring quiet in the car mismatched the holiday serenity of the neighborhood. Daniel kept hearing inner echoes of Gianni's snarling vituperation. Eyes riveted ahead of him, he tried catching a glimpse of his friend's expression without being obvious. Suddenly Gianni braked the car and pulled off the road underneath a street lamp. They came to a halt.

"I'm sorry, buddy," he said as he softly pushed the gearshift into neutral. "I shouldn't have said that to you. There's just this bad anger inside me. I don't know what to do with it. I'm helpless."

Daniel remained silent.

"Listen Danny," Gianni tried to explain, "this kind of thing is going to happen with me now. You're going to have to ignore it and just be my friend. I'm being jerked all over the place. It may as well be July Fourth as Christmas Eve."

"Things are happening with my family, too, and I don't take them out on you."

"But it's not—" Gianni began and then broke off. "You're more together than I am," he finally said.

"I know what you were getting at." Daniel spoke in a growl. "You were going to say my situation isn't the same as yours."

"I didn't say that!" Gianni said defensively.

"You certainly began to."

"I'm not sorry about what I didn't say. But I'm sorry about yelling at you."

"But don't you see," Daniel agonized. "It's not fair to compare the situations. They're completely different. I mean, I thought that was the nice thing about us. That we were helping each other through things and not saying who was worse off."

"I know," Gianni said softly. "I know."

Out of the quiet, dark hollows of the street emerged a group of people. As they passed the car, someone thumped lightly on the windshield with a gloved hand. Startled, Gianni and Daniel recognized the high school glee club treading across the wide, snowy lawns of the wealthy Jewish neighborhood. Wearing bright ear muffs, long hand-knitted scarves and high winter boots, the carolers stopped in front of a lighted house where there was obviously a holiday event in progress. "Certainly know what side their bread is buttered on," Gianni remarked.

Then he suddenly grabbed Daniel by the arm. "Don't turn off to me," he pleaded. "I need you right now." Daniel remained silent, overwhelmed and alarmed by Gianni's wanting, something that he was aware of within his own self but kept furtive.

"What are you worrying about?" he scoffed. "You got plenty of friends. You got Debbie Lerner wrapped around your finger."

Gianni laughed. "I'm wild about Debbie Lerner, but it's not the same with her. She doesn't know the right thing to say to me about what I'm going through now with my mom."

They heard the first tentative notes of a carol and soon a warm rush of youthful harmonies piped through the stillness of the night. Gianni continued, "I mean, Debbie tries to say comforting things; she even offered to come over and cook for the family. But she doesn't understand. She tells me how sorry she is and then, right after, wants to cuddle and be fondled. It's like we always fall into that, fooling around with each other. We keep getting distracted by our attraction."

Thoughts of Julietta suddenly cut through Daniel's emotional disarray. Even though he basically decided not to pursue her any further, he had been distressed to learn that she remained totally absorbed in the football player. Although Vito had given her the okay to start seeing Daniel again, she was quite happy the way things were. So of course when her preference was made clear, Daniel felt more strongly about getting involved with her again. More and more he had found himself dwelling on her, in lustful fantasy. He felt that her sexual power was unbridled and consuming; in a way perhaps she was a female equivalent to Gianni Scaravento. Maybe that was why Gianni had been attracted to her. But Gianni had to be in control—so did Julietta; and with Gianni she must have sensed that would be impossible. After all, Gianni won over Debbie Lerner, the princess of high school, who was now completely besotted by him. Daniel glanced over at his friend. What was it about him? He scoured the angles and the planes of Gianni's imperfect, rough-hewn face, wondering if his power over women was due purely to his animal magnetism. And why couldn't Daniel possess the same quality?

Gianni was looking at him, his dark eyes perplexed. "What are you so quiet about, man?" he whispered.

"Nothing. Nothing at all."

Gianni sighed. "I wonder if it's just that me and Debbie aren't really suited to each other. Or am I just learning about something that happens between men and women that will keep happening to me the rest of my life?"

"Learning what?" Daniel asked.

"That sex"—Gianni broke off—"that sex creates a distance between people. Keeps people from really getting to know each other. I mean, I feel like I know you much better than I know Debbie Lerner. And I've been friends with both of you the same amount of time. But if I had to choose one over the other there wouldn't be a question of which friend I'd choose."

"It's ridiculous to worry about having to make a choice, Daniel said. "It'll never come down to that."

"Oh yeah?" Gianni said. "I'll bring a tape player next time I go out with her and record when she complains that I spend too much time with you."

Daniel was taken aback. "I didn't realize she was jealous."

Gianni sighed. "Yeah, she gets jealous." He sounded morose. He was staring across the street at a dimmed house whose front lawn was canopied in a virginal blanket of snow. "She keeps tying me up in knots. When what I really need to do right now is concentrate on Angie. That Angie gets better. That Angie will come home." He bowed his head.

As he agreed with Gianni that Angela's convalescence was indeed the most important concern, Daniel realized that his friend was afflicted with a sort of dispassion toward women. Perhaps women were attracted by dispassion, were challenged by it. Perhaps ambivalence created a stronger sexual pull than honesty.

Just then he grew aware that the twinkling he had been noticing all evening on the windshield was not radiating from a piece of ice. Daniel leaned closer to the scintillation of light; the spur sustained several weeks ago had begun forming a crack. The crack had described a small loop and then started its descent down the windshield, its length no more than a half inch.

"Is your father going to pay for it?" Daniel asked.

Gianni shook his head. "My family seems to have gotten tired of this car. They think it's temperamental. Before she went into the hospital, my mother claimed the car had taken on my personality." He paused. "They want me to trade it in for something more dependable."

"Why haven't you told me this before?" Daniel demanded.

Gianni shrugged. " 'Cause I knew it'd piss you off."

"But selling the car won't change *you*," Daniel pointed out. Gianni did not react. "But you can't let them get rid of it. We *love* this car!"

Silent for a moment longer, Gianni began to softly pummel the steering wheel with the large, calloused palm of his right hand.

"Why don't you try and make the money to replace the windshield?" Daniel suggested.

"I thought of that. But my mother already convinced my father that the car is too dangerous for someone like me. He's dead set on my selling it. He said something about the spring. And right now there's no arguing with him."

18

It had been Vito's plan to introduce Daniel to his mother before the holidays. Unfortunately, Maria Polanno decided to make her yearly visit to Italy in the middle of December. According to Vito, she wanted a break from the pressure of the holidays and felt that she would be best off with her own relatives. The Polanno brothers spent an uneventful Christmas with Julietta and her family and Daniel didn't hear from Vito again until the end of January.

Apparently, while in Italy Maria had gone to Livorno to see a gypsy woman renowned for her psychic abilities. She asked the gypsy point-blank if her sons had murdered the animals. The woman offered a deck of Tarot cards, asking Maria to cut them twice and then to choose three cards from the pile. Studying the Tarot without comment and then interpreting the configurations of tea leaves in the bottom of Maria's cup, the gypsy finally delivered her verdict. Her gnarled, painted face wrinkled up, revealing rotten teeth, and she admitted to being unable to make head nor tail of the contradictory impressions she was receiving, impressions that both supported and denied the premise that Vito, Mario and Mickey killed the animals.

For a while, supposedly, hope had supplanted Maria's doubts. She began wondering if indeed her sons were telling the truth. But then one of her ultra-religious aunts suggested that the Lord

had purposely intervened and created a diversion; relying on clair-
voyance was, after all, taking a shortcut from the longer road of
seeking knowledge through perpetual prayer. Maria finally returned to New York with renewed doubts although, luckily, family life in Italy had agreed with her enough to add some pounds
to her gaunt frame. She didn't worry nearly so much as she did
before she left.

"But we still want you to come over and have coffee with her,"
Vito said one day after school when he had caught Daniel walking
down the cement steps en route to the parking lot. "See if you
can get her on the conversation without sounding obvious."

"But has she been going on about it the way she was before?"
Daniel asked.

"No, not like she was."

"So why do you want to stir things up again?"

"Look man," Vito said impatiently, "I just want to know that
I can rely on you if I need you."

Daniel hesitated. Throughout the past two months he had been
regretting his decision to help the Polanno brothers. In fact, he
was now unsure of what led him to even consider helping them
at all. "I already told you once I'd help you," he said irritably. "I
don't go back on my word."

"You know something, Fell," Vito said somewhat respectfully.
"You're pretty tough-mouthed. I hope you can fight as good as
you talk."

"But I don't have to worry about fighting, do I?" Daniel said,
reminding Vito that in exchange for his favor the Polannos were
now supposed to guarantee him protection.

"Is that what we said?" Vito laughed. His face was looking
especially pointy and homely, his teeth stained from smoking too
many cigarettes and chugging black coffee. "By the way, you still
hanging out with Scaravento?"

Daniel nodded.

"Hear his mother's been pretty sick. My mom went to see her
the other day in the hospital."

Daniel scrutinized Vito. "Are you sure about that?"

Vito turned his hands palms up. "Unless she turned into a liar
while she was back in the old country."

"Funny, I thought Angela wasn't seeing anyone."

•

"Probably isn't. But Maria insists on going over there with her rosary beads."

Frowning, Daniel wondered if he was the only person Angela Scaravento was refusing to see. That couldn't be. She really had no reason to avoid contact with him.

A few days later, the day before Daniel's father moved to his new apartment in Manhattan, Daniel received a phone call. He was in his bedroom, trying to finish a paper on *Crime and Punishment* that he was writing for an independent study project. Gianni was supposed to swing by at eight-thirty and they were planning to drive around until ten. Alexis answered the phone and entered Daniel's room with a perturbed look on her face. "You won't believe who's waiting to speak to you on the phone?" she said.

"You got me."

"Vito Polanno."

When Alexis saw her announcement provoked at best a meager shrug from her brother, she grew shrill. "What, are you friends with *him* now, too?"

Daniel put aside his book of criticism and note pad and trotted to the hallway phone. "That's about as low as you can get," Alexis called after him.

Daniel held the phone out. "Why don't you talk a little louder. . . ?" he said, smiling.

Alexis shot him the finger and returned to her bedroom.

"Hello Vito," Daniel said. He could hear screeching in the background. "What can I do for you?"

"Who was that answered the phone?"

"My sister."

"So the mouth runs in the family?"

"Just tell me what you want."

There was a pause and the shouting grew even more audible. "Hear that," Vito said in a low voice. "Danny, she's gone nutso again. Every time she goes to see that Mick priest she comes home like a fucking scourge."

"You mean, she's accusing you again?" Daniel winced inwardly, knowing now what was forthcoming.

"Ah Jesus. Her face is all red and the jugular vein is sticking out. She looks like she's going to bust. Hold on a second. Now listen to that."

Daniel could hear someone in Italian calling Vito a killer and ordering him to put down the phone. She used the verb *uccidere*. "At least she's not using a stronger verb like *ammazzare*," Daniel told Vito.

"Come on, stop computer geeking my head. Heh?"

"Okay, so what do you want from me?"

Vito whispered, "Can you swipe your mother's car and get over here?"

"It's eight o'clock at night. And anyway, I got plans. Gianni's coming by."

"Postpone Scaravento, will you? Come on. Here's the address."

"I know the address," Daniel said. "Everybody knows where you live, Vito. But can't I do it tomorrow or some other time?"

"I'm telling you, she's whacked out. Look, I'll make it up to you, somehow."

"For my sake, I hope you don't have to," Daniel told him.

He tried calling Gianni at home, but the line was busy. He asked the operator to interrupt the conversation, but she came back on and claimed the party refused to give up the line. A moment later the phone rang. It was Gianni. "You got some nerve doing emergency interrupt!"

"Prick!" Daniel heard Frank Scaravento shout in the background.

"My dad was on a business call to Oregon, for Christ's sake. What's wrong?"

"I got to go over to Vito's. Maria is flipping out again. She just got back from seeing the priest."

"Do you want me to come with you, buddy?" Gianni asked.

"No, but I want you to tell me why Mrs. Polanno gets to visit your mother in the hospital and I don't. And who else gets to visit her besides Mrs. Polanno?"

There was a lengthy pause and then Gianni sighed into the phone. "Danny, I don't know what to say. She just started having other visitors. But she's asked not to see you. I don't understand it either."

"But how am I supposed to interpret that?" Daniel agonized.

"My Dad says she's afraid for you to see her all laid up like that."

"But why should I make any more difference than any of you? I've seen how she looks when she gets distraught late at night."

"What can I say, buddy," Gianni said. "I'm sorry. I can't try to explain her."

In contrast to his irate behavior on Christmas Eve, Gianni could now be magnanimous; Angela's refusal to see Daniel left him little cause for jealousy.

All the homes on the Polannos' street still displayed their Christmas decorations. As Daniel pulled up in front of their house, he reflected on yet another difference between the Italian and Jewish populations of Houghton. Many of the Jewish people, contrary to religious dictates, displayed outdoor lights and menorahs and even in some cases a splendidly adorned evergreen—referred to in Jewish jargon as a Hanuka bush. But after New Year's, the decorations came down all over the ridges and there was never any trace of holiday ornamentation after January second. Many of the Italian homes left their lights up until the middle of February, and some even longer than that. Daniel wondered if this was done out of laziness or lingering sentimentality.

The Polannos were no different. The wrought-iron railing leading up the flagstone steps to the front door was festooned with colored lights. Anchored to the middle of the front lawn was a plastic Santa Claus and a sled drawn by leaping reindeer. It was difficult to imagine that Vito and his brothers would have taken the time to decorate the railing and the hedges with lights; or to trim the Christmas tree that stood blinking at the bay window that overlooked the street. Maria Polanno must have conjured up the spirit of Christmas before departing for Italy.

Even from where he stood in the street Daniel could hear the shrieking. A woman from across the way, wearing a fake fur coat, stood in the cold on her front porch. She was obviously listening to the disturbance. That was another thing about the Jewish neighborhood. You would never catch someone on their front step eavesdropping. Granted, the properties were broader and it would be more difficult to hear anything, but no one wanted to be known as a busybody. Daniel remembered the word for it in Italian: *ficanaso.*

He walked up to the front door and pushed the bell, which was the sort that rang out in chimes. Almost immediately the door swung open and a small, frail woman who resembled Vito was squinting at Daniel. "What do you want?" she said softly.

"Uh, I . . . I was trying to find Vito."

"He's busy now. He'll be at school tomorrow," she said, shutting the door.

"Ma!" Daniel heard the brothers cry out in unison. Then the door swung open again, this time Vito answering. His face broke into feigned surprise. "Hey, guess who came to see us?" He yelled to his brothers. "Danny boy."

He opened the door wide so that Daniel could see Mario and Mickey perched on the high back of a green sofa that was protected by a transparent, plastic covering, their legs casually draped over the side. "How about that?" Mario said gleefully. "The kid comes to see us." Mickey just laughed. Some charade, thought Daniel. Spare me, he said under his breath.

Maria Polanno stood in the middle of the living room, hunched over herself, chin resting on her left hand and her left elbow propped on her right hand. She was wearing a long gray cardigan that reached halfway down her black house dress. Her face was long and sad, her dark eyes shrewd and intelligent, and she had silvery hair worn in a braid. Definitely a trace of the aristocrat in her countenance. A bit of flesh folded inwardly in the middle of her chin, some sort of scarring. Beyond Maria rose a fake fireplace filled with a cement log and a rotary of orange lights that were supposed to resemble flames. Above the fireplace was an oil reproduction of a two-dimensional medieval Christ in the act of blessing. The house was warm and smelled of a laundry cycle.

"Heh Ma, isn't this amazing?" Vito said.

"This is the kid you asked us about," Mario said. "The kid who knows Mrs. Scaravento. The kid who speaks Italian."

Silent now, Mrs. Polanno smiled cautiously.

"Heh Danny, so where's tomorrow's homework?" Vito said.

"Tomorrow's homework," Daniel repeated, momentarily bewildered. But then he caught on. "I thought you wanted today's homework?"

"No, I wanted tomorrow's. I did today's."

"Oh, well, then I must have misunderstood you. I only brought today's. It's in the car."

"Why didn't you bring it up with you?" Mrs. Polanno asked, her eyes darting inquisitively back and forth between Daniel and Vito.

"Well," Daniel said, "to be honest, I heard some yelling and I didn't know if it was the right time to drop by."

Because Mrs. Polanno was so absorbed in scrutinizing Daniel, Mickey was able to throw his head back in a gesture of glee. Daniel thought how lucky the Polannos were that he was quick on his feet.

"That's okay," Vito said, looking meaningfully at his mother. "She was just scolding us for something. It's over now, isn't it, Ma?"

"*Per il momento*," Mrs. Polanno said. Then she turned to Daniel and continued in Italian. "So I hear you spent the first ten years of your life in Padova."

"*Si*," Daniel said.

Mrs. Polanno had only passed through Padova once or twice. Her family was from Rome and she attended the University of Bologna for two years. Her bearing and education certainly had not rubbed off on any of her children, over whom she obviously had little control. Perhaps she was forced to throw temper tantrums and refuse to eat; it was as if she had to take desperate measures in order to get through to them. Unlike Mrs. Scaravento, Maria Polanno had little control over her family.

She asked Daniel to come with her into the kitchen and have a glass of tea. Daniel glanced at Vito and then shyly accepted. As they all headed toward the kitchen, Daniel made a quick appraisal of the house. It was without a dining area, populated with all sorts of old chairs, some with burst seams. There were worn plain wooden stands lined up against the walls on which were piled stacks of thick books and magazines—no doubt the books belonged to Mrs. Polanno. The magazines: car and road racing manuals and back issues of *Muscle Fitness* obviously belonged to the brothers. Daniel was suddenly startled by a terrible thumping upstairs. Mrs. Polanno wearily raised her eyes to the ceiling, speaking in a dialect that he had difficulty deciphering. However, he knew she said something about low-class fools. It made him wonder exactly how this educated woman regarded her profligate sons.

"Our great aunt lives upstairs," Vito explained.

The kitchen was rather small, cramped with old appliances, and included a disproportionately large eating table.

Mrs. Polanno put on the tea kettle and bid Daniel to sit down at the table. The brothers, meanwhile, spread themselves around the kitchen. Mickey sat on the counter next to the stove. Mario leaned against the oven and Vito, the most agitated of them all, kept walking tight concentric circles around the table.

The conversation was at first perfunctorily in Italian. Daniel could tell that Mrs. Polanno stood more on ceremony than Mrs. Scaravento. She used words that Daniel had heard before but did not know the meaning of. And sometimes she spoke so quickly —yet always articulately—that Daniel missed some of what she said.

Finally Daniel asked how Mrs. Polanno came to America.

She smiled and said wistfully, "I fell in love with their father. He was from Barre. A beautiful man. A construction foreman. He had always wanted to live in America and finally an opportunity came our way." She cast down her eyes, momentarily demure with private memory, and stirred her tea. She smiled thinly at Daniel. "Unlike Angela Scaravento's family, my family didn't make a fuss over his being southern. We are Romans," she said proudly. "Romans are always more tolerant. After all, Rome is in the middle of the country and is populated by all sorts of people.

"Coming here wasn't difficult for me. I had studied English ever since I was a young girl. I had even worked as an interpreter and a translator."

"Yes," Daniel said. "Vito told me."

"Unfortunately, I could never find work."

"Did you ever try the U.N.?"

"I tried everything. I even went to one of those headhunters who find jobs for people with obscure talents. Nothing worked. Then their father died. Did the boys tell you about that?"

Daniel nodded. "Yes, Vito told me."

"He was a drinker," Mrs. Polanno said.

"Come on," Mario broke in angrily. "He was not."

Daniel looked over at Mario in amazement. "How did you understand all that?" he said in English.

"You must be joking," Maria continued in Italian. "That one

understands everything. That one could have been the scholar of them all. I know." She fervently nodded her head. "You wouldn't think so. You'd think Vito, the talker, would be the scholar. But Mario is the most intelligent of the boys. He always tests well on aptitude exams. And look at him. He's throwing his life away."

"Leave me alone, Ma, I am not."

"*Disgrazia*," Maria Polanno enunciated with disdain. "No conscience. No motivation."

Daniel noticed Vito standing behind her, flapping his hands. He obviously wanted Daniel to broach the controversial issue with his mother. Daniel managed to raise his eyebrows without Maria's noticing, indicating that he felt it was not quite the appropriate moment. However, he now knew in his heart that it would be impossible to lie.

"I hear that you've gone to see Mrs. Scaravento," he invoked a new subject, ignoring the subsequent grunt that issued from Mario. Mickey clucked his tongue, but Daniel ignored that too.

"I saw her yesterday. She seems to be doing much better. Gained some weight. No trace of anything in her lower tract now. She gets to go home tomorrow."

"I wouldn't know. For some reason she won't see me," Daniel said sadly.

"But that's absurd," Maria said. "She . . . I mean, up until yesterday she referred to you . . . in some way. Let me see, what did she say?"

"Please try to think of what she said," Daniel insisted.

Mario Polanno glanced at him. "Oh, she's very fond of you, that's for sure." Then she put a hand against her cheek and looked upward reflectively. "I know she's very happy you've become a friend of Gianni's. She thinks you've already improved his attitude." She shook her head. "I can't for the life of me understand why she wouldn't want you to come visit."

Daniel shrugged, although he felt relieved that at least Angela was recommending him to other people.

A long, troubled silence followed and during it Mrs. Polanno caught Daniel and Vito exchanging glances. Her eyes narrowed as she asked Daniel how long he had known her sons. Was their friendship recent?

"Na, we knew each other from last summer, right, Danny?" Mario said.

Mrs. Polanno was scrutinizing Daniel's face. He nodded fervently. "Yep, we hung out a little bit last summer," he said in English.

"Oh, that's nice."

"Yeah and we used to go swimming up in Croton reservoir," Mickey said.

Now Vito and Mario were slyly motioning to Daniel that this was his cue.

Daniel gave up trying to do things his way. He turned to Mrs. Polanno. "Signora Polanno," he began, "I probably should have come to see you earlier."

Mrs. Polanno's face turned grave. It was as though she already suspected what Daniel was about to say. "About what, Daniello?" she asked.

"About," he began and faltered. "About the . . . animals."

Maria Polanno suddenly grew extremely agitated. Her hands fluttered spasmodically and she seemed to have trouble controlling them.

"Are you trying to protect them?" she asked, indicating her sons with a flick of her head.

"No," Daniel blurted "We were together . . ." he faltered. "That night."

"I thought as much," she said, the pitch of her voice rising. Then she began to speak shrilly and incoherently in dialect. Something about "You don't mean your parents let you out so late on a week night? You really should be at home and in bed. I have to get back to my sewing. It's so important for me to keep my hands busy. And you should go see some Italian plays in New York City. Good way to keep up on your language. Oh, yes, it's so nice to speak Italian with an American boy who has such respect for the language. And you speak it marvelously, really, just a trace of accent, but what of it?" She was speaking so rapidly now that Daniel was having trouble understanding.

Then Maria rose abruptly from the kitchen table, her face flushed crimson. "Who are you trying to fool?" she hissed.

"What do you mean?" Daniel said, alarmed.

"How dare you do this!" She suddenly reverted from the sophisticated, well-modulated conversationalist into a wild woman. Her teeth bared themselves and spittle from her mouth flew all over the kitchen. "How dare you insult my intelligence in such a way!" Mario slapped himself on the forehead and Vito muttered, "Shit to hell" under his breath. Daniel closed his eyes and wished he could evaporate.

"Ma, calm yourself!" Vito ordered while Mario and Mickey rushed to either side of their mother and began telling her not to get too excited and that she had been getting excited all evening and hadn't the doctor said she wasn't supposed to get excited.

"Excited because the three of you are killing me!" she shrieked.

"Ah come on, Ma!" They pleaded with exasperation.

"The three of you get out of here now!" She yelled, clapping her hands together. "Come on, Vito. Take them out of here and leave me with this boy."

Mickey and Mario slunk out of the room and then Vito stalked after them, casting a murderous glance at Daniel.

Maria Polanno waited until they were in the living room. Then she turned to Daniel, glowering. "What, did they bribe you to say this?"

Daniel scrunched his shoulders together and looked down at his feet.

"I don't understand." Maria placed her small frail hands on the kitchen table, leaning toward him. "What could they have done to get you over here? Did they threaten you? Come on. Tell me!"

Daniel still could say nothing.

She spoke more softly, trying to draw him out. "You mustn't let people threaten you into being dishonest. You only shame yourself in the end. Now, you're not their friend, are you?" she said.

Daniel shook his head dejectedly.

"And you have no idea where they were the night of the animals?"

"No, Mrs. Polanno."

He now glanced up at Maria's face, which was contorting miserably. Part of a small vein protruded from the right side of her forehead and he could actually watch it pulsating rapidly.

"Please, don't disappoint me anymore," Maria said sadly. "Just go home now."

Daniel got up from the kitchen table and walked into the living room. The Polanno brothers were sitting three in a row on the sofa like admonished schoolboys.

"You're dead meat, Fell," Vito whispered angrily. "You better get yourself some protection. Some better protection than Gianni Scaravento."

Daniel shrugged and went out the door. As he walked down the flagstone steps towards his car, he wondered how difficult it would be to get hold of the Barzinnis.

19

In the early morning before Daniel would get out of bed, things always seemed at their worst; even minor problems took on mammoth proportions. Today his throat was cracked and sore from repeated swallowing during the night and his head throbbed from lack of sleep. When he arose, stretched and looked around the window shades at the barren trees and the two inches of crusty snow that glazed the lawn—which had been stained yellow in spots by neighborhood dogs—he was not reassured by the presence of the world at large. By then he had heard shuffling noises and his mother's voice, high-pitched with tension, warbling throughout the upstairs. By then he knew that his father was in the act of bringing all his belongings downstairs.

Last night he had offered to help Harold cart down the suitcases and boxes, but his father had preferred to carry everything himself. Irene was making her famous light waffles, the recipe which other women in the neighborhood—particularly the mothers of Alexis's friends—had unsuccessfully vied for: a blending of sour dough starter into the flour and a special method of folding in egg whites. She had given the family several choices for breakfast and they all independently opted for waffles.

A knock sounded on Daniel's door. Harold entered, dressed immaculately. He went to raise the window shades, admitting the sallow light of the overcast morning. He sat down on Daniel's bed. His cheeks were smooth and pink from a fresh shave, blotched red in places where he had been too ambitious with his razor. His bristly hair was plastered down and he reeked of musky after-shave, something he normally did not wear. His tie, however, was crooked. "Your mother just went down to put on the waffles," he said. "She made the batter last night."

Daniel frowned at his father. "Are you hungry or something?" He sat down on his pillows and cocked his arms behind his head.

"Not at all," Harold said. "And I haven't even had a cup of coffee."

"So why are you telling me all this about the waffles?"

"I was warning you that breakfast would be ready soon. And I was making an attempt at conversation."

"Why, is it so hard to talk to me?"

Harold smiled sadly. "When you get like this it is."

"I know. I question everything, don't I?" Daniel said.

"You'd make a good lawyer."

"Or a manipulator."

"A manipulator?"

"Oh that's just Gianni Scaravento's notion."

"Gianni Scaravento," Harold repeated. "When will I ever get to meet this Gianni Scaravento?"

Daniel shrugged. Now that his father would no longer be living in the house a meeting would be more difficult to arrange. "I guess we'll have to come into the city sometime and visit you," Daniel said.

"You mean you're only going to come visit me sometime?" Harold asked in a hurt voice.

"No, Dad, I meant that Gianni would come *with* me some-time."

At a momentary loss for words, Harold rubbed his chafed, stubby hands on his trousered knees. Daniel took the opportunity to straighten his father's tie. "I guess I'm afraid that you won't want to come and visit me," his father said, "what with the apart-ment being so small."

"Now wait a second. Alexis was the one who complained about the apartment being small."

"Well, it is small. But it was the cheeriest apartment I could find."

"Dad, if I told you once I've told you a hundred times the apartment is okay. That's the least of it."

Harold suddenly leaned forward and stared at Daniel's chest. "Looks like you're getting in a few hairs there."

Daniel stuck his chin to his chest, trying to see the hairs his father referred to. "Maybe I'll end up being as hairy as you."

"Then again, you might take after your mother's father. And be bald by the age of thirty." Harold laughed.

Daniel rolled his eyes. "Something to look forward to."

They heard noises in the hallway: someone pattering into the bathroom and a door slamming. "Sounds like Alexis is up," Daniel said.

"Oh, shit. I was going to go get her up too."

"Best to knock on her door in a little while. If you go in and start pulling up *her* shades she'll get suspicious and think it's too much of a gesture."

"It would be," Harold said, standing up and moving to the window. He tapped lightly on the cold glass; then made a halo of mist with his breath and drew a large ring with his squat index finger. He sighed. "I guess I just don't feel as close to her as I do to you."

"Dad, I know it's your last morning in the house, but you shouldn't say that—out loud."

"Why not?"

"It makes me feel badly for Alexis. It might change. And besides, it makes me feel responsible."

Harold turned back from the window, looking dejected. "Responsible for what?"

"Not to let you down."

"That would take a lot of work."

"All I'd have to do is drop out of school."

Harold's eyes widened.

"You see what I'm saying?"

They were silent again. Harold seemed at a loss and kept glancing toward the door. Wishing to relieve the sudden awkwardness, Daniel said, "Go on, Dad, talk to Alexis for a while and I'll see you downstairs."

Harold peered at Daniel, noticing his eyes were filmed with tears. "You all right, Danny?"

"Why shouldn't I be all right?"

"I'm just concerned."

"Well then, I'm not all right. I feel lousy."

"It's okay," Harold said, "to feel lousy." He now hesitated at the doorway.

"Would you go on, Dad?" Daniel told his father, who reluctantly continued out into the hall.

Soon the smell of coffee wafted upstairs, blending with the toasty fragrance of feather-weight waffles and the grilled odor of sausage. Daniel got up and dressed and then crept down the stairs where, unbeknown to his mother, he stood outside the kitchen. He wanted to spy on Irene as she bustled through the preparations for breakfast. He watched her face, daring her to smile, but she looked genuinely downcast and remorseful and that made him feel better.

The kitchen table was heaped with homemade jams and honey butter Irene had made as well as a plate of sausage. A stack of freshly made waffles was being successively raised two inches by each steaming golden batch that she removed from the waffle iron with a fork. Irene was chattering out loud, reminding herself of the number of waffles and timing each preparation in the waffle iron. She'd glance at the stove clock and then peer up to the ceiling, as though wondering when the rest of the family would descend. Daniel watched her spoon batter from a large blue mixing bowl on to the open waffle iron. The resulting hollow sizzling sound, normally an inspiration to his appetite, depressed him. "They should get down here," Irene murmured under her breath.

"I'm here."

She jumped, dropping her cooking spatula on the counter. "Jesus, you startled me. Good morning, Danny," she said. "I was just talking to myself."

"Like always."

Irene looked at him balefully.

"I don't think you should make any more waffles. Wait and see how much everybody wants. I for one am not hungry."

Irene dipped her head forward and her hair tumbled over her eyes. She raked it away with quick, anxious strokes of her doughy hands. "Don't worry. You'll get hungry once it's before you," she assured him.

And she was right. When everyone assembled at the table, Alexis was the first to dig in and then Daniel followed suit and soon Harold was eating. Ironically, Irene ate nothing. She sat rigidly at one end of the table, gripping her favorite turquoise coffee mug that had chips and crevices from its everyday use, her fingers still bearing traces of waffle mix. They talked about Alexis's history teacher coming down with hepatitis, which prompted an inquiry after Mrs. Scaravento's illness. Harold complained of a difficult client and of a newly hired secretary who was turning out to be insolent. All of it was just filler for the gap that was about to open up in the family circle after years of unity. This idea grew more and more apparent to each of them as the meal progressed until finally it cast a pall on conversation, which soon came to a standstill. There was only the munching sound of waffles and sausages and Daniel's slurping of his coffee for which Irene scolded him and then she ignored it.

The collective sound of their eating reminded him of when they first came back from Italy and how his father would take him to a Dairy restaurant on Second Avenue for raisin French toast made from challah bread. Just the two of them alone on a Sunday; they would drive in and have breakfast and then go to a movie or a matinee. The restaurant consisted of a yellow counter with red vinyl stools permanently attached to metal columns. Hemmed in on either side by hungry patrons, Daniel would listen to the munching of bagels and eggs and the slurping of coffee. Part of the reason why Harold liked going to the Dairy restaurant was talking to a middle-aged man named Larry who had been running the place for twenty years and who was famous for his nasty mouth. Apparently, there had even been a line in a famous Broadway play about "If I need abuse I'll go to the 2nd Avenue Dairy restaurant."

Larry had a terrible limp and in order to walk between the grill and the kitcnen he needed to lean heavily against the counter and hoist himself along. Throughout his herky-jerky movements, his head swiveled and he eyed customers as though defying their pity. He yelled at Daniel on his first visit to the restaurant and Daniel started to cry into his French toast and couldn't eat any of it afterward. Then Larry called him a rotten kid, winking at his father. But Harold wouldn't defend Daniel, and later on explained that was how people were and that one had to grow a tougher skin. However, Daniel figured that his father admired Larry for some reason. Or maybe he just felt sorry for him.

After Daniel got to be known by Larry, he wasn't treated so shabbily. Sure, he was treated gruffly, but he often saw a smile lingering on the face of the bald man who didn't shave everyday. He eventually discovered that underneath all this bluster beat a soft heart. And he even began to look forward to Larry's abusing people. The more Larry demeaned the customers, the better the food seemed to taste, and that degree of abuse also augured well for the rest of the day: the movie or matinee seemed more exciting or there would often be an ice cream vendor outside the theater.

Only once did Daniel see Larry come out from behind the counter. He was actually a lot shorter than he appeared alongside the black griddle and as he hobbled along, using the outer edge of the counter for support, one of his legs dangled, practically lifeless. Once revealed, his disability was distressing to Daniel. Larry talked to a man who sounded like a doctor about some condition that wasn't getting any better. Daniel assumed the condition had to do with his crippled legs. He asked his father what the condition could be, but Harold said he didn't know and that it would not be polite to ask.

When they came in the following Saturday, Larry wasn't working. Daniel asked one of the Puerto Rican cooks where he was and the cook matter-of-factly said that Larry had died on Thursday. "Oh, come on," Daniel said, "you're just fooling me."

"Heh," the cook said. "He died Thursday. Okay, punk?"

"He died?" Daniel cried out. Someone eating a ways down the counter told him to be quiet. "He really died?" Forks continued to stroke plates and glassware kept on chattering. Shouldn't it all stop?

The cook clucked his tongue and didn't answer. Daniel glanced up at his father, who could only give a pained shrug. Tearful, Daniel regarded the steaming pots of Wheatena and split pea soup, and then stared at a framed picture on the wall of Larry with this very Puerto Rican cook who had gone on to make matzoh bri. Then he noticed the people sitting at the counter, people he had

seen every Sunday, who had probably been coming to the 2nd
Avenue Dairy longer than he. The news did not seem to trouble
them. In fact, a few of them were curiously watching his reaction,
while continuing to shovel food in their mouths. Daniel missed
Larry's heckling. French toast never tasted the same when it was
made by the Puerto Rican chef. And within a few weeks they
stopped going to the 2nd Avenue Dairy restaurant.

What else was there to do, he now thought to himself. Those
people had been right. You couldn't stop living. You couldn't not
eat. Daniel looked down at his plate of sausage rind and little flecks
of waffle saturated with maple syrup. This morning he just wanted
to see some telltale faltering among the members of his family,
for them to share a moment of recognition of what was about to
be lost. But here they all were—him included—stuffing their
faces. He pushed back from the table and closed his eyes.

"You sick or something?" Alexis asked.

Daniel shook his head. "Leave me alone."

"Danny," Irene said softly. "Open your eyes."

"I can't," he said, his voice shaking.

"Just let it come out," she said, words he remembered her
using when he was younger as she held him while he vomited
into the toilet bowl.

He now looked at his mother, who gazed back at him with
sympathy. "This all seems so dumb to me." He wept a little and
then withdrew into the wound. "I just don't understand it."

Alexis was regarding him as though he had just said something
insane. She was shaking her head back and forth and then set her
jaw and stared down at her plate. He knew she was resentful and
maybe that was a simpler reaction to have.

"What don't you understand?" Irene asked.

"How this has happened."

Harold reached across the table and covered Daniel's hand
with his. "This is not the end, Daniel. We're all going to still see
each other. Right, Irene?"

"Absolutely," Irene said. "We'll be relatively close by. I'm
sure we'll have meals together."

"Okay." Daniel tried to take them at their word. "I'll help you
clear, Mom," he said.

"No, that's okay. I've got it."

But he felt hapless and unwanted. "Let me do something."

"You can help *me* in a few minutes," Harold said. He glanced at each of them as though rounding up their attention. "I was going to say . . . I was going to make a speech to both you and Alexis and reassure you that I'm still your father, although I might not be living here. But I guess that would sound stupid. I guess you know that."

Daniel and Alexis stared at him vacantly and said nothing. Then Alexis burped.

Harold fidgeted for a moment longer and then rose from the table. He went into the dining room, where he had temporarily stowed his belongings, not wanting them to be visible in the kitchen while the family was having breakfast. Daniel followed. But when he entered the dining room he stopped short. There were only two large suitcases, two garment bags and four small boxes. He turned to his father. "What are you leaving behind?"

Harold shrugged. "Nothing. This is all my stuff."

"What about your books?"

"There aren't that many. And the shelves would look bare without them."

Daniel once again studied the luggage and boxes. It seemed so little for twenty years of life in various households. Then he glanced over the dining room, whose walls were adorned with several oil paintings and pastel drawings; at the mahogany dining chest with pewter candelabra on top. Without another word to his father, he stalked into the kitchen. Irene was scrubbing the Teflon pan in which she had cooked the sausage.

"What's going on here? Doesn't Dad get anything at all in the house? What, you get to keep it all?"

"Now wait a second," Harold said, following him in the kitchen.

Irene stopped scrubbing. She dropped the pan into the sink with a clatter, turned off the faucet and wrung soapy water from her hands. The kitchen beat with the silence of urgency. "I told your father he could have whatever he wanted to take."

"And I turned down her offer," Harold broke in.

Irene switched on the water, as though needing to buffer herself with continued domesticity. Daniel detested their last minute conspiracy and preferred to see them do battle. It would make more sense. He turned to his father. "But why? Why don't you want anything?"

"I've only taken the stuff that you, Alexis and your mother

have given me personally. The rest of it, the household stuff, I'd prefer your mother kept. I want to furnish my own place. I don't want . . . well to be—" He looked helplessly at Irene. "Is 're-minded' the word?"

"I'm not sure what you're intending to say, Harold," she said softly.

Alexis spoke up from where she still sat, rigid at the kitchen table. "But Dad, why don't you want to see stuff you and Mom shared?"

He turned to her. "Sure, honey, I want to. I guess I'm not explaining it very well."

"You're doing okay," Irene said. "It's just hard for them to understand."

"But we want to understand," Daniel fumed.

"Okay," Harold said. "It's just that the future is vague for me now. I'd like to try and fill it up with new things instead of things from a life I'm no longer living. How's that?"

"Oh my God," Daniel groaned. "When is this going to stop? How much do we have to take?"

No one said anything else after this. Each of them regarded the others in bewilderment and then the critical moment passed without any spoken reassurances.

Daniel helped Harold carry his things out to his new Buick Skylark. Together, in a stalemate of silence, they loaded the car. When they were walking back inside Daniel happened to realize that it was Groundhog Day. He looked up through naked branches to the overcast sky. No shadows to be found in such grim weather. Maybe spring would soon come and by spring he'd be more used to things.

His parents hugged and his father kissed Alexis on the top of her head, Alexis who still sat stiff and immobile at the kitchen table. And then Daniel asked his father once again if he was sure there wasn't something in the house he'd rather take with him.

"Would that make you feel better?" Irene asked, folding her arms across her apron front. "If your father took something else?"

Daniel nodded.

"Then what should I take?" Harold said.

Daniel didn't have to think about his answer. He wanted his father to take something that his mother wanted at all costs to keep. He wanted her to pay for their separation, because he felt she wasn't paying dearly enough. He walked into the living room and stood before a three-by-five-foot marble mosaic his parents had bought in Florence and which they considered to be the most valuable piece of artwork they owned: a pastorale of the hills and farmland of Fiesole. Red earth tones were heightened by the cerulean sky and a low mist clung to swales in the valleys. For a moment Daniel stood before it in awe, but then his appreciation was corrupted by a wicked glee; he knew how much Irene loved the piece. He dragged one of the winged back chairs across the room and situated it below the picture. He stood on the chair. As the picture was quite unwieldy, he had to struggle to unsnag it from the hanger. Daniel was careful not to bump into the walls when he walked with the mosaic back to the kitchen.

His choice provoked horrified gasps from both his parents. Irene averted her eyes and grimaced; she was obviously crushed. Harold looked stunned, panicky. But Alexis was smiling. She winked at Daniel, as though she knew all along that would be his choice.

"I can't take that away from your mother," Harold finally said.

"She said you could have whatever you want," Daniel reminded him. He caught his mother's daunted eye, glad that his arrow had struck its mark. "Possessions aren't supposed to matter," he said coolly. "Take it with you to New York. It's not as though you're going to sell it. Mom can come and visit it if she misses it. Just like . . . just like we'll keep having meals together," he said indignantly.

Harold shrugged, searching Irene's face for approval, but she gazed back at him dejectedly. He took the mosaic from Daniel and held it for a moment, looking vanquished and feeble. Thus weighed down, his goodbye kiss to his son was delivered awkwardly. And Daniel would always remember watching his father maneuvering the artwork through the doorway and down the narrow walk to the garage. At one point the corner of the frame hit the house and sounded as though part of it got chipped. Irene fled the room without finishing the dishes. Alexis sighed.

20

Daniel and Gianni were in the midst of one of their nocturnal drives in the Triumph, having one of their talks. Gianni was upset. Today his mother had come home from the hospital, looking weak and debilitated. Shortly thereafter the mail arrived with letters from two Ivy League schools that declined to give him a football scholarship. His potential as a starting quarterback had been evaluated and both schools (in almost identical phrasing) felt that his aptitude was not quite high enough to merit an athletic scholarship. He would now have to apply on the strength of his academic performance—although special consideration would be given to his case, being that he was an athlete.

"It was the lousy Rye game," Gianni fumed. "When I blew those couple of plays. There were scouts there that day. I don't know why they couldn't come to the New Rochelle game."

Daniel agreed. "It's a bad break."

"Maybe I shouldn't have eaten that strawberry shortcake when we went up to Bedford to see Vito. I was feeling a little queasy while I was playing. That may have had something to do with it. Imagine a piece of strawberry shortcake ruining my whole college career."

"Now wait a second," Daniel said. "One snack doesn't make that kind of difference."

Gianni turned to him angrily. "Hey man, what do you know about nutrition?"

"Okay, maybe I don't know enough about nutrition, but you're making me feel responsible for your eating the strawberry short-cake."

Gianni frowned. "You're paranoid, Danny. It was my choice to go up to Bedford. I knew what I had to do that day. I'm just saying it's very unfortunate."

Daniel pointed out that Gianni still had one Ivy to hear from as well as Michigan State. But Gianni explained that the remaining Ivy had less athletic money available than the other two Ivies and a full scholarship there was unlikely.

"What did your parents say?" Daniel asked, wondering if Gianni were going to invite him over to see Angela.

Shaking his head morosely, Gianni fumbled for a joint in his coat pocket.

"Do me a favor," Daniel said. "Don't get stoned right now."

"Okay," Gianni said and put the joint away. He then admitted that despite the fact that his mother had lost twenty pounds in the hospital and now looked frightfully drawn and frail, she was still capable of giving a strong, well-considered opinion of his two college rejections. "She said she knew all along I didn't have a snowball's chance in hell of getting into Princeton. That I was dreaming if I thought I could actually get in. That I wasn't com-mitted to football enough and that I better decide what I wanted to do with my life before my life decided what it wanted to do with me."

"Jesus," Daniel said. "What about your father?"

"He always goes along with what she says. What, you don't think that sounds like her?"

"No, it does," Daniel said. He knew that Angela Scaravento would do whatever she could to force Gianni to face the possi-bilities of his future before she grew too ill to exert any influence over him. For her, Daniel realized, it was a race against time.

They were heading through downtown Houghton and Gianni braked the Triumph as they passed in front of the Oaks, outside of which the Polannos' black Trans Am was parked at a haphazard angle. It was odd how during the last few days since Daniel's meeting with Maria Polanno that the brothers had not even tried to make good their threat of turning him into a piece of "dead meat." Sure, Gianni had stuck close by him in an attempt to offer some protection. However, there had been plenty of occasions between classes when the brothers could have stalked Daniel— as had been their pattern with other people. However, nothing happened. No one approached Daniel to warn him of anything; there was no foreboding aura in the hallways.

Once he even had passed by Mario and a group of his friends loitering outside a bathroom that was notorious for cigarette smoking. When Mario noticed Daniel, he turned away, actually dismissing Daniel's presence. Daniel had never thought the Polanno brothers capable of such subtlety as a snub.

When it was obvious that he no longer served a purpose to the Polanno brothers, Daniel had begun wondering about Julietta: if perhaps she might be willing to get together with him again, maybe even dump the football player that everybody said was no great shakes. In school a few days after Mrs. Polanno had banished him from her house, Daniel spied Julietta coming out of the girls' room, followed by a gust of forbidden cigarette smoke. She glanced nervously at him, gave her wild mane of hair a toss and began to slither away in her muscular womanly walk that had always been a topic of conversation in the boys' locker room. "Could you hold up a minute," Daniel called after her, and was surprised to see how she froze in midstep.

Daniel approached her and they stood close together—not quite as close as they had stood for a few months but still closer than two people who had never shared an intimacy. She smelled faintly of cigarettes. Would Julietta become one of those people who smoked like a fiend all throughout their twenties and thirties, turning into a raspy-voiced, middle-aged woman? "I thought maybe we could have a talk."

Julietta's mouth curled up. "We don't have nothing to talk about."

"Why don't we have anything to talk about?"

"Because you're just like every other jock in this dumb school."

"You seem to like jocks."

She smiled a mocking smile and her two front teeth grazed her lower lip; they were like pearls appearing out of the dark jungle of her mouth. "You don't have much choice in this school.

It's either jock or computer geek. Or liar," she added with bitterness.

"Liar?" he repeated.

Julietta threw her head back. "Why did you have to go and
insult my aunt like that? She knows you never hung out with my
cousins."

"Maybe I was trying to help them. Maybe they convinced
me."

"They did not. And if they did you're stupider than I thought
you were."

Just then the bell rang. The intense silence of the hallways
was disrupted by a clattering of heels and a cacophony of voices
in many different registers. A few of Julietta's friends found them
and immediately formed a phalanx behind her, daring Daniel with
their predatory eyes. Julietta surprised him by turning to them.
"You girls got someplace to get to?"

"Sure Julie," a few of them said.

"Well then get there!"

Daniel saw a momentary glimmer of a smile in the midst of
her scowl. She obviously relished the command she had over her
girlfriends. He wondered if she was in complete control of the
football player. Maybe the football player was easy to count on,
easy to second-guess. She didn't seem to be the sort of person
who liked her men to be unpredictable.

Daniel resumed the conversation. "Now that everything is over
with, I was hoping we'd be able to talk to each other again."

Julietta looked perplexed.

"The brothers told me that they asked you not to have anything
to do with me while all of it was going on," Daniel explained.

"They told me they were after you," she said, "but they didn't
say they were getting you to lie for them."

"But you must've known that. After all, you're their cousin
and you're close to their mother."

"Well, Danny, you figured wrong."

It was certainly clear Julietta didn't want to see him again, he
thought with a sinking feeling, and on such tenuous grounds, too.
How did any relationship survive, Daniel wondered. Even his
parents were getting divorced on what seemed to be merely his
mother's whim. Look at this relationship, thwarted by a silly

misunderstanding. Even if both he and Julietta wanted to clear things up between them it still seemed impossible to do so.

The late bell rang and as the students retreated into their classrooms the unsettling silence that had begun the conversation returned. Julietta had stopped fidgeting in place, had ceased sending body signals that she had someplace to get to. She probably was missing a class.

"Julietta," Daniel said, "when they told you they were after me, why didn't you ask why they were after me or at least try to stop them from being after me."

She looked skeptical. "They'd never listen to me. They're a bunch of greasers, for Christ's sake."

"And you couldn't wait until it all blew over, before going out with somebody else?"

"Danny, you know they take their time, the brothers do. Here we are in February and it's still going on. This is my last year of high school. I don't want to wait around for anybody. I want to have some fun."

Nodding his head, Daniel looked down at his shoes. What more could he have said?

Gianni had continued to survey the entrance to the Oaks and finally inched the car ahead. Then he found something objectionable at the side of the street and the Triumph came to a squealing halt.

"That lousy . . . ," he muttered.

"What lousy?"

"Debbie," Gianni growled, indicating Debbie Lerner's silver Audi Fox. "She went to the bar. Just to burn me."

"Is that one of the limits of your relationship: she can't go to the Oaks alone?"

"Come on, Danny, don't dig in," Gianni said. "Would you let your girlfriend go alone to the Oaks?"

"That all depends on who my girlfriend was. I certainly don't think Debbie would go off with somebody. She knows it would get back to you."

"But that's just what she wants," Gianni groaned. He slipped the car in first gear and started off slowly, as though part of him yearned to burst into the Oaks and make a scene if anything untoward was happening between Debbie Lerner and another guy. "We had a big fight."

"About what?"

At first Gianni declined to answer and channeled his mounting frustration into driving. He sped up to pass through an intersection whose traffic signal already had turned yellow and went red before they got through it. Daniel noticed a turquoise patrol car on the opposite corner. He shut his eyes and gritted his teeth. Suddenly he felt cold air purging the car. He glanced over at Gianni, who had rolled down the window and was motioning to the cop, to let him know it was the "quarterback" who ran the red light. The cop responded with a saluting beep of his horn and remained stationary.

"Jeez," Daniel said. "If you don't get into an Ivy you should run for local office."

"Too young," Gianni said with a trace of pride in his voice; he was obviously thrilled to have held sway over a patrolman. Perhaps it compensated a little for the blow dealt to his ego by the college rejections. And as though to verify his immunity to local traffic laws, Gianni shot up to sixty and blistered through the remaining downtown zone of Houghton, making a right turn on a red light, which was illegal in New York State.

Soon they were gunning along the road that led to the Scaraventos', Daniel faintly hoping that they would be stopping in to see Angela. "So you never told me what you and Debbie are having a fight about," he said.

"Oh, you know the old razzmatazz about how she and I should be spending more time together. That if she sleeps with somebody it's serious and she expects a serious amount of time to be spent together. She says it's very Italo-American to spend more time with your buddies than with your girlfriend—"

"Buddies meaning me," Daniel interrupted.

Gianni nodded. "And that's how come the Jewish girls don't usually go out with Italian guys."

"Interesting," Daniel said.

"What is?" Gianni said.

"Either she's right and you don't spend enough time with her or you just don't make her feel important enough."

"Probably the second," Gianni said.

"Let me go out with her. I'll make her feel like a princess. Jewish-American boys have a tendency to do that to their women."

"Cut it out, Danny!" Then Gianni began nodding his head rhythmically as a thought dawned on him. "I bet she'd go out with you. Just to claw at me," he fumed.

"I can't believe you worry about that," Daniel said. "On one hand she's claiming too much of you and on the other hand you're afraid she's going to hook up with somebody else."

"Girls have been known to do that."

Daniel remembered Julietta and the football player. Don't I know it, he thought to himself. "But Gianni, she's absolutely crazy about you. I wish I were so lucky."

Gianni's face turned purposeful. "I really, really like her man," he said.

"So why aren't you with her then?"

"I told you we had a fight."

"So go apologize."

"No. I just don't think I'm wrong. I think we spend plenty of time together." Gianni frowned. "Wait a second, let's say you had a girlfriend like Debbie, would you spend more time with her than I spend?"

"Damn right," Daniel said. "I wouldn't let her out of my sight."

"Come on," Gianni said. "You're exaggerating what it's like to have a girlfriend. Having a girlfriend can be quite a headache."

"Then bring on the headache," Daniel said.

They drove on for a while in silence. Finally Daniel spoke up. "Maybe you don't really like Debbie that much."

Gianni turned to him angrily. "When did you turn into such a know-it-all. You're practically a virgin—"

"There's no 'practically,' " Daniel defended himself. "Either you are or you aren't."

"Well, you certainly know the ins and outs of going out with girls."

Daniel was annoyed. "Go ahead, you little shit. Patronize me."

"What does patronize mean?"

"Patronize is the reason why you didn't get into an Ivy. Patronize is what they did to you when they told you your application wasn't strong enough."

"Fuck you, buddy," Gianni said softly.

"Let me ask you something," Daniel said in a seething voice. "How many times do I have to get laid until . . . you'll listen to my opinions about when people get involved with each other. If I took the train to New York and went to bed with fifty whores would you listen to me then? Believe me, my opinion wouldn't be any different."

"All right, I'm sorry," Gianni said. He shook his head in sudden perplexity. "I don't know. Listening to you makes me wonder if . . ." There was a look of anguish on his face. "I mean I know I don't have the hots for guys or anything. I just like to make love with Debbie and take her out and treat her really nice and not go out with anybody else. I'm faithful. I just don't want to spend every waking hour with her." Now in the midst of driving, Gianni was staring at Daniel. He peered at him for such a long time that Daniel got nervous they'd run off the road. Gianni sighed. "You think I'm shallow or do you think maybe she's not the right person?"

Maybe it has nothing to do with being shallow or Debbie being the right or wrong person, Daniel thought. Maybe you're just not willing to give yourself. "How do I know?" was all he said.

The Scaraventos' street was now upon them and Gianni slowed the car down and put on his turn signal.

"We're going to your house?" Daniel tried to sound matter-of-fact.

"Yeah, Angie wants to see you."

Daniel tilted his head back and shut his eyes. The image of Angela's kitchen blazed in the back of his mind. "Why didn't you tell me this before?"

" 'Cause she's pissed off about something," Gianni said, pulling into the driveway. He looked at Daniel, indifferent. "And don't ask me what it is, 'cause she didn't tell me. Only to bring you over when I had a chance," he said, cutting the ignition. The last drone of the pistons shattered the late night silence of the early-to-bed-early-to-rise Italian neighborhood. Every other house on the block was pitch dark. The Scaraventos', by contrast, was flooded with light.

"So she's angry with me, huh?" Daniel said, brimming with sudden anxiety.

*   *   *

The first thing he noticed, upon walking into the kitchen, was an enormous roast beef set out on a wooden cutting board and a carving knife jutting from its mass. Frank Scaravento was in a pair of navy-blue silk pajamas, sitting slumped over at the kitchen table, eyeing the roast beef as though it were the last food left on earth. His hair for once was askew. Angela was in her quilted pink bathrobe, her head buried in the refrigerator.

"They're here," Frank told her, but she remained at her post, scouring the vegetable crisper. "Here's a tomato," she said, standing upright. Her head was wound in a magenta scarf, hiding the loss of hair. Still facing the refrigerator, she said, "I can't believe I forgot to order tomatoes today." She eventually turned around, shuffling a few steps with her head bowed before looking up at Daniel, whose heart was pounding. And even before he endured the shock of seeing her face, he could feel that somehow Angela was an altered woman. The few movements she made in his direction were halting and subdued, as though part of her already had given up on surviving. Then she looked at him, or rather through him. Her mismatched, questioning eyes were now set within a sunken, metallically pale face and seemed abnormally large, like the eyes of a starving child. The size of her body had been winnowed down by weeks of intravenous feeding, and the flesh drooped from her frame.

"Hello," she said, clutching the large tomato in a withered claw of a hand. "Hello Daniel," she said without much emotion.

Daniel crossed the room to kiss her. She offered him a dry, sunken cheek, creating a barrier between them with her tomato-filled hand. "Sit down," she said stolidly. "Can I fix you a roast beef sandwich?"

"No thanks, I'm fine," Daniel said. He was contending with his shock at her changed appearance and his apprehension of whatever her anger stemmed from.

"Gianni, how about a roast beef sandwich?"

"Sure, Ma, fine," Gianni said, sitting down at the kitchen table opposite Frank. Daniel remained standing.

"Angie, let Gianni make it himself," Frank said, staring across the table at his son. Gianni rolled his eyes instead of answering back his father.

"That's okay. I'll make it. Daniel will help me," Angela told Frank. "And no arguing between the two of you," she warned. Frank shrugged and narrowed his eyes at Gianni. He began picking away waxy droplets that had melted from a dinner candle on the kitchen table. "Daniel, get me the mayonnaise," Angela said.

On one hand Daniel was glad to help, dispelling his discomfort in activity. On the other hand he was somewhat insulted by being recruited into making snacks for Gianni and Frank. As far as he knew Angela never asked either of her sons or their father to help make anything.

In spite of her lethargy, Angela's fingers were nimble. Within a few minutes, she had cut uniformly thin pieces of roast beef, shredded lettuce and perfectly sliced the damaged tomato. She told Daniel to get dinner plates from the cupboard for the sandwiches, garnished the sandwiches with pickles and then put them on the table. "Okay, the two of you," she said. "Gianni take your sandwich into your room and Frank go into the den."

Father and son looked at her with misgiving. "Go on," she ordered. "I want to talk to Danny. And I want privacy. Get out of here, both of you," she shrilled when they didn't make an immediate move to leave the room.

"Ah Angie, for Christ's sake," Frank said.

Angela tapped her foot and waited.

Frank got up slowly and took his time lumbering out of the room. Gianni managed to smile at Daniel before retiring to his bedroom.

For a moment Angela remained in the middle of the kitchen, her back toward Daniel. "I have no more patience for them," she whispered to the room at large. She turned to Daniel, looking puzzled. "You think I would, huh? I mean with things being pretty finite as they are. You'd think I'd want to be nice to them. To make it easier on everybody." She looked away. "But I don't want to. Not right now."

"Then maybe you shouldn't do what you don't want to. Probably saps your energy," Daniel said quietly.

Angela nodded. "Right. Probably does." She peered at him shrewdly with her wan countenance. "You're a smart young man, Danny," she said. "And that's what bugs me. I guess I want you to be smart all the time. Not stupid like them." She pointed to

Frank now in the den down the hall, occupying his armchair, already hypnotized by the television, eating his roast beef sandwich in slow motion. "You sure you don't want anything?"

Daniel looked at her unhappily. "I'm a nervous wreck, Angela. How could I eat something? Would you just tell me what's going on?"

At this she slammed a frail fist on the kitchen table. "What the hell is wrong with you?"

The muscles in Daniel's throat constricted and for a moment he couldn't even draw a breath.

"Why did you go over to Maria's house and tell her those lies?"

Daniel plopped down at the kitchen table, leaned on his elbows and rubbed his face with his hands. He had given in to Vito, figuring it would help set people's minds at ease. He just should've followed his original instinct and not gotten involved. He had served only to inflame the situation and now was getting it from all sides. Perhaps it was best to say nothing and just allow Angela to unleash her anger.

But she had no intention of doing that. Standing there amid a blaze of fluorescent light, she merely insisted he explain why.

He was unable to look her in the eyes. "Because they said she worried herself sick over the whole business. They said she was insomniac. And the doctor warned she'd give herself a stroke if she kept on worrying like that."

"That's her problem if she wants to give herself a stroke. If she's that self-destructive."

"They kept saying they had proof they didn't do it. They kept insisting. Even Gianni was believing them after a while."

Angela put wilted hands on hips that now protruded as a result of her recent weight loss. "Don't bring Gianni into this. He has nothing to do with it."

"He advised me."

"You're responsible," Angela insisted. "It was your choice to go over there."

"I know it was. And I guess I made the wrong decision."

"I guess you did. I guess you don't recognize the devil when he lusts after you."

"Now wait a second," Daniel said. "I figured it was no big

deal helping them out. The police didn't suspect them so it was just a matter of convincing their mother so she wouldn't drive herself crazy. If the police haven't blamed them it's not for me to."

Angela now sat down at the kitchen table and leaned toward him, her one good eye narrowing and widening malevolently, her glass eye nearly shut. "You know about the police in this town," she said with disdain. "They'll protect their own kind." She went on to say that Daniel of all people should understand how Italian-Americans stick together when it comes to matters of reputation. They might jettison their culture and their heritage but would try at all costs to maintain their honor and their pride. Particularly if threatened by bad publicity, they'd bend over backward to keep from prosecuting one another.

"I'm sorry," Daniel interrupted, "but I don't agree with that part. I think you're being hard on your own people."

"Then you're a fool," Angela squawked. "And even more of a fool to help a bunch of animal killers . . . hoodlums! And I'd be even more disgusted if you had been able to convince Maria they didn't do it!"

Daniel's head reeled from the rapid-fire reprimand. He had to close his eyes and take a few deep breaths before he could even begin to collect his thoughts. It was strange how when Angela yelled at him, his reaction was to be submissive and yield to her point of view. With his own mother he had always fought back. Speaking softly, he reminded Angela that he had his own problems, too: the separation of his parents and his father's moving out.

Angela's face softened a little bit. Daniel wondered if he was finally eliciting some sympathy. But he soon discovered the change in her countenance was just another brand of disdain. "I know it's been hard for you," she said, resting her chin on her elbows. "And don't think my heart doesn't go out to you over all that. But it still doesn't give you the right to meddle in another family's affairs, especially when they're in a crisis. You should know from your own family what it's like to be in a crisis. Would you like Gianni butting his business into what's going on between your parents?"

"No, I wouldn't," Daniel said.

Angela sat back in her chair. "Maria's got to deal with those kids the best she can. That's her lot in life. And your interfering, especially"—Angela paused, her ire rising once again—"the way you spoke Italian to her and expecting that to help your story, because you could do it in her own language, as though it would give credence. It's the most revolting thing I've heard in a long time. It's almost like prejudice. Like going into a black woman's home and talking black talk to worm your way in."

This last remark thrust deep inside Daniel, touching off a fundamental doubt. Angela made it sound as though he wormed his way into mothers' lives, sapping their affection, feeding off their misfortune.

"Stop it!" he cried out. "Stop it! Don't you understand why I did it? I did it because of you. Because she's your close friend. And because . . . she made me think of you. And because I couldn't do anything to help you I thought maybe I could do something to help her."

Angela put both hands over her eyes. "I know," she intoned. "I know that's why you did it. And that's why I feel so ashamed." She looked menacingly at Daniel. "Because you pity me so much." And then she collapsed on the table, ringing her head with a pair of pale, emaciated arms. When she spoke again her voice was muffled. "You can't just treat me like a woman you've grown fond of. And that's why I didn't let you see me in the hospital. You treat me like somebody who's dying."

"That's not true," Daniel said as he got up and rushed around to the other side of the table in an attempt to soothe Angela.

But she stiffened when he touched her. "Stay away from me," she warned, looking up at him with a gloss of hatred in her eyes, a look identical to that which Daniel had witnessed in Gianni. "Just keep away. I don't want you to touch me with your Jewish pity."

A moment later Daniel was out of the Scaraventos' back door, clutching his jacket, which he had grabbed as he fled their kitchen. He was so caught off guard by Angela's remark, so hurt that she would bring religious difference into their disagreement. He had let down his guard and she had struck him at a tender, internal place. Her anger seemed overblown. Something else was feeding it, some jagged fear had emerged. As he walked toward the front of the house he could hear Angela's sobs jabbing the quiet of the neighborhood. Then Gianni's voice filtered out, low and comforting, and Frank was saying, "Now what's the matter?" And as Daniel stood there, pondering the meaning of Jewish pity, the cold night enveloped him, permeating his distress until he was shivering.

21

Alexis was still awake that Friday night when Daniel arrived home. She answered his knock on her bedroom door, wearing a body stocking and a pair of blue jeans. Daniel was so intent upon telling her what had just happened at the Scaraventos' that he barely noticed that Alexis seemed to have something on her mind. Finally she stopped him and said, "I'd like to talk to you about this, Danny. And I'd like to talk to you about something else, too. But I want you to take me skating. On the lake near where we rented that house."

"This late?"

Alexis moved to a window and raised the shade. "The moon's almost full," she said in an awed voice. "There's plenty of light for night skating."

"But we don't even know if the skating has been good this year."

"Danny, look how cold the winter's been. It's been frozen for weeks. Mom and I drove by there the other day and plenty of people were skating. Come on, take me," Alexis said. "And we'll talk about everything. And we'll put bourbon in Dad's flask and bring that too."

Alexis got her way. It was not necessary to tell Irene, who had gone to a party in New York City and would not be returning home until quite late. Daniel went down to the basement, got his skates out of their cardboard carton and dusted them off. Alexis already had been to the local rink several times that winter and had been maintaining her skates with white gloss.

When Daniel climbed back to the top of the basement stairs, Alexis was there waiting for him. She had put on a beige skating skirt over her body stocking. She had borrowed Irene's mink chubby and a pair of rabbit earmuffs, which now hung around her neck.

They drove by the house they had occupied for several months while waiting for the house they now lived in to be renovated. It seemed a lot smaller now. It *was* smaller but appeared even more so because Alexis and Daniel had grown. Daniel remembered the comfy feeling of its informal decor of maple furniture and tartan sofas; in tone it had been similar to the Scaraventos' house. The Japanese maple trees in the front yard had noticeably matured since their departure.

"I liked my bedroom in that house better," Alexis mused, looking back at the unlit house as they kept on driving. "Even though it *was* smaller. It had a nicer view than I have now."

"It feels weird to see it now," Daniel said. "But then that was a weird year. Beginning with Dad announcing we were being transferred back."

"Mom screaming like a stuck pig."

"She did have a point," Daniel said. "I mean, he took the transfer without discussing it with her."

"He just figured she'd want to come back."

"He can be so thick sometimes," Daniel said. "He should have known better."

"I didn't even realize she wanted to stay there," Alexis said.

"Well, *I* did."

They arrived at the lake front and found a parking space on the street between the driveways of two houses that fronted the water. They grabbed their skates, put on their mittens and scarves and walked toward the bank. There had been a dusting of snow the previous evening, coating the crust of the ice. The surface of the frozen lake absorbed the moonlight, creating an illusion of dawn and suspending it over the ice—when in reality it was only half-past midnight.

Alexis laced up her skates and ventured out onto the pond. Her legs were short and muscular like Irene's and she had a low center of gravity. She stood there uncertainly like a deer testing the wind and then shot off across the ice. Alexis skated balletically. She had been taking lessons on and off since Italy. "Don't go too far out," Daniel called after her. "You could hit a soft spot."

"Come on," Alexis yelled back to him. "Don't be so chicken. It's perfectly safe."

Soon she was gliding back toward him, and as Daniel skated out to meet her, she extended her gloved hand and caught his. They twirled centrifugally around each other and then let go, each getting thrown outward, Alexis's squeals of laughter continuing in waves of echoes. Daniel's cold legs and feet began warming to the exertion. He skated hard for several minutes, passing the middle of the pond and heading toward the other side. He stopped at the opposite shore, panting and catching his breath; he hadn't had a good workout since his last soccer practice. He suddenly remembered Alexis said she had something to discuss and wondered what that could be. He looked at the frozen attenuated branches of the weeping willows, gleaming in their sheaths of ice beneath the moon. It was hard to imagine they would explode with beautiful minnow-shaped leaves during the spring; they now looked so chaste, so hopelessly barren.

He looked back across the pond toward Alexis, whom he could barely make out but whose skates he could hear scraping the ice as she practiced her figure-eights. He began skating toward her. He kept his eyes on her the entire way but suddenly she seemed to disappear. Just as he began worrying she emerged from the darkness and was skating right next to him. Her hair was bunching up around her earmuffs, her eyes were sparkling with vigor.

"So tell me about Mrs. Scaravento," she said.

As they continued to skate along Daniel explained the whole story of the Polannos; why Vito had called him; how the story had percolated down to Mrs. Scaravento; and her angry remark about Jewish pity. Part way through the explanation, Alexis took his hand and began leading him toward the middle of the pond. When they got there, she continued a few yards, did a pirouette and then backward crossovers in a slow, wobbly fashion.

"Mrs. Scaravento is really fond of you, Daniel," Alexis said when she returned to his side. "Especially since she was too embarrassed to see you while she was in the hospital."

"But if she liked me she'd want to see me?"

"And I'm saying if she didn't care so much she wouldn't be embarrassed."

Daniel considered this for a moment and said, "But now I think she's unfair to get so mad. I mean, Vito kept bothering me. I admit, he was persuasive. I never meant any harm in what I did."

"Did your going out with Julietta have something to do with Vito asking you to speak Italian to his mother?"

Daniel skated forward awkwardly and then unsuccessfully tried to do backward crossovers. "Yes and no. She mentioned something, but Maria Polanno already had heard about my Italian from Angela."

"I told you not to go out with Julietta."

"Look, are you going to talk to me, or are you going to be smug?"

"I'm just pointing out that I gave you good advice."

"I took your advice. Eventually. I never really got involved with Julietta."

"Ha!" Alexis said. "You mean she never really got involved with you." Then her tone softened. "Anyway, I'm sure by now Mrs. Scaravento regrets what she said. She'll probably call you tomorrow. I wouldn't worry about it until you don't hear from her."

"I don't think I *will* hear from her," Daniel said sadly.

"She must realize people make mistakes. You can't be perfect."

"But you know, it's like she wants me to be perfect in a way," Daniel said. "Almost . . . because she's disappointed in Gianni." This statement actually marked the first occasion the thought crossed his mind.

"You make it sound like she's given up on him," Alexis said.

"I think maybe she has." Daniel turned to his sister. "I guess she almost considers me like a sort of son."

"She probably thinks you need a mother. Come on, let's skate a little more," Alexis said. "Let's skate like Olympic pairs."

Alexis showed Daniel how to take one hand behind her back and the other in front. Soon they were whirling along the perimeter of the frozen pond. Alexis suddenly let go with one hand, applying a steadying pressure with the other, and extended her right leg into an arabesque. Her neck was arched, the mink fit snugly around her waist; she looked professional. Then she bent her torso lower and using Daniel for a balance, her hand pressed harder and trembled more. Her leg squeezed higher up in a penché. Then she closed her legs again, stood upright and then did an arabesque in the opposite direction, skating backward on her other leg. "Now lift me up," she said. Daniel lifted her; she did a midair split and then landed awkwardly. She slipped and fell on the ice before he could try to save her. For a moment she just sat there, laughing. Then a look of doubt rippled over her face and she frowned. "Pick me up," she told him.

Alexis brushed the snow from her tights and then faced her brother.

"Mom's going to have a garage sale," she announced in a voice still panting from her unexpected fall. "She hasn't had the opportunity to tell you about it yet."

"But why would she have a garage sale before selling the house?"

"Oh, she already has somebody who wants to buy the house. You know Mom, always one step ahead of everybody."

The implications began to sink in. "How could she already have found somebody who wants to buy our house?"

Apparently a wealthy Venezuelan man drove by a few years ago and noticing that the Fells had more land than the rest of their neighbors, actually telephoned to inquire if they would ever consider selling the house.

"I guess she didn't throw away his phone number," Alexis said.

She went on to say that Irene planned to sell almost everything that would be too difficult to ship to Italy. Their father's apartment would be unable to accommodate any more furniture.

Daniel stood there, dumbfounded.

"Mom's still planning on living in Italy?" he whispered.

"That's what *she* says."

He had always hoped that once disentangled from her marriage to their father, Irene would eventually realize it was unnecessary and pointless to go clear to Italy in order to justify her personal freedom. He thought about his and Alexis's conversation on the way to the lake and wondered if there wasn't some vindictiveness in his mother's decision to return to Italy. After all, Irene had always felt that she had been wrenched away from a place where she had intended to stay.

Daniel remained motionless and uncertain. "So what do you think. About her going to Italy?"

Alexis stopped skating and stood rigidly before him. She shivered and crossed her arms. It did seem to be getting colder suddenly. It was also getting very late.

"I don't want to move into the city and live with Dad and give up all my friends. Go to some private school and start over again." Wrinkling her nose, Alexis peered up at the moon and sighed. "I feel like we've been doing that our whole lives, picking up and starting over again. I'm tired of all these changes. You'd think at least they'd let me just keep going to the same school."

"I suppose you can always commute back to Houghton."

Alexis looked doubtfully at Daniel. Then she blew out a plume of frosted air. "And living in that cramped apartment. I can't imagine having to cook my own dinners because Dad can't cook."

"That's the least of it," Daniel said.

"Not to me. I think about who's going to cook dinner, about making new friends, what my bedroom is going to be like and maybe having to do more homework than I do at Houghton. Mom says we'd see each other at least four times a year. And that I'd spend summers over there. I guess it'll be like going away to boarding school," Alexis said wearily. "Except she's the one who's going away."

For several moments, they both inwardly reflected on the situation. The wind picked up and slapped their faces rudely and made them feel even lonelier. Daniel had certainly known for a few months that his mother wanted to sell the house, but he never dreamed it would happen this year. So soon! And beyond that he never really accepted that these changes could actually occur. He had just filed away the possibilities—they were too difficult to deal with—and continued as he had before. What else was there to do?

Now suddenly everything seemed to have coalesced, become more definite. He looked up and saw clouds shredding over the round blade of the moon. His toes had gone numb. He slid his skates to and fro to revive them. The pond creaked beneath his weight. He wondered how thick the layer of ice was and if it were thinning out already as the world was pulled toward spring. He moved his legs again. The lake groaned.

"I think we've pushed our luck enough with skating tonight," he told Alexis.

"I don't want to go home yet," she said. "It makes me feel better being out here."

Daniel studied her in a different way. "You look so much older in Mom's fur."

Alexis giggled.

"I haven't seen you happy in a long time."

She shrugged. "I hate my life this year. But I love to skate," she said, taking off once more across the ice. Daniel was sure that he could hear the ice creaking beneath her weight. He took off a mitten and held his finger to the air. It wasn't all that cold. As he watched the figure of his sister growing smaller with distance, he thought he saw something under the ice, a moving shadow of monstrous proportions—had a dreaded pocket of lake water gurgled up suddenly to a weak spot in the surface? By the shore, branches rattled like hollow bones. He was suddenly afraid for Alexis, afraid that the ice would cease to support her, that she would fall through. He knew it was his responsibility to protect her. He couldn't lose Alexis. It would destroy him. Would leave him little recourse. How would he be able to face his parents if she plunged through the ice and drowned?

He took a deep breath and shouted "Alexis!" His voice cut through the sound of the wind and the sifting granules of snow sweeping across the ice. It had a desperate and unearthly ring and he saw the effect this had on his sister, who stopped abruptly in her flight, turned and homed back to him. His heart whipped in his chest until she reached him.

"What's wrong?" She asked in alarm.

"Nothing," he said as he embraced her. "You went out too far. And it worried me."

"Oh rats," Alexis said. "You sounded like you were sinking into the ice."

"I was," Daniel said.

Alexis quickly studied the area around her brother's skates and then looked at him doubtfully.

"I mean, I thought I was."

"What's wrong, Danny?" she said.

"I want to go home now," he said. "Okay?"

"Sure," Alexis said. "We can go home."

They were back in the car and the heater was blasting. The cold windshield kept fogging up from their breath and Daniel had to keep the defroster on. They passed the flask of bourbon back and forth, taking tiny gulps until they felt warmer. It took a long time for the interior of car to shed the cracking chill and it had barely heated up by the time they arrived home.

Daniel braked the car to a stop in front of the house. The kitchen was welling with light, as was the master bedroom: Irene had returned. They just peered at the house for a while, each of them dragged down by the weight of inner sentimentalizing, which seemed to be the effect of realizing that this place would soon no longer be their home. Daniel forestalled pulling into the driveway.

"If I was where you are in high school I'd go to Italy," he said finally.

"You speak Italian better than I do."

"Still. It'd probably be easier to get into college. All the Ivies would be impressed with your continental upbringing."

"That's too far in the future," Alexis said. "When we first moved in here Dad and Mom swore up and down that we'd stay."

Daniel shrugged, switched off the ignition and the motor sputtered and died.

"Well, they couldn't predict what was going to happen."

"I'm not saying they could," Alexis said. She had bent her head into the fur jacket and her last words were muffled by it. Rousing herself, she stared once again at the house. "There's Mom." She indicated a shadow moving across the kitchen. "You ready to go inside?"

Daniel sighed. "Ready as I'll ever be."

They found Irene hovering over the kitchen stove, scrambling eggs. She still wore her evening clothes: a gray angora dress with a cowl neck and a black silk turban. She turned to them when they came in the door, her eyes artfully shaded with kohl, her face weary yet composed, turning radiant with a smile. Sometimes Daniel found her beauty astonishing, and this exhilaration juxtaposed against the knowledge of her future plans gouged him deeply. Here she was, making eggs at one o'clock in the morning. Unlike other parents, she didn't seem at all disturbed that her children were missing when she arrived home. It was only when she saw them holding their skates that Irene frowned.

"Is the rink open this late?"

Daniel and Alexis glanced at each other. Then Alexis walked matter-of-factly past her mother, through the kitchen and over to the cellar door. Daniel and Irene listened to her trotting down the cellar steps.

"We didn't go to the rink," Daniel said finally. "We went skating on Maury's Pond."

Irene, who had been absent-mindedly prodding the jiggling mass of eggs, abruptly stopped. She turned to Daniel, gripping the spatula tightly. Part of her black turban had slipped down her forehead and cut across one of her eyes, giving it an exotic angle it did not normally own. "What, are you nuts?" she said. "You're not supposed go pond skating at night like that."

"You're right," Daniel said, dropping his skates by the back door. "While we out there the ice started to crack and we nearly fell in."

Irene dropped the spatula on the formica. "For Christ's sake!"

"What do you care? You're selling the house and going off to Italy."

"Stop guilting, Daniel."

He glared at her. "That'd be impossible."

They heard Alexis clumping back up to the top of the basement steps. When she stepped out into the hall light she found both of them staring at her. She was still wearing Irene's chubby, the rabbit muffs dangling around her neck. Her face was flushed from the climb.

"Come here, honey," Irene said in a coaxing voice. "We're talking about something."

Alexis kept her distance. "What are you talking about?"

"About moving."

Alexis made wavering gestures with her hands. "I'm going to bed."

"Alexis!" Irene ordered.

"I said I'm going to bed," Alexis insisted sternly. She hurried to the stairway and climbed the carpeted steps two at a time, using the bannister to hoist herself along.

"She's really got the right idea," Daniel said, "by refusing to discuss anything."

"Oh, she'll discuss it when she's alone with me," Irene softly explained. "She doesn't like for you to see her get upset."

Daniel turned to his mother. "She told me about the garage sale."

Irene inclined her head and peered at him. "You know I usually tell her things first. Because she takes longer."

"I'm not objecting to that," Daniel said. "But why can't you at least wait another year."

Irene sighed. Glancing indifferently at the Teflon pan and its contents, she picked it up and dropped it in the sink. She turned water on the eggs and ruined them. Daniel saw droplets of butter floating on the surface of the mess.

"I guess I did in your appetite," he remarked snidely.

Irene ignored his sarcasm. "I just started making the eggs because . . ." She paused, sticking a manicured fingernail under the turban and righting it on the top of her head. "I got home. You two weren't here. I got nervous and bored."

Daniel sat down at the kitchen table. "Mom, that doesn't make any sense."

Irene turned to him with a frantic glimmer in her eyes. "Why not?"

He suddenly realized that she was in a state of extreme agitation, almost to the point of distraction.

"What are you going to do in Italy if you miss us?" Daniel asked. "Take a midnight flight to New York? Arrive at Dad's apartment all frumpy?"

"You probably wouldn't even be there," she said. "You'd probably be at college."

"So."

"So Danny, what about me? Don't I get a chance to do something for myself?"

"Yes, but why can't we get used to the divorce before you sell the house?"

Irene approached the table and after a moment of hesitation sat down next to Daniel. "Why not?" she said in a hoarse voice.

"Why not?" Her throat was seized by fit of gulping. "You wouldn't be any more used to it a year from now. You'd be ready for your second year of college. Alexis would be finishing ninth grade. And your father and I had already decided to put her in private school next year. In Manhattan. So she'd be making that change whether or not we moved."

"And she's got no say in what school she goes to?"

"The schools around here are so godawful."

Irene glanced away. "Look Danny, we've got to sell the house."

Irene and Harold would divide the proceeds from the sale of the house, money they both needed for their respective lives; Irene would hold on to whatever she could collect from the sale of the furniture and artwork. Later on his father would confirm to Daniel that, indeed, they did need to sell the house no matter where Irene decided to live.

"You still don't have to sell everything and move to Europe. You could very well live in New York City and not give up your custody. To go so far away—it's selfish!"

"I agree with you," she said. "I *am* selfish. But I have to be at this point right now. Because . . . I need to save myself."

"Save yourself," Daniel mocked her. "By going to Italy?"

She seemed to anticipate this reaction. "That's right."

"Then I don't understand."

She dipped her head for a moment and when she looked up at him he saw the film of tears in her eyes. "If I'm unhappy now. And if I really believe that living in a certain place will make me happy, why shouldn't I live there?"

Daniel fell silent. He saw a strange sort of chasm opening before his eyes, huge and fathomless, a wretched place where nothing could come to any sort of fruition.

"Do you know why I go into New York all the time?" Irene asked.

Daniel shrugged.

"Because I can't keep still here anymore. I know this will sound ridiculous because I want to move to Italy, but I have trouble dealing with the idea that you're going to college. Because I feel like I have nothing to fall back on. That's why I want to go somewhere. . . ."

It was then that Daniel, who all along had wanted to say,

"You're our mother and you should be near us," suddenly saw that Irene's extreme unhappiness had made this responsibility expendable to her. "*In quel caso, buon viaggio*," he said, rising from the table, leaving the kitchen, leaving the unresolved disturbance of their conversation and his brooding mother in his wake.

22

Certain things were beyond discussion. This was the conclusion Daniel came to as the winter broke apart around an early spring. The sudden transfusion of warmth was unforeseen in light of the constant cold that had beleaguered New York State since autumn. No longer was weather predictable the way it had been when he was a child in Italy or even when the family first returned to America. Winter used to arrive on schedule. Spring came in April. And there always seemed to be snow on Christmas.

He did not return to the Scaraventos' house after the night Angela rebuked him; Alexis was wrong: Angela never called to apologize. Her withdrawal from him took a while to set in, to make itself completely understood. As the weeks elapsed, the rejection rankled more and more, particularly since the time Daniel spent with Gianni was now confined to driving around aimlessly in the Triumph, or cruising up to the Bedford diner and ogling patrician beauties or drinking pitchers of beer elbow to elbow at the Oaks. Gianni was reluctant to broach the subject of what had occurred between his mother and Daniel, making it seem that any discussion of Angela's anger would only interfere with their friendship. Which Daniel found all the more frustrating. The Scaraventos' house remained informally off limits to Daniel, who just assumed he was no longer welcome. And as the term of his exile lengthened so did his distress.

It started with insomnia that began plaguing him around the
vernal equinox. At first he thought he was kept awake by the
changing of seasons, the gradual lengthening of the days, the
prolongation of light. Daniel realized there was something about
the idea of daylight seeping further and further into the evening
that was disturbing to him. Longer days seemed also to reinforce
the reality of certain painful events to come: his mother selling
the house and taking flight in the summer; Mrs. Scaravento's anger
lingering into a warmer season. Daniel would find himself wide
awake at three in the morning and even got to know the degrees
of night; he could read time without consulting a clock. He knew
that when a graininess superimposed itself upon the dark, it would
be five and that a wan flickering of blue meant it was seven and
nearly time for school. Sometimes as he lay awake reading or
listening to his radio, he would picture Mrs. Scaravento in her
pink quilted bathrobe, sitting in Mr. Scaravento's armchair, one
eye brooding, one eye dulled and cold. He saw her standing vigil
over the early planting of her L-shaped garden, having hired someone to sow the seeds and vegetables that he had helped her order:
Daniel knew that her displeasure with him would never interfere
with the schedule of planting she had mapped out early in the
winter. He began wondering if his insomnia could be sympathetic
insomnia. Perhaps if Angela knew he was sleepless too she'd admit
him back into her life; then they might stay up late and suffer
insomnia together.

One thing Daniel discovered, however, left him hopeful of
eventually regaining Angela Scaravento's favor. Shortly after she
vilified him for visiting Maria Polanno, Daniel learned the reason
why the Polanno brothers had been ignoring him. According to
Gianni, Angela had asked Maria to come visit her and then warned
that if her sons laid a single finger on Danny that she would never
speak to Maria again, even on her deathbed. Apparently, Maria
took this threat to heart. She phoned her brother-in-law in Brook-
lyn, who promptly arrived in Houghton and slapped the brothers
around until he was satisfied that they would become more at-
tentive to their mother's wishes. Daniel Fell was now definitely
off limits.

In the middle of April, Daniel was accepted by Princeton and
Amherst and chose the latter because it was smaller and because
it had a better undergraduate philosophy department. He decided

to pursue philosophy, thinking it would perhaps give him a better perspective on life's unpredictability. Philosophy would give him various approaches to thinking, alternative explanations of the meaning of existence and of dying.

Gianni was accepted by Michigan State; provisionally, however. Although the football team wanted him to play, his grades were too low to gain him a full acceptance. The university asked him to attend its summer session and in so doing he'd be better prepared to meet their requirements. The dean's office wished to remind him from the start that his college education would be as important as his playing football.

At the end of May, Daniel took Gianni Scaravento to meet his father in New York City. The meeting was arranged because Harold had spent a year in Michigan and offered to share with Gianni some pros and cons about the campus. But Daniel felt that his father had lived in Michigan too long ago and what he remembered probably would not coincide with the changes that had occurred since his student days. Harold was just curious to finally meet Gianni Scaravento.

The night they drove into Manhattan, Gianni was wearing a navy-blue shetland sweater which Debbie Lerner had bought for him at Christmas. Debbie had drummed it into Gianni's head that he looked best in darker colors. And she was right. Navy blue toned down the evidence of his frequent bouts with acne and accentuated his dark, moody handsomeness.

Gianni was driving in his typical maniacal manner on the various connections of highways that led into Manhattan. The Triumph dodged in and out of traffic openings with roaring precision. Daniel reminded him several times that they had plenty of time to get to his father's apartment, that the restaurant reservation was not until eight o'clock. But Gianni was still intent upon reaching Manhattan in record time. His spirits seemed buoyant. Having accepted the fact that he would now attend a Big Ten instead of an Ivy, he obviously had relinquished the fear that he'd end up working for the town sanitation department. He was truly bound for higher education, and even, eventually, law school.

At one point a car in front of them stopped short, avoiding one of those inevitable pot holes that punctuate the well-traveled urban highways. Gianni swerved into the middle lane. It was a close call but he pulled off his maneuver with rapid-fire confidence. Daniel reflected that driving with anyone who had less than Gianni Scaravento's lightning reflexes would have landed them in the emergency room of some Harlem hospital.

"Will you slow down, Gianni?" he complained for the umpteenth time.

"Don't worry. Nothing's going to happen to us. We're fucking invincible. We're out to rule the world. Heh man, look how beautiful it is," Gianni said, sticking his arm out the window and pointing to trees newly garlanded with leaves. Spring in the suburbs was not quite so turned out as it was in Manhattan, where flowering always occurred a few weeks in advance. "Smell that sweet air, Danny," Gianni said infectiously. "We got our whole lives ahead of us to think about."

"Speaking of the future," Daniel said. "When do you leave for Michigan?"

"A few days after school's out. I guess I'll find a place to live for the summer. It won't be so competitive then. And I'll keep it through the year."

"Aren't you going to live in the dorms your first year?" Daniel asked.

"Na," Gianni said. "I don't want to live in a dorm. I want to have my own place. My father said he'd pay for it. That way Debbie can fly in and spend the weekend with me." Debbie Lerner was bound for Ithaca College.

"I thought they put all the football players together."

"If they do I don't want to be a part of those animals off the field." Gianni turned to Daniel. "You going to come visit me this summer, buddy?"

"Sure. But if my dad gets me this filing job down on Wall Street, I won't be free until the middle of August."

"That won't be a good time," Gianni said. "I start football practice in the middle of August."

"You mean you'll be too tired to do anything else?"

"Remember this is the Big Ten," Gianni said sarcastically. Daniel admired the fact that Gianni still felt somewhat cynical about playing football.

Daniel drew a deep breath as he always did before asking a question concerning Angela, which he did a lot these days, and which Gianni had learned to anticipate. "So what does she think about all this?" he said.

"Don't we get off at Seventy-second Street?" Gianni hedged answering the question.

Daniel looked at him squarely. "No, Fifty-third."

Gianni's face screwed up. "You sure, buddy?"

Daniel looked out the window. "Go any way you want," he said flatly.

"Oh shit, all right. She's not wild about me playing football in college. But you know that, so why are you asking?"

"Just bringing it up?"

"Figures," Gianni scoffed.

They dropped into an awkward silence, but then their attention was drawn to the sight of an ambulance flanked by two police cars, the whole entourage sundering the traffic on the East River drive in the opposite direction.

And then Gianni tensed up. There was a slight body odor present in the car that had a deep, fearful scent.

"She went into a slump, Danny," he said finally.

Daniel waited a moment, trying to conjure up an image of a slump. "What do you mean?" he asked.

"She got this thing called shingles. It's a nerve thing."

"I know what it is."

"She had to go and stay in the hospital for a few days. She's over that now, but she's really depressed. Hardly talks to anybody."

"When did this start happening?"

Gianni hesitated. "Recently," he said finally.

They were just entering the tunnel that gave out to the sharp off-ramp to Fifty-third Street. Daniel told Gianni as much and then fell silent waiting for him to go on. But Gianni seemed unable to continue.

"Why haven't you told me . . . about her being sick? Don't you think I—"

"Danny, man," Gianni broke in, "she's only got a few more months."

A droning sound reverberated in the tunnel, amplified rubber tires impacting upon concrete. The noise and the words split Daniel inwardly and left him feeling raw and tight and winded. When he turned to look at Gianni, Gianni's eyes had grown wide and fearful. The green lights in the tunnel kept strobing over his face, disjointing his anguished expression.

"The doctor told us. He's says everything that is now happening to her is predictable. Higher stages. All that. And she knows it without being told. We try to lie to her and say we'll all get through it together, that we're in it together like a team. But she knows." Gianni shook his head in bewilderment. "I always thought I'd have my ma, Danny. I figured my dad would go before she went 'cause he drinks and smokes. She was always so healthy when I was a kid." He began blinking. "Ah Danny, she's going to die on me."

Despite the sudden escalation of emotion in the car, Gianni managed to catch the Fifty-third Street exit. As soon as they were off the highway, however, he pulled over to the side of the street in front of a fire hydrant, put his forehead on the steering wheel and wept. Tears welling in his own eyes, Daniel slipped his arm around him. While comforting his friend, he found himself peering at the crack in the windshield, which at the end of February had made a sharp turn in the glass out towards the passenger side and zipped back across to the driver's side, looped and began plunging down toward the bottom.

Gianni's body shook and rippled with his misery. He eventually got himself under control, wiped the tears out of his eyes and looked at Daniel again.

"She's been mentioning you lately, buddy," he finally admitted, nodding his head like a little boy who is full of important information.

Seconds after they knocked, Harold opened the door with an apron on. Miffed, Daniel squinted at him and then said automatically, "I know we're fifteen minutes late. But there was traffic and . . . can you still hold the reservation?"

A silly grin spread across Harold's face. Gianni was shifting uncomfortably at Danny's side, waiting to be introduced. But for the moment Daniel had forgotten all about Gianni. "What, are you blind?" Harold said. "Don't you see what I'm wearing?"

"I see that," Daniel said. "But you said we were going to a restaurant so I just . . ." and then his words failed him.

Harold turned to Gianni and extended his hand. "Harold Fell," he said and then turned to Daniel again and shook his head. "You're so literal. Why don't you both come in?"

"Your father's cooking," Gianni told Daniel when Harold took a step backward and began opening the door. Now they could smell the simmering food odors.

"It was all a hoax, there was never a reservation," Harold explained as he led them past an Oriental screen into the foyer, where flush to the wall, an oblong mirror had been placed above a black lacquer table. "I wanted to surprise you." On the table stood a cut-crystal vase filled with fresh yellow irises. Daniel's mouth gaped when he continued into the kitchen and saw mounds of chopped greens and scallions and the bottles of spices out on the counter. "All you need is a chef's hat," he cried. "Where did you learn how to cook?"

"I took one of those courses you suggested. At the New School."

"You're joking," Daniel said, lifting up the lid of an expensive-looking Revere-ware pot that was heating on the stove. "Umm, this smells great. What is it?"

"Basically veal shanks with rosemary," Harold said, beaming behind them. "I made it because I know how much you like veal, Daniel." He turned to Gianni. "And you've got to keep up your strength for football at the University of Michigan. Congratulations."

"Thank you, Mr. Fell," Gianni said.

"Call me Hal. Please. Don't stand on ceremony. I feel like I know you."

Daniel laughed uncomfortably. Harold, meanwhile, was looking carefully at Gianni. "Your eyes look all irritated," he said. "You want some drops or something. Are you allergic—"

"Dad, he's been crying, all right?" Daniel said irritably.

Harold turned to Daniel. "Sorry you don't like my solicitude."

"I like your solicitude. But you're being so hyper and we just came from this intense conversation."

"Jeez, Danny," Gianni said. "You didn't have to tell him I was crying, did you?"

"He's my father," Daniel said.

Harold turned to Gianni. "Heh, don't worry about it. We understand. The Fells are all big criers. Nothing like a good cry. Danny, why don't you show your friend the apartment—the view—while I get the rest of this together."

Daniel led Gianni out of the room, ostensibly to show him the view from the living room, but stopped short when he found the natural burl dining table beautifully set with china, silver, silk place mats and tall wineglasses stuffed with linen flags. There was a finely chopped salad in a crystal bowl in the middle of the table as well as a vintage bottle of red wine that was already breathing. "Dad," he cried out, "I don't believe this. You're turning into a caterer."

A pot clanged in the kitchen and Harold came running out. "What did you say?"

"Look at this table," Daniel said.

"Why, what's wrong?"

"It looks like *House and Garden*."

"Well, I've had to entertain. It's the best way to meet people."

Gianni shot Daniel a strange look. "I suppose," Daniel said.

"Do women go nuts when you make them dinner," Harold bragged. "A man cooking dinner is like good stage lighting. I'm suddenly no longer this boring accountant-type guy who divorced, but this urban exec who's got flair. Panache."

Gianni laughed. "Maybe I should learn how to cook. That would flip out Debbie."

"Who's Debbie?" Harold asked.

"His girlfriend."

Suddenly the doorbell rang. Daniel looked at his father inquisitively. Harold broke into a big grin. "Perfect timing. This is somebody I've been wanting you to meet," he said.

This somebody must be a certain woman. Daniel glanced at the dinner table and suddenly realized it had been set for four. He was unsure how to react and felt himself inwardly squirming with embarrassment. Daniel and Gianni kept their eyes glued to the door, which Harold opened to reveal a tall, very attractive blond in black slacks who wore wire-framed aviator glasses. She couldn't have been more than twenty five. Kissing Harold on both cheeks, she said, "You must be Daniel. I've seen pictures of you. I'm Sylvie."

"Nice to meet you," Daniel said stiffly. He was unprepared to meet a new woman and felt his father should have warned him. He introduced Gianni Scaravento, who was having trouble concealing his admiration.

Harold took Sylvie by the hand and asked her to come into

the kitchen and see what he was cooking. He then reminded Daniel
that Gianni had not yet witnessed the wonderful view of the East
River.

"She's certainly a gorgeous tomato," Gianni whispered to Daniel when they were alone.

"I guess she's all right," Daniel conceded.

"Your father's been on the move," Gianni said approvingly.

"Something I'd rather not see."

"Well buddy, you have to realize it's going to happen sooner
or later," Gianni said as he headed to the living room windows.
He framed his eyes with his hands, looking out over the East River
and the highway drive and then southward along the extremities
of buildings that fronted the water, an ongoing curve that resembled the pleats of a curtain. "Wow," he murmured, moving from
window to window, taking in the 180-degree panorama. "You'll
be in heaven living here."

"I'll be in purgatory," Daniel corrected him.

Gianni's eyes held the view of Manhattan for a moment longer.
Then his brow wrinkled. "What *is* purgatory?"

"It's a lot like going to summer school," Daniel explained.

23

Irene enlisted Alexis to help make an inventory of the furniture and artwork in the house. Out of the thirty-three paintings and drawings hanging on the walls, she decided to keep only a third. She offered to buy the marble mosaic from Harold, who insisted on giving it back to her as a parting gift. Of course he had to ask Daniel's permission, but Daniel refrained from making any objection. He felt that he had already made his point with his mother. By now he had realized that his father's possessing the mosaic would have little affect on the final outcome of his parents' separation. And Harold admitted that because he never felt right about owning the mosaic, he was never able to bring himself to hang it. Better that someone should enjoy the picture than exiling it to some dark closet.

In early June there was a reunion week up at Amherst to which incoming freshmen were invited if they hadn't already seen the campus. Daniel had passed through the campus once a few years ago but never properly visited it. He borrowed his father's Buick, drove up to Massachusetts and arranged to stay in one of the fraternity houses. There was a double purpose to his visit.

At the end of his two-day visit on June 3, Daniel turned eighteen. He deliberately arranged it so that no one in the family could get hold of him at Amherst and had led them all to believe that he'd be back home in time to celebrate. Phone calls inundated the campus switchboard, which referred them to the fraternity house. But he was never there to receive them. Once or twice the night of his birthday people knocked on his door. As he ignored them, he indulged himself by imagining his mother and Alexis running to the phone amid their preparations for the garage sale. He pictured his father clamping the lid down on one of his culinary masterpieces, picking up the phone as he looked out on the night barges and on the diamond lights of distant Queens, cursing his inability to reach his son. Being incommunicado was a wonderful way of causing the rest of the family distress, Daniel thought, and what a way to show them just how rotten he felt. Childishly, he vowed to himself to do the same thing on his twenty-first birthday, if he felt similarly disgruntled.

The morning of June 4, he emerged from his room to find a sheaf of messages taped on the outside of the door. "Irene Fell called at 10 A.M. Please call back. Harold Fell called at 9:45 A.M. Please call back at office. Alexis Fell called at 1 P.M. Please call back. Irene Fell called at 6 P.M. Happy birthday, Danny." Below the message was written, "Why didn't you tell us?," obviously scrawled by some college student who had lingered on after graduation. "We'd have celebrated with you." Another message: 7 P.M. Harold Fell. "Sorry to have missed you. Happy Birthday." 8:30 P.M. "Wishing you Happy Birthday, but please call home. Mom!" 11:30 P.M. "Cut the crap, Danny, and call us already! Alex."

He arrived back in Houghton at twelve-thirty in the afternoon. Unfamiliar cars were lined up in front of the house and were blocking the driveway: Volvos, Ford LTDs, Country Squire station wagons. A few contained children's car seats. He spied a hand-lettered sign on a telephone pole with a red arrow, FURNITURE AND GARAGE SALE, and realized that for the last few blocks he had peripherally noticed smaller versions of this sign on several telephone poles. For some reason, perhaps his general unwillingness to accept the garage sale, he had confused the dates and had thought it was to begin the following day. If he had known it was today he would have stayed away. Unfortunately it was too late to escape. Soon Alexis was poking her head out of the upper window and peering down at him. She appeared upset. He hoped that she wasn't angry about yesterday. She had no right to be.

He was entitled to spend his eighteenth birthday in whatever manner he chose, particularly if he didn't feel like celebrating.

As Daniel prepared to park on the street, he noticed that the front door was wide open; a strange woman wearing a yellow rain slicker was scaling the staircase.

His mother emerged onto the porch, escorting another woman, who was carrying a black fur over one arm; how surreal to see a fur coat in the summer. Then Daniel realized that it was his mother's mink coat. He couldn't believe she had sold it! The woman opened the passenger side of her car, laid the coat over the front seat, then crossed around and climbed into the other side. By now Irene had spied the Buick and remained where she was standing, waiting for Daniel. She was wearing a cream-colored linen skirt with a matching jacket and a pale-blue blouse. A silk scarf was wound around her neck and she had on her diamond earrings. Daniel pulled into the street space vacated by the woman who had bought the mink coat, grabbed his bag and got out.

"Well," said Irene as he approached her, "what do you have to say for yourself?"

"About what?" he said.

Irene inserted one of her fingers between the scarf and the bare skin of her throat. "Why didn't you call us back?"

"I didn't get the messages until this morning."

"You were gone from morning until night?" she asked skeptically.

Daniel shrugged. "Mom, there's a lot to do up there." After saying this he wondered why he didn't just blurt out the truth and explain he had ignored the phone calls when they were announced. No, better to have her think it didn't really matter to him if he talked to anyone in his family on his eighteenth birthday. That would give her a twinge.

"But you knew we wanted to get in touch with you," Irene went on.

"I fell asleep in one of the student lounges and didn't wake up until late."

"We were up late getting things arranged."

"How was I supposed to know?"

"You know how busy we've been."

"You're saying it like I should've been around to help."

"Well, you could have cleaned up your room before you left," Irene grumbled softly.

"Mom, you know I don't approve of this. So why should I help out?"

"Daniel, I explained to you that your father and I have to divide everything. The only fair way is selling it all." Irene's voice rattled. He sensed that her nerves were already frayed from the stress of it all. Good, he thought. This should unnerve her.

"Mom, just because you *have* to sell everything doesn't make it any easier for me. I mean you're selling things that are familiar to us. In fact, I think you should go inside and keep your eyes on some of those ladies. They might lift something valuable and then you won't be able to move to Italy."

Irene winced and then whispered his name admonishingly.

But the tension building between them was short-circuited by the woman in the yellow rain slicker whom he had noticed earlier and who was now holding out a pair of ceramic Foo dogs that Harold once used for bookends. "How much?" she said.

Like an emotional chameleon, Irene suddenly turned charming. "The price tag should be on the bottom," she told the woman, bending toward her solicitously. Daniel noticed his mother was wearing a gold nugget on a long delicate eighteen-karat chain, which swung expansively to and fro as she upended the Foo dogs and indicated a price written—in what he recognized as Alexis's scrawl—on a white sticker with an indelible marking pen. One of Irene's rings made a hollow tinkling sound against the porcelain. "Says right here 'Three hundred for the pair.' "

"Hum," the woman said. "It's actually a good price. They sell them in the city for five hundred."

"I've had appraisers in," Irene told the woman. "We're underpricing everything. That's what makes a garage sale."

"Absolutely," the woman said. "Will you take a check?"

Irene nodded, her hair bouncing around her shoulders in lustrous auburn scrolls.

As Daniel watched her he remembered when he went to camp in Italy and she came to visit him with Harold and how all the counselors kept murmuring how lovely she was. She had been wearing this short golf dress, showing off her hard, shapely legs.

Sometimes the dress blew up and you could see the place up close
to her crotch where she had a bikini wax. He used to love having
such an attractive mother. But that was a transitory feeling. Her
stunning appearance had now become an anathema; looking lovely
would no doubt fetch a greater profit from the sale. She was
already working against him, plugging for her new life, leaving
him to plug for the old.

He sat down on the front steps, waiting until Irene was done
with the woman. She turned toward him, a green check scissored
between her index and middle fingers. "I want to finish this discussion," she said.

"There's nothing more to say."

"There's a lot more to say," she disagreed.

Daniel indicated the swell of browsers picking over the house
like scavengers. "It's already in motion." The bright sunlight suddenly caught the gold nugget around Irene's neck. "What about
your jewelry, Mom?" he said. "You going to sell that, too?"

"No, I'm not going to sell it," she said. In this conversation,
Daniel knew that he could get to her in a way he hadn't as yet,
even more than when he asked his father to take the marble mosaic.
He was now in a position to rake his fingers over her heart.

"I'm just confused about all of it, Ma" was what he actually
said instead of digging his claws in. "That was the reason why I
wanted to be away."

"You don't think I realize that?"

Daniel shrugged. "I just need to sit here for right now. Why
don't you go back inside. And we'll talk about it in a while."

His mother obeyed, leaving him to occupy the front steps for
another twenty minutes. Floral smells perfumed the air. Tree
peonies Irene had cultivated for years were in full bloom, emitted
waves of intoxicating fragrance. A rash of delphiniums were arch-
ing over themselves in the flower bed at the side of the yard, and
the house's brick flanks oozed with newly bloomed wisteria. Bum-
ble bees swarmed the rhododendrons. Daniel watched the gardener tending the tulips and the pansies and the white azaleas.
He could smell the earth, the raw, rich fecundity of growing
things. A burst of happiness briefly surged through him; summer
was arriving. But then he knew that he would be spending most
of the summer in his father's apartment, sleeping on the couch;

there were only the two bedrooms. Harold, of course, was overjoyed at this prospect. But the city was so syrupy and unbearable during the summer and it perpetually reeked of garbage. If only he had been on good terms with Mrs. Scaravento he could have asked to occupy Gianni's room while Gianni was in Michigan.

"Danny," Alexis called down from her bedroom window.

"What?" he said, not looking at her.

"Aren't you coming in?"

"Not right now."

"Please come up here. I need to talk to you."

Daniel looked up through the sunlight to his sister's window. She appeared pale and stricken. "Please come here." Her voice quavered.

A moment later, he was on his feet and plunging into the house. His eyes had difficulty adjusting to the abrupt change of light and he actually bumped into a wall on his way to the staircase. The house was brimming with women and children, many of whom were neighbors he recognized from their seven years in Houghton but whom had never spoken to. No doubt they were using the garage sale as an excuse to look over the inside of a house, whose exterior they had always known, a landmark in their daily comings and goings and which probably gave off certain impressions that may have been contradicted by its interior.

He bolted up the stairs, brushing against several people on their way down. A small group was hovering outside Alexis's closed bedroom door, Irene among them. She turned to Daniel, her face pinched with worry. "Alexis won't let me in. She slammed the door a while ago and refuses to open it."

"She's probably upset," a neighbor said.

Daniel felt it was inappropriate for all these strangers to be witnessing something so intimate and disturbing. He addressed them. "All of you please go downstairs and let me talk to her."

Irene, taking her cue, began herding people toward the staircase.

"But I was interested in something there," protested a dumpy, middle-aged fellow, one of the few men who had actually ventured into the house.

Daniel met his eager gaze with a glower. "Then you'll just have to wait a while."

Taken aback, the man edged toward the others. "Uh, okay," he said.

"I'll be right here," Irene said softly as Daniel knocked. "It's me, Daniel," he announced and then turned to his mother irritably. "Just go downstairs for a bit and let me talk to her."

"Are you sure?" She looked doubtful.

"Please, Mom!"

As soon as Irene had left, the door cracked open, showing Alexis's fearful eyes. She let Daniel in quickly and then slammed the door again. The shades were now drawn and a rigaux candle was burning. The room reeked of Christmas. "What's wrong?" Daniel said.

Alexis was wearing one of Harold's old tattersall shirts and a pair of khaki pants. Her eyes were wild. "She's going to sell my rocking chair."

Daniel glanced around the room, unable to locate the piece of furniture. "Where is it?"

"I put it in my closet."

"Well, there's no use hiding it, Alexis."

"I don't want her to sell it. Let her sell everything else. But I want to keep it."

"So tell her."

"I told her. She said it was an antique and that it wouldn't fit in my bedroom at Dad's apartment?"

"When was *she* there?"

Looking even more distraught, Alexis explained that Irene had gone to visit the apartment. She had given Harold some suggestions about fixing up the guest room in a more personal way to suit Alexis.

Daniel went over and opened Alexis's closet. The rocking chair was suspended amid a jumble of clothing and a stack of board games like Monopoly and Scrabble and Go to the Head of the Class. "I can't believe you were able to get the door to close," Daniel said.

"It wasn't easy."

"You know, Alex." He tried comforting her. "It's an old rocking chair. Probably nobody will want it."

Alexis shook her head resolutely. "Did you see this man out there: the one with the big mouth and beady eyes?"

"Yes."

"Well, he's interested in it," Alexis said. "I waited until he left the room and then I locked him out."

"Oh God," Daniel moaned. Then something inconsistent occurred to him. "I don't understand why you helped Mom with the sale. I mean, you objected to it as much as I did."

"What was I going to do?" Alexis wailed. "I don't have a license to drive off and escape everything like you do."

Daniel said nothing. He knew this was true.

"Please, Danny, please don't let her sell it," Alexis pleaded helplessly.

Daniel rubbed his face with his hands. "God damn her," he growled. "Just stay here," he said as he flew out the door and yelled, "Mom! Where are you?" No answer. "You downstairs, Mom?"

"In the den," she finally answered.

Daniel passed perhaps twenty browsers on the way to the den. His purpose lent the house a soft, furious blur. The fact that every available flat surface was being employed as display area for things such as old silverware, jars of glass beads, carved jade bookends, a toaster oven only increased his fury. Their home was being turned into a panderer's den, and this showcase of price-tagged possessions was a vulgarity.

He found Irene standing on a high kitchen stool, reaching toward the first editions of Somerset Maugham kept on the top shelf of the bookcase. Harold had purchased them in London. Her waist was at his eye level. She tugged a book from the collection and then looking down on Daniel, asked, "Did Alexis open her room?"

"We're not selling the rocking chair, Mom!" he shouted.

Irene shut her eyes for a moment, inwardly composing herself. Meanwhile, the half-dozen people present in the den made a quick exit. Daniel shut the door after them. "Danny," she said plaintively, "sweetheart, why are we discussing this now? Didn't you say before—"

"But she wants to keep it," he insisted. "And if that's important to her, you shouldn't sell it. It's not going to make that much of a difference."

Irene was peering at him strangely. She sensed that he would not back down and doubtless was trying to adjust herself to this idea. After all, he was interfering with something that she already had arranged. The moment was delicate; she seemed at a momentary loss for how to handle it.

"But your father's—" she began.

"Don't give me that shit . . . that fucking shit about Dad's apartment." Daniel lunged for the telephone extension. "I'll call him right now to see if it's okay with him."

"Don't you talk to me like that!" Irene hissed, climbing down from the chair. She was clenching a first edition with both hands, her knuckles blanched. "Don't you bring that foul mouth to me." They now stood within a foot of each other. This close her beautiful face was distorted by purpose and fear and for a moment she was as strange to him as the people invading the outer rooms, lured in by the garage sale signs.

"Well now, you're overdoing it!" Daniel snapped.

"The chair is mine too. I bought every single piece of furniture in this house."

"Then you're being selfish. You're being a bitch!" Daniel said.

She slapped him across the face. Although his cheeks smarted, the stinging vented some of his muddled anger, and for a moment his thinking clarified.

"Get out of this house!" Irene suddenly shrieked, the chords in her neck straining her silk choker. "Go on. Get your things and go to your father's. And don't come back in here, you horrible kid."

Daniel bolted from the room. Many of the browsers were huddled by the door listening and his abrupt exit startled them into a multi-directional sprawl. "Get out of here, all of you!" Daniel screamed to them. "Leave this house. Nothing is being sold!"

"No!" Irene shrieked from the den. "*You* leave this house!"

Then it occurred to Daniel what he must accomplish to have his way, to prevent Irene from selling the rocking chair, to chase away these awful people. It became so clear that he felt saddened; for in his mind their confrontation had already reached its denouement, and he could even contemplate the aftermath. He rushed into the kitchen, opened the cutlery drawer and selected a small, sharp grapefruit knife. His mother, meanwhile, had trailed behind, still commanding him to leave the house. As he brandished the knife, he saw her face twitch in stupefaction. The stain of outrage drained from her face and then she squawked in short bursts. "Put that down. Are you out of your mind? Put that down!"

"It's not for *you*," Daniel growled. "I wouldn't waste my time. I don't care enough about *you*, you cunt!"

Irene gasped.

In a moment he had lurched past her and was bounding up the stairs. His purpose was single-minded. He could think of nothing else. Alexis had once again shut and secured her door. Daniel banged on it frantically. "Open up!" he cried out. "Open up."

"All right, all right," Alexis said. "Wait a second."

Then he wedged his way in. She was so taken aback by his unaccustomed belligerence that she could only follow him in dazzled confusion. He went to the closet and yanked out the rocking chair, causing Monopoly and Scrabble and the rest of her games to fly apart. Colored boards opened up, revealing stenciled faces of prim schoolchildren, drawing cards and plastic wonder wheels, the treasures of Alexis's childhood scattering all over. A dice cube struck Daniel in the eye.

"Oh, no!" Alexis cried out. "Stop it. Don't do that. Ahhhhh!" She screamed at the top of her lungs. Gripping the knife firmly at its handle, Daniel dug the blade deep into the chair. The wood was soft and aged and easily accepted the stab. Ignoring her, he gouged a long slit down the widest panel of the rocker's headboard and then made a curve that connected one end to another, sloppily etching D for Daniel. The knife slipped from his fingers.

Hands balled into fists, Alexis rushed at Daniel, who fended her off. She dug her elbows into her sides, letting loose a harrowing cry; then threw herself down on her bed in a frenzy of weeping.

Daniel turned to face the doorway, where Irene was now standing, her eyes wide with shock. "Here it is," he said demonically. "Go sell it now. I hope you get lots of money for it."

But then his mother suddenly slumped and she seemed to understand the tragic absurdity of what she was trying to do. Bowing her head, she drew in a sharp breath and began to cry.

At that moment Daniel knew how deeply he loved her. And that it all seemed so pointless: the garage sale, the argument, gouging the rocking chair. And suddenly a realization managed to cut through the hysterical tangle of his thoughts. He should have carved an A in the chair, an A for Alexis, and then his intent would have been clearer.

Daniel heard Irene intone something in the midst of her sobbing. At first he couldn't believe his ears, but then she repeated it. "I'm sorry, Danny," she whimpered. "I'm sorry."

Alexis was amazed to hear Irene apologize. Sniffling, she managed to raise her head off the bed. Bits of her hair, moist with tears, were sticking to her forehead as she gazed at her mother in bewilderment.

Daniel went to hug his sister, who at first resisted fiercely but then collapsed in his arms. "I'm sorry," he whispered to her. "Maybe you can keep it now." He glanced at Irene, who groaned in response.

"But I don't want it any more," Alexis said. "You ruined it!" Her voice was muffled by his shoulder.

"Of course you want it," Daniel said.

"No I don't," Alexis insisted.

"Of course you do," Daniel soothed her. "Of course you do."

24

No browsers remained in the house when Daniel went downstairs. For a moment he wondered if they had been frightened away by the ugly scene and the garage sale was now doomed to fail. As he stepped outside the front door, however, he saw a group of people hovering at the end of the driveway like vultures waiting for a kill to be vacated. Glaring at them, he climbed into the Buick and drove away.

At first he didn't know where he was going, but then found himself driving toward the Italian neighborhood. He felt so raw. And there seemed to be no further danger of increased distress if Angela Scaravento turned him away from her door. He figured he couldn't possibly be made any more miserable than he already was. Now he was willing to take the risk of rejection in order to see her.

He parked a ways down the street and slowly approached the house. Gianni's Triumph was parked in the driveway. As he continued walking toward the kitchen door, Daniel couldn't help stopping to admire Angela's garden. Along the back perimeter of the yard, he spied small green ruffles of early Swiss chard; tufts of tomato plants poked up along the left property line. In the middle of the lawn was an islet of the green iris Angela had been so keen about ordering. A cluster of striped, purple clematis thrived along the side of the house. And next to the clematis flourished a tangle of thorns and green leaves that protected the nascent buds of the Albertine roses. Even though it was bright outdoors, Daniel could see inside well enough to trace Angela plodding around her kitchen. She had a scarf cap on her head and was listlessly pushing a dust mop along the floor. He could tell by the way she limped along that her joints were aching. And when she finally noticed him and drifted to the window and smiled, he felt a terrible burden being lifted.

Throwing the back door open wide, Angela said quite matter-of-factly, "*Ma non hai ricevuto il mio messaggio?*"

"No," Daniel said. "*Quando mi hai telefonato?*"

"We called you yesterday for your birthday and even today. Why didn't your mother tell you?"

Daniel explained about being away. A terrible silence followed this first exchange and during it Daniel shifted back and forth in place. He claimed he had come to say goodbye to Gianni before Gianni's departure for Michigan. Angela said Gianni was not at home.

"He leaves tomorrow morning. Why don't you come on in and sit down. I'll fix you a sandwich. I've got turkey and roast beef."

He was awed at how she easily reverted to their old rapport, after having decided almost on whim to accept him once again. He followed her into the house and as he drank in its familiar smells of laundering clothes and marinara sauce, a welling ache opened up within him. He sat down at the kitchen table, pressed his forehead against the cool wood and wept. He felt the kitchen floor vibrating as Angela made her way toward him.

She stood above him patting his head, saying, "I'm so stubborn, aren't I? I was too hard on you, wasn't I? I'm sorry, Daniel. Now, don't cry anymore. Have yourself a nice turkey sandwich and a fresh cup of my coffee."

But the offer of food made Daniel even more miserable. Only then did Angela begin to suspect that something more than her own rebuffing was plaguing him. She went over to the tea kettle and put it on and then sat down next to him at the table. He sat back up and leaned over to hug her, not crying so much now. She smelled of that slightly perished odor he had smelled once before. As though now aware of it herself, Angela was wearing more perfume.

When Daniel finally regained his composure, he explained

what had just happened at his house, carefully recounting the
conversation between him and his mother and what he had done
to the rocking chair. Halfway through the story, Angela got flustered and asked him to stop. He seemed to have upset her in a
very fundamental way. For several moments she was unable to
give voice to her reaction, just sitting there with her breath coming
fast and shallow. When Daniel asked if she were feeling okay,
Angela nodded her head and waved off his concern. Eventually
she got up from the table and rescued the tea kettle, which just
then had begun to sing. She fiddled with the cups and saucers,
poured the boiling water into a ceramic pot and then abruptly
stopped her preparations.

"*Vergogna,*" she said softly in Italian. "Shame."

"*Perché lo dice?*" Daniel said. "Why are you saying this?"

"Because of what always seems to happen in the pinch," Angela
said, turning toward him with a tray and the pot of tea and the
cups. "It's so clear to me. I suppose because I'm not a member of
your family," she said, sitting down at the table. "As I imagine
what's clear to you about me because you're not a member of
mine."

"Nothing is clear to me," Daniel said definitely. "Nothing at
all."

"What are you talking about, you fool?" Angela said. "You
don't give yourself enough credit. You were the only one in your
family who saw what was happening. Your mother is so busy
trying to protect herself, she doesn't stop and see how much she
is hurting you and your sister. I'm certainly not condemning her
for it. Because I'm as guilty as she. Toward my own children.
Even toward you."

Angela poured Daniel a strong cup of black currant tea. As
she did so a sudden exhaustion filled him.

"I never saw it until now," Angela went on, folding her withered hands. "Our two families. The similarities. Sure, the situations are different. But they aren't really." She took a sip of tea
and turned to Daniel, reflective. "I know you and Gianni argued
once about this very thing. I know he told you that you couldn't
compare what he was going through with me to what you were
going through with your family. But he was wrong."

Angela took a deep breath. "Your mother and I are both ailing.
We're both about to do something neither of our families can

understand. She is dying out of one life and being born into another. At least she knows where she's headed. But she's not doing it with much dignity because it's all she can do to get through it." Angela looked off through the kitchen window into her backyard, now blazing with plants and flowers of the season Daniel was missing. "I always thought that at the end of this whole rotten illness I'd at least have some dignity, at least have a clear understanding of what was happening to me. But there's no dignity, Daniel. No understanding. The same thing goes for your mother, I'm afraid." She regarded him purposefully for a moment and then fixed her gaze out the window again. "It's just a process that for the most part won't allow a better view of life. No last-minute wisdom."

"You don't really know that," Daniel said. "I mean, it's not the last minute yet."

"How dare you?" Angela started. But then her mood changed and she laughed. "There it is. You understand it. Why is everyone else so nearsighted? They're all trying to lie and make it easier. But they'll never hit on the truth even after it's all over." She blinked nervously as she peered at him. "That's why I haven't wanted you around. Sure, I was angry about Maria. But Daniel," she said, leaning closer to him, "you remind me of it. Much more than anyone in my family. I forget how well they delude me. I even start to believe them about getting better."

They were silent for a while, sipping their tea. Then Angela got up, hobbled over to the cabinet and took out a package of anise cookies. Daniel could see how badly her health had deteriorated over the past few months, but wary of disturbing her contemplative mood, he was reluctant to inquire about it.

On a plain white plate, Angela arranged the cookies like wings on a pinwheel. Daniel took one and dipped it in his tea. "I hope there are some of these left for Gianni," he said.

"They'll be enough until tomorrow," Angela said. "Then my food bill gets cut in half."

Daniel laughed.

"Go ahead and laugh. That kid has got a bottomless pit for a stomach." She frowned at Daniel. "How come you don't eat so much?"

"I do sometimes. But the problem for me is I get nervous and lose my appetite."

"Me too," she said.

"You *have* lost a lot of weight, Angela."

"I'm size eight. Must've been a size twelve when you first knew me. When I was young I was dying to be a size eight. Up, there you go. Just twenty years too late." She grew tearful for a moment but then forced back her distress. Barely recovering her composure, she went on, "I must say I'm glad they have those cafeteria eating plans at universities. The students can have as much as they want, right?"

"That's how it usually works," Daniel said.

"Good, he won't starve." Angela laughed. "Sound like a Jewish mother, don't I. Jewish. Italian. We're really all cut from the same fabric. We're good mothers. We're bad mothers." She tssked. "I can't believe Jews and Italians can't get along in this town. But then again, in Italy some Italians don't get along with other Italians. So go figure.

"People are petty," she said after a bit. "That's the problem. Pettiness. I see it in my immediate family. Frank and Gianni, jockeying around me, telling lies. And yet, they're already making plans for you know what. I've overheard them."

"That's hard to believe."

Angela looked hard at Daniel. "I don't trust them, Danny. Maybe I'm overly suspicious. I guess maybe I'm paranoid. But I always had good instincts." She pointed to her glass eye. "It was losing this," she said, "which made me realize I was at a certain disadvantage and determined me to develop other ways of seeing."

There were noises in the hallway, the trace of a voice. "It's Tony," Angela said wistfully. "My little boy," she whispered. "He understands so little of this and yet it affects him much more than the other ones because he can't close himself off to it."

Tony stalked into the kitchen holding one of Gianni's memorabilia footballs that was signed by each member of the New York Jets. He seemed to have grown taller since Daniel last saw him and was entering the gawky phase of pre-adolescence. He had lost some of his baby fat and now resembled Gianni even more than before. When Tony saw Daniel, he frowned mildly at him. "Hey, what're you doing here?" he said.

"He's visiting your mother," Angela said.

Tony turned to her. "I thought you don't like him no more?"

"Now, did I ever say that?"

Tony shrugged. "Well no, but you said something."

"What did I say?"

"I don't remember. But it was something like 'too smart for his own good.'"

Daniel chuckled.

Angela smiled warily at him. "I suppose that could be taken as a compliment." Then to Tony, "Now honey, don't gossip like that."

Tony put his arms carefully around his mother and pressed his cheek to hers. It was as if he were worried that she might break apart in his arms. "I'm sorry, Ma," he said.

"That's okay. Now, when you set the table I want you to set another place for Danny."

"Okay." Tony started counting on his fingers. "So that makes, let me see—"

"Don't count honey, just set one more place."

"But there's more extra people than one. There's Debbie," Tony said.

"Debbie? Who said Debbie was coming?"

"Gianni, Ma. Gianni said Debbie was coming."

"Set one more place, Tony. Debbie is *not* coming."

Tony looked perplexed.

"Just do what I said," Angela insisted softly. "Run along now." She waited until Tony left the room. "I don't like that girl," she complained to Daniel. "I don't care if she's gorgeous and her parents *are* rich."

"Why?" Daniel said. "She's nice."

"I know that kind of pretty girl. That kind is only interested in her own looks and keeping herself attractive. She doesn't have enough heart for Gianni."

"She doesn't strike me like that."

Angela shook her head sadly. "Now Danny," she said. "That's one area where you might not have any objectivity."

"You'd be surprised," Daniel said.

"Nothing surprises me anymore," Angela said.

Gianni betrayed no surprise when he came home later on and found Daniel with Angela, huddled at the kitchen table among long shadows cast by the enduring daylight. After a brief skirmish

over having Debbie Lerner come to supper, Gianni acceded to his
mother's wishes. With Angela and Daniel as witness, he phoned
Debbie and claimed his mother wasn't feeling too well, that he'd
see her later on and they'd also see each other before his departure
the following morning.

When Gianni mentioned the part about being ill, Angela threw
Daniel a "Can you believe this?" look. Gianni noticed it as he was
speaking and shrugged; he apologized as soon as he got off the
phone. "I couldn't think of anything else to say," he lamented.
Angela waved him off and ambled slowly down the hallway to
watch television in the den. Her house slippers shuffled heavily
against the wood floors and the rugs.

"She's really having trouble getting around now, isn't she?"
Daniel said after a moment.

"Oh yeah," Gianni said miserably. "I don't know, man," he
went on, his eyes still on his mother. "Somehow I feel bad about
going away now. In case something should happen while I'm
gone."

"Well, you're going to be away in the fall anyway. Besides,
nothing is going to happen this summer," Daniel said.

Gianni turned to him annoyed. "How the hell do you know?"

Daniel was actually as surprised as Gianni by his comment.
"I don't know how I know," he said incredulously. "Something
just made me say it."

Gianni sighed. "Anyway, buddy, I'm glad you came by. I'm
glad you got tight with Angie again."

Daniel smiled. "I'm glad too."

"But now can you come outside with me? There's something
I want to show you."

Just as they were stepping out of the back door, they heard
the ringing of the Good Humor ice cream truck. Gianni asked
Daniel if he wanted ice cream and Daniel declined, realizing he
hadn't eaten a single thing since the previous evening and that his
appetite was anesthetized. Strangely, he had no desire to discuss
the garage sale with Gianni, as he normally would have. Angela
understood these sorts of things far better.

They walked over to the Triumph. The crack in the windshield had paved its way to within an inch of the bottom of the
glass.

"Dad says that's it. No more Triumph. I'll be using his station wagon. He'll either sell the Triumph or trade it in for something else. It won't move another foot until then."

Studying the crack, Daniel said, "You don't have any say over what he buys next?"

Gianni shook his head. "Nope. The station wagon is my car now. I'll be using it to bring my stuff to Michigan."

His friend's imminent departure for a distant place suddenly made Daniel very sad. "I guess I won't be able to come visit you," he said. "My dad got me that job."

"Ah, you can come," Gianni said. "We'll work it out somehow. But you're definitely going to live with your father?"

"Looks so."

"Be pretty cramped."

"I don't mind."

Gianni hesitated and then traced his finger along the crack in the glass, along all its strange diversions and malignant turns, as though subtly recapitulating the autumn, winter and spring. "You could stay in my room whenever you want."

"I could?" Daniel asked.

"It's going to be lonely for Angie." He paused. "I'd be happy if you did," he said, averting his eyes.

They fell into awkward silence there by the Triumph, which for so long had been the forum of their friendship, where they had spoken about so many different things. Daniel looked at Gianni. "You don't seem sad to give up the car."

Gianni said, "I am a little."

"You seemed sad about it during the winter when we first found out."

"I was. But Danny, I got used to it."

"I never did," Daniel said. "I still love this car."

"Why don't you buy it from my father?" Gianni said poignantly, a trace of excitement, of dreaming, creeping into his voice. "Buy it from my dad. He'll give you a good price. And then you can drive *me* around when I come home from school."

They stood there looking squarely at each other. There was a question between them now that was not the question of whether or not Daniel should buy the car, but of something else, something farther reaching. But neither knew how to identify or answer the question. And neither could locate words to tell the other that they knew something important must be said.

"Fucking Vito Polanno," Gianni broke the silence. "If he hadn't peeled his car out on that gravel driveway we'd still be flying around town smoking J's."

"It wouldn't have made any difference. You'd have to take the station wagon for the summer," Daniel pointed out. "And we can still go for a drive."

"Sure," Gianni said. "But you know in that big bomb of a station wagon it won't be the same."

That was true, Daniel agreed. It certainly would not be the same.

25

The moving vans came to collect Daniel's and his sister's personal belongings and bring them to New York City. Although Irene was supposed to be tying up loose ends for the house to finally close a few days later, she insisted on driving her children to Harold's apartment. Since their father was still at work she took it on herself to direct the moving men when they arrived at his apartment in Manhattan, making sure they didn't damage anything while ferrying around the boxes. She seemed particularly anxious when the rocking chair, swathed in padded material, was brought in and placed in the second bedroom.

Then Irene phoned Harold and invited herself to dinner. Harold was taken aback. She claimed she wanted to buffer Alexis and Daniel's first night away from Houghton. Although he couldn't resist gently pointing out that she was really trying to make it easier on herself, Harold didn't object. Daniel was certain this forced a change of plans with his girlfriend. Lucky that his father was a good sport.

After the boxes had been unloaded, Irene began buzzing around the kitchen, talking about making dinner for the four of them. Daniel explained that Harold liked his kitchen just so and would want to have charge of dinner. His honesty deflated his mother's jolly mood, and looking chastened, she went to sit down on the living room couch.

"What's wrong with you, anyway, Mom?" Daniel asked as he approached her.

She uncrossed her legs and recrossed them in the opposite direction. "I could very easily cook us all a nice meal. I'm sure your father wouldn't get bent out of shape if I took it on myself to go to the store."

"Mom, it's just that he told me he was planning to make something special."

"So I suppose that leaves me out of it," Irene sulked. She suddenly reached over to a rosewood box on the glass coffee table, filched a cigarette and lit up.

Daniel watched her in amazement. "What are you doing? You don't smoke."

"I'm taking it up," she said slyly, dragging on the cigarette. Daniel waited to see how much she actually inhaled. When an enormous plume of smoke issued from her mouth he began to worry.

"Mom, I don't understand you sometimes."

She shrugged. "If I can't make dinner I don't know what else to do with myself."

Just then Alexis entered the living room. A sickened expression riddled her face when she saw her mother puffing jauntily on the cigarette. "That's really healthy for you."

"It's not going to kill me," Irene said.

"So now you're going to start smoking too?"

Irene looked inquiringly at Alexis. "What else am I doing?"

"Try moving to Italy."

Irene flicked a long ash into a spotless ceramic ashtray. Daniel wondered if Harold would resent the residue of smoke in the apartment. Then again, cigarettes were provided. But suddenly his mother said something that ripped these thoughts from his mind.

"Maybe I won't go," she announced, looking down at her Italian shoes.

"You must be joking," Daniel said.

"Don't kid us like that," Alexis said.

"It's cruel," Daniel agreed.

"Oh, of course I'm going to Italy," Irene told them. "I guess I'm just a little apprehensive." When she looked up at them they both sensed her uncertainty.

Daniel went to the window and leaned against the sill. "Here we are sitting in Dad's apartment that he had to buy because you didn't want to be married. We have to live here because you wanted to sell the house. And now after all this you tell us you're nervous about going to Italy."

Irene looked at him in bewilderment. "I'd be nervous about any change. That's all I'm saying."

"Well then, don't go," Alexis said.

"I just thought you'd feel satisfied to know that I don't exactly feel like rushing off," Irene told Daniel.

Alexis was so confused by the conversation that she suddenly inflated Irene's anxiety into a change of heart. "But I have to go to this private school next year. Where I hear they give you tons of homework. And I could be going to Houghton High?" She turned to Daniel for some explanation, but he looked as miffed as she did.

"Honey, you'd be at this private school no matter what," Irene said. "So stop with that."

Alexis fled the living room for the bedroom she was now to live in. She threw herself into her mutilated rocking chair and Daniel and his mother could hear it creaking furiously. After a moment, Irene sighed, got up and went in to talk to her.

Daniel plopped down in the place where his mother had been sitting. She had left a warm spot, which felt good and soothing to him. Soon the rocking chair stopped its complaining and the apartment drew on a hush. After a while Daniel could hear his mother murmuring something, unintelligible to him, but which he assumed was having a soothing effect on his sister. He heard a round of laughter coming from the bedroom and then his mother returned to the living room with a satisfied look on her face.

He waited until she reached the sofa. "Was this all a trick, going to Italy? I mean, to get us to live with Dad so you could be alone?" he asked.

Irene shook her head mildly. Her eyes were mocking and beneficent all at the same time. "Of course it wasn't. You know I'm not like that." She seemed honest and resolute in her answer, and Daniel was able to cast off his doubt.

The house closing was on Saturday and right afterward Irene left for Padua as planned. Daniel began his filing job on Wall Street and hated it. Harold gave him permission to quit and promised to pay for a trip across the country. But Daniel was determined to stick things out. Besides, he had promised Gianni to keep an eye on Angela.

Indeed, before leaving for Michigan, Gianni arranged for Daniel to sleep over at the Scaraventos' at least one night a week. Angela was now too weak to be insomniac and usually nodded off in the armchair around 2 A.M. The evenings Daniel stayed up with her would leave him totally fatigued the next day. His exhaustion did not escape the notice of his father, who began to resent his absences because of their obvious effect. It was difficult for Daniel to explain to his father his closeness to Angela and the responsibility and willingness he felt to spend time with her. And Harold was unable to understand that Daniel could treat Angela in any way other than as a surrogate parent, which he felt was only a result of neglect on Irene's part. There was no way Daniel could dissuade him from believing this and eventually he stopped trying to do so. Soon his father began worrying that when Angela died Daniel would be devastated.

Frank and Tony plainly resented Daniel's intrusion and unlike Gianni, their resentment was not softened by their fondness for him—as it had been in Gianni's case. They tolerated Daniel because Angela and Gianni wished them to. But as she weakened so did their tolerance.

One night when Daniel arrived at the Scaraventos' after work he found that Angela was gone. According to Frank, earlier that day she had been admitted to the hospital with breathing difficulties. He and Tony were both in the den, Frank occupying the armchair that Angela normally sat in. Oddly, father and son were afflicted by the same stiff, restrained manner and answered Daniel's questions in barely civil tones: Tony kept glaring at Daniel's overnight bag. Finally, Daniel glanced at his watch and saw that visiting hours would be over by the time he could reach the hospital. Dejected, he drove back to the city.

As soon as he got into the apartment, he tried reaching Gianni in Michigan. There was no answer. He kept trying unsuccessfully to get hold of his friend until three in the morning. Then he remembered this was the week that Debbie Lerner had gone to visit Gianni; they were probably out late. Daniel went to bed and tried calling Gianni once again the following morning. But there was still no response.

Close to noon that day, a phone call came into work for him. It was Angela, her voice sounding weak and scared.

"Can you come see me?" she said. "When you get off work. I need to talk to you?"

"Where are you?" he said.

"At home. I'm not feeling good."

"You're back already? I was there last night . . . they said—"

"They lied. I was here. I was in bed asleep. For once."

Daniel was shocked by Frank and Tony's duplicity. "I'm weak and this is jabbing me," Angela said.

"What's jabbing you?"

"Oh honey, I'm not quite myself. Can you tell? They won't come back, will they? They won't take me later?"

"They, what do you mean by they?"

"You know," Angela said.

Was she incoherent? "Are you okay, Angela?"

"Come and see me when you get off work." Angela put down the phone without saying goodbye.

Daniel pleaded a family emergency and left work immediately. He retrieved his father's car from the building garage and raced up to Houghton. The new Oldsmobile Frank had recently purchased was absent from the driveway. Thank goodness, thought Daniel. The Triumph was parked on the street, a "For Sale" sign taped to its window.

The back door was wide open, and expecting no one home but Angela, Daniel walked right in. He yelled for her, but there was no answer. "Tony?" he asked. Nothing. He ventured in a little farther and then noticed a small person hurrying toward him from the den, demanding "Who is it?" Her voice sounded oddly familiar. Daniel stopped, spooked by the presence of Maria Polanno. "What's wrong?" he demanded in a fright.

Smiling frigidly at him, Maria said in English, "Angela's in bed. Sleeping. You'll have to come back later."

"She called an hour ago and asked me to come up here," Daniel rattled off in Italian.

Mrs. Polanno shook her bony head and insisted on speaking English, which Daniel found off-putting, not to mention patronizing in light of their first meeting. "Impossible," she said. "I've been here for three hours. No one has talked to her since then."

"I think you're hard of hearing," Daniel said, now in English. "Because I've been yelling hello for the past five minutes and no one answered."

"The television" was Maria's lame excuse. Perhaps faulty hearing induced her voice to be so shrill.

"*Maria, che c'è?*" Angela called out faintly.

"*Il ragazzo. Quel Daniello,*" Maria said disdainfully.

"Send him to me. I want to see him."

Maria gave a resigned jerk of her head toward a hallway.

"Why are you here?" Daniel asked Mrs. Polanno. "Where are Frank and Tony?"

"They flew to Michigan," she said quickly and went to sit back down in the armchair. Her unexpected presence there in the Scaraventos' boded something ill Daniel felt he was unready for.

He had never visited the master bedroom before. For a place shared by man and wife it was surprisingly feminine. The furniture was antique white with blue corduroy cushions. The curtains were of a worsted beige fabric and the bed had a scrolling canopy above it, hemmed with voile.

Angela lay in bed propped up by pillows. She was wearing her quilted pink bathrobe. There were several large serious-looking bottles of pills on her night table, along with a single glass of water pierced by a drinking straw with a crenelated strip that allowed it to bend.

"What's going on?" Daniel said nervously, sitting down next to Angela. "Why did they go to Michigan?" He scrutinized her haggard face. One eye was closed, one opened, and at first glance he figured that her docile, glass eye was shut. But then he noticed that her good eye was closed and the eye that actually gazed at him could not see him.

Angela proved this when she began groping for Daniel's hands like a blind person. Finally getting hold of him, she gripped tightly and shuddered. Then she bit her lower lip. "I want you to call Michigan," she said in a low rasp, "and talk to Gianni and have him explain it to you. I can't talk about it. I'm completely worn out."

"But what happened?"

"Ahh, Daniel, that boy was driving crazy again. He had to be driving crazy. I'm just glad I made him get rid of that little car. I can't imagine what would have happened in that little car."

Daniel's imagination was suddenly fueled by several feverish scenarios. "But is he okay, is he okay?"

"He's fine. *She's* in the hospital."

"Debbie?"

Angela nodded.

"How bad?"

"Cracked her hip."

"Oh my God. Oh my God," Daniel groaned. He wished Angela would open up her good eye and see him.

"*I* went to the hospital," Angela said in a dreamy voice. "When I heard it. My breathing. You know how my breathing gets bad. They had to give me oxygen. But I didn't stay overnight. Thank goodness. I'm taking these pills now," she said, indicating one of the capped bottles on the night table with a roll of her head. "I don't even know what I'm taking. And I do feel strange. Sort of heavy and light. At the same time. Maria still here?"

"She's in the den."

"They didn't want you to see me." Angela was beginning to sound winded. "They told her not to let you in. Luckily she told me. I said that she'd pay to God if she didn't let you in. I told her"—a silly grin broke over Angela's face—"why, I told her that you and I were going. Driving though. That we were going in a limousine. But we'd get there in time . . . ." Daniel realized that she was probably talking on the effects of whatever strong medication she was taking. Angela continued, still grinning. "We'll get there in time for Gianni's first game, just in time to see him squashed. So he won't squash other people. People like you," she said, her face crashing into sadness. "That rotten . . . sweet lovable kid . . ." Angela's voice trailed off. Her eye fluttered and closed and soon she was dozing.

Daniel went to the kitchen phone and dialed Michigan directly. This time he got Gianni. "Buddy," Gianni yelped. "What a mess I got myself into, buddy. Can you come out here to see me, buddy?"

"Your father and Tony are on the way." Daniel paused, de-

ciding not to mention anything about how they had deceived him
the night before.

"You're my buddy," Gianni said slowly and jerkily. Daniel
realized now that his friend was drunk. "My best and only buddy."

"What happened, Gianni?"

There was a pause full of static. Daniel repeated his question.
When there was still no response, he thought he could faintly hear
something in the background. At first it sounded like water running into a cistern and then it sounded like a pair of marimbas
softly shaking. And then he realized that Gianni had abandoned
the phone momentarily. Daniel waited a few more moments before
saying, "Talk to me, Gianni, please?"

Gianni finally returned to the phone, his voice noticeably
strained. "She's so beautiful. And I hurt her so bad. The most
beautiful girl I've ever been with. And she'll never ever forgive
me. She said so right when I took her to the hospital. I carried
her in cause I didn't want anyone to hurt her anymore."

That was foolish, thought Daniel, carrying Debbie into the
hospital. "Gianni, please tell me what happened."

And what came next was rather incredible.

There had been some kind of massive rock concert at a race
track in the farm belt outside the campus. Daniel remembered
hearing advertisements for it over WNEW radio. Many of the big
bands had been slated to play and the last time Gianni had spoken
to Daniel over the phone they had discussed who was going.
Daniel never realized that the concert would occur the week of
Debbie Lerner's visit.

Gianni had chauffeured a load of his new Michigan State friends
to the concert, which was to continue for several days and where
they all had planned to camp out. The station wagon was piled
with camping gear and a keg of beer and on the way to the concert
everyone in the car got completely drunk, including Gianni. There
was a line of traffic on the two-lane road out of town and it was
tough going, with plenty of bottlenecks. Eventually the people in
the car began to get sick from all their drinking. One of Gianni's
football player friends threw up all over the back seat and his
retching soiled the camping gear and some of the exposed provisions of food. By then Debbie Lerner had lost patience with the
overcrowded situation and could no longer bear the smell in the

car. For her, the only solution apart from abandoning the excursion altogether was sitting on the hood, which she decided to do. She had Gianni pull over, situated herself against the windshield in a bikini top and took sun as the traffic crawled the rest of the way.

When they finally arrived at the concert site they had to drive around on the race track, which was surrounded by dense pine woods, until they could find a large unoccupied grove of land to set up camp. At some point in his journey around the race track—and this part of it was blurred because Gianni was unsure of what exactly happened—another carload of students from Michigan State pulled alongside. "We'll drag you," somebody yelled out the window as the car sped off.

By now Gianni was quite drunk and dangerously impatient from the long, frustrating drive. His competitive urges took over. He wound up to sixty with Debbie Lerner on the hood of the station wagon. Somehow—if it was possible—in his drunken frenzy he actually forgot that she was out there. There he was drag-racing with Debbie Lerner shrieking in terror and pressing herself crucifixlike against the windshield. She began banging furiously against the windshield, imploring him to stop. The intoxicated kids in the car were alternately egging Gianni on and shouting for him to slow down. Daniel could just picture Gianni's eyes glued maniacally on the road ahead of him, looking over at the other car to see who was inching ahead. And when Gianni suddenly realized Debbie was exposed like that he froze, overreacting as he braked the car. She fell off at around thirty miles an hour.

When Gianni finished the story, Daniel realized with a shock that he was still in the Scaraventos' kitchen, staring at the crockery jar where cookies were kept and into which Gianni automatically stuck his large hand whenever he came home. He was remembering how scared he had been that first night he had ever spent with Gianni when Gianni turned off his headlights on 684. "I don't believe it," he said. "I can't believe you did that!"

"Heh man, I don't need any more shit about it, okay? I told you I feel like the worst shit I've ever felt in my whole life. I feel like my life is over."

Daniel knew he should now be comforting to his friend, but the words just wouldn't come. He couldn't help but feel galled by Gianni's recklessness. "So self-destructive," he muttered. He stretched the phone cord out of the kitchen and walked into the den, where Maria Polanno sat in stolid silence. He peered out the window into the street at the Triumph with its "For Sale" sign. It seemed ironic now that Frank forbade Gianni from driving the car on account of the windshield. It would have been impossible for Debbie Lerner to lie on the snubbed hood of the Triumph.

"Look," Gianni continued in a frightened voice. "I need your support. I need my best friend."

But Daniel was disillusioned. "I don't know what to tell you."

"Can't you be supportive to me?" Gianni agonized.

"I'm trying," Daniel said.

"Then get on a plane and come out here," Gianni said. "Okay, buddy?"

A ferocious longing filled Daniel. The longing frightened him because it took on such a vast dimension, one that he had never suspected existed within him. And for a moment he worried about the rest of his life and what he would say when people he loved commanded him to do things that were in his worst interest. He shut his eyes. "I can't come now, Gianni. I have to work."

"You can take off work. Tell 'em it's a family problem. Tell 'em it's an emergency."

"I don't want to leave New York right now."

There was a short explosive pause. "You mean you won't help me?" Gianni sounded incredulous.

"Not with this, Gianni," Daniel said.

"Well then, if you can't help me, then you can go . . . screw a wall," Gianni hissed. "I heard my father left word with Maria not to let you in the house. Good. I'm glad I didn't argue with him. And if I have anything to do with it you'll never see my mother again. Why don't you stop going where you're not wanted? Why don't you stop sneaking around other people's mothers. You got your own mother. You fag." At this, Daniel slammed down the phone.

26

One rainy afternoon in early October Daniel was in his room at Amherst when someone appeared at the door and told him he had a long-distance phone call. As soon as he started to walk toward the extension he got a feeling of an irrepressible foreboding. He hoped he was wrong; but he wasn't: Alexis was on the phone. Patrick Riordan had called her in Manhattan, trying to reach Daniel. He wanted to make sure Daniel knew that Mrs. Scaravento had died of pneumonia in the hospital. Her passing had been kept quiet; few people learned about it before the obituary was printed in the local newspaper. The funeral had taken place the previous day.

"I can't believe they didn't call me," Daniel exclaimed.

"Maybe they're not thinking clearly right now."

That the "they" no longer included Angela was inconceivable. She no longer had the capacity to think or judge; she had departed the earth. No longer able to support himself, Daniel leaned against the wall. A cold draft was invading the hallways and he shuddered from its chill, from the knowledge that Angela had ceased to exist. He had the impression that his perceptions were turning extra-sensory. Through the wall he felt he could detect the sound of leaves in their death cascade toward the ground, that he could smell the spectrum of autumn smells. "The Scaraventos must want to hurt me," he finally murmured.

"I don't think it's that, Danny. I don't know what's going on, but I know it can't be to hurt you."

Long-distance was purring. His mind was jumbling into his gut. He wanted to weep but was unable to locate an emotional avenue that would allow tears to flow. "Are you okay?" Alexis asked tentatively.

"I feel like jumping out of my skin."

"Why don't you come home this weekend," she suggested. "Just be with Dad and me. And then you can meet Karl." Karl was Alexis's new boyfriend. He was Daniel's age and according to her owned four leather jackets. The last thing Daniel wanted to do right now was meet Alexis's boyfriend and speculate whether or not she was sleeping with him.

"I'll see," Daniel said.

"Can I call you later to see how you're doing?"

"Sure. That'll be okay."

"And you'll think about coming home?"

"Yes."

"Oh yeah, and Patrick was hoping you'd call him. He'd like to talk to you. He's coming home for the weekend, too."

Daniel returned to his room, stood before the window and looked down and across the picturesque campus that was strewn with a brilliant quilt work of colored leaves, and through which students tracked their way to and from classes. He was relieved his roommate was absent so he was able to have a few moments to himself. At first he tried to play back some of his conversations with Angela; but strangely his memory drew an oppressive blank. His head was freighted with numbness and eventually he had to lie down.

Then the room started to take on irritant qualities. The sheets on his bed scratched and each time his cheek grazed the blanket, he would get a tart, shriveling feeling in his mouth as if he had been sucking on lemon rinds. He envisioned huge metal dumpsters full of rainwater hovering above his head. He got up with the intention of leaving his room but felt dizzy and constrained. How ridiculous, he thought, of course I can leave. But when he opened his door and stuck his head out into the corridor, it seemed cavernous and forbidding and he had to duck back inside. By now he was sweating. He didn't know what to do. He ended up missing his afternoon class. When his roommate finally returned and Daniel had someone to talk to, he calmed down a bit. The next time he lay down on his bed, he was able to think more clearly.

He wondered what could be going through Gianni's mind right now and whether in denying their friendship Gianni had ceased to have any feelings at all for him. Gianni had rejected him in order not to be rejected, or at least that's what Daniel assumed. But when you cut yourself off from somebody how can you cauterize your emotions? Admittedly, Daniel had always expected that Gianni would get back in touch, or apologize, but when that didn't happen he had forced himself to write off the friendship for the time being. But now, denying him the right to attend Angela's funeral almost seemed like a malevolent, vindictive act on Gianni's part. Could the decision not to contact him possibly have been left up to Frank? No matter, Gianni still could have tried to get a hold of Daniel; there was no excuse for the news of Angela's death to be withheld from him. This absolutely convinced Daniel that his friendship with Gianni would never again be resumed.

At some point during the early evening, his roommate, a practical, sandy-haired boy from the Midwest named Martin, brought Daniel a potent vodka screwdriver and ordered him to drink it. After sipping the cocktail for a while, Daniel's inner coiling began to unwind. For the time being he managed to set aside his anger. He lay on his bed, his thoughts clotting into a rabid nonsense, and eventually he slipped into a heavy sleep.

He dreamed that a healthy, vibrant Angela was running along the top of a speeding passenger train, holding a rubber mallet in her hand. She was angry with Daniel for not bringing her a pot of black currant tea while she was ill. Now that she was better Angela would take revenge.

As she chased Daniel, Angela skipped effortlessly atop the swaying cars. Daniel, in turn, had to scurry along on all fours or else he was certain to fall off and be killed. But somehow he managed to keep ahead of Angela, who every so often would throw herself prone on the roof of the train, lean over and smash at the windows below with her mallet. At one point when she turned toward Daniel, he saw with a shock that her eyes were gone, replaced by black, fathomless hollows.

Daniel awoke trembling and in a dense sweat. He had slept far into the night. The clock read four-forty-nine. His roommate on the bunk above was snoring. He felt terribly disoriented and confined by the small, dark room. Then he grew aware of a purpose rising up within him. A voice, growing stronger and stronger by the second, kept ordering him to drive home. And after several moments of indecision, he got up and started getting dressed.

In the midst of donning his clothes, he noticed Martin gazing at him, wide-eyed. "What are you doing?"

"I'm going to the funeral," Daniel said matter-of-factly.

"I thought you missed the funeral."

"There's another one in a couple hours," Daniel muttered.

"You're not making any sense," Steven said.

"That's because I need to go home. And then I will."

"Will what?"

"Make more sense."

"I give up." Martin turned himself over and went back to sleep.

It was a frantic drive and as Daniel drove, the night gradually slackened its stranglehold and the hilly contours of Massachusetts bloomed from their dark obscurity. By now, Angela's death had become a spinning clot of anxiety that had taken up permanent residence in his throat. He kept the Buick going eighty-five the entire way, glad that his normal responses were somewhat deadened. Otherwise he was afraid of being disturbed by more dreams of Angela pursuing him or that the car would suddenly seem claustrophobic and he'd flip out in the middle of the parkway. He needed concentration. Concentration would keep him sane. As he drove southward, the vibrant tides of autumn appeared visibly less advanced; it almost seemed as though he was driving back into the recent past—into the tired, sighing green of late summer. Part of him even began to believe that there was a funeral to attend. That would make it all right, he thought.

He made it to Houghton in two and a half hours. The day was starting out grim and overcast and half-promised rain. First he drove slowly past Patrick Riordan's house. It was completely dark. He wondered if Patrick had arrived home yet for the weekend. Probably not. Daniel smiled to himself. He always figured that at some point in time they would be able to resume their friendship. Probably because there wasn't so much at stake to begin with. In friendships of lesser magnitude, people go through phases; things shift rather than fall apart.

Daniel finally pulled into the Scaraventos' street and parked his car a block away from their house. Lights were already burning in the house; everyone must be awake. Then again, they probably had not slept. He walked along the sidewalk until he stood in front. He recognized the blue light in the den, shadows shifting and shrinking there, televised images cast on the walls by early morning news programs. All during his drive he had entertained fantasies about knocking on the door, bursting in and vilifying Gianni for treating him so shabbily, for banning him from Angela's funeral. But now as he found himself contemplating other houses on the Scaraventos' street, which in their state of slumber looked uninhabited, Daniel realized with a chill that for him Houghton was becoming a ghost town. He had no compulsion to do anything other than continue his journey into Manhattan.

And just as he was turning to walk back to his car, Daniel saw what he first thought was a hallucination: the Polannos' black Trams Am sidling down the street, puffing out exhaust into the still morning air. The car pulled up next to him and the driver's window rolled down. There was Vito, all alone. He was dressed in a suit, white shirt and tie.

"What are you doing here, Fell?" Vito said.

I was about to ask you the same question, Daniel thought. "I'm headed home to the city for the weekend. I was just passing through Houghton."

"The city, huh?" said Vito, exhibiting what Daniel felt was a common suburban attitude toward Manhattan, a composite of respect and mistrust.

Vito hesitated. "You going in or what?"

Daniel shook his head.

"Go ahead. They're all there. And they're awake. My mom is making them breakfast. I'm here to pick her up."

Daniel turned to look at Angela's kitchen window but in the difficult light was unable to detect any telltale movements. "No, I got to get going," he said, taking a step away from the Trans Am.

"Hold on a minute," Vito said. "I want to talk to you."

Daniel shrugged and faced Vito once again. "How come you're all dressed up?" he asked curiously.

"I'm working." Vito grinned proudly. "At an insurance company in White Plains."

"I'm impressed."

"I'm just an office boy right now. But I'm hoping to get my sales license one day."

"A good way to make money."

Vito grinned nervously. He didn't make a move to continue the conversation, purposely bringing on an awkward moment. Daniel watched his narrow, pitted face and let the silence gather.

"I know you probably still think we killed the animals," Vito said finally.

Daniel rolled his eyes. "I don't think about it, to tell you the truth."

"Well, *I* think about it."

"Oh, I don't doubt that."

Vito fidgeted in his seat. His flinty eyes were trained carefully on Daniel. He gripped the steering wheel and then folded his lean hands and put them on his lap. "Look, I wasn't being completely honest with you last winter. I know I kept insisting you had to help us out and I know that I insisted too much."

"Something like that," Daniel agreed.

"Well now, I want to explain something." Vito glanced at the Scaraventos' house for a moment and then continued. "First of all, Mickey, Mario and I don't always hang out together. I know it seems like it. Lots of times cause of the tinted windows it seems like we're all in here, when it's just those two."

"What are you getting at, Vito?"

"What I'm getting at, Danny, is that I didn't kill the animals. But my brothers did kill them."

Daniel started, more in surprise at the fact of the confession than at the actual confession itself. He had always believed that the Polannos were involved in the carnage one way or another. But hearing it now all over again made him terribly sad, as it had when he had just heard it for the first time. And yet he was relieved that Vito had no part in it; it didn't seem quite so awful now.

"I guess you don't expect me to go to the police."

"I suppose you could." Vito flashed a sinister smile. Daniel knew Vito assumed that reporting their conversation to the police would be pointless, would in fact probably be considered hearsay, the word of one "kid" against that of the Polannos.

He looked at Vito curiously. "Why are you telling *me* all this?"

Once again Vito glanced toward the house. "Because I finally told my mother it was them and not me. She's been able to live with it now . . . and she wanted me to tell you."

What difference would it make to Maria, Daniel wondered, if he knew the truth, although he said to Vito, "Then I'm glad she feels better about it."

Vito nearly said something else but then held back, as though editing his words. "Mom wanted me to tell you because . . ." he faltered. "I don't know. I guess because Mrs. Scaravento was really nuts about you. And Mom felt she owed something to her."

Daniel smiled an artificial smile and said nothing. He felt a little sick.

Vito made a sharp flourish of his hands in order to end the conversation. "Well." He stuck his arm through the window and shook Daniel's hand. "It's been nice knowing you."

"Yeah, it's been nice," Daniel said.

"Sure you don't want to go in with me?"

Daniel took a step backward. "I'm sure."

Vito parked the Trans Am, got out and went around to the kitchen door. As Daniel watched him go in he managed to get a sideways glimpse of Angela's garden. It was looking barren again, the clematis and iris and vegetables plants all withered. The beloved Albertine roses had long since perished, ghosts of their former selves.

27

Irene seemed happier to be living in Italy, or perhaps more comfortable would have been a more accurate way to describe her state of being. She rented a modest house outside Padua and took up painting in a studio that had been built on the edge of her property. "I started out small and now I'm doing four-foot canvases," she told Daniel in a transcontinental phone call. He asked her what sort of subject matter she was focusing on and Irene said, "Oh, mostly geometric stuff."

"That sounds too easy for you."

"I'm getting warmed up for things like landscapes," she explained.

"Have you been seeing people?"

"A lot of people have moved," she reported. "But yes, I've been going out to dinner and that sort of thing. I'm also enjoying my solitude."

Daniel felt too uncomfortable to ask if his mother had had any dates, assuming that she probably went out with men. He asked instead about changes in the city.

"They redid the Pedrocchi. Now it looks like one of those garish coffee houses you'd see in little Italy. The traffic is even more horrendous. There are these communist rallies all the time, which cause road blocks. And the frescos in the Scrovegni have faded even more."

"But you'd still rather be there," Daniel said.

"It would be nicer if I had you here to translate for me," Irene said coyly. "You could always transfer to Padua University. They've got a great medical school."

Daniel said nothing for a moment. "Maybe junior year."

Irene didn't mention Marcella Auguri during those first few telephone calls, and finally in a letter Daniel asked how much his mother had seen of her friend. The reply came. "Marcella dropped me. As soon as I told her I had gone ahead and gotten divorced."

Part of Daniel felt that his mother deserved to be rejected by her friend and part of him felt Marcella was being unjustifiably rotten.

Irene flew back to New York for Christmas and stayed with a friend just a few blocks away from Harold's apartment. His girlfriend, Sylvie, had family in Oklahoma with whom she spent important holidays and so the potential conflict about having a lover and a former wife at the same Christmas dinner was avoided. Not that Irene would have been unwilling to take part in such a mixed occasion.

After arguing over the menu and over who would cook, she and Harold ended up preparing the meal as a joint effort. He made pheasant with cornbread stuffing; she made a standing rib roast and a penne pasta dish with snowpeas. Harold had bought some wonderful wine on a tip from a cooking school instructor and by the time dinner was over, the family had polished off four bottles. Alexis got tipsy and fell asleep on the couch; Irene was afflicted with a case of the giggles. Throughout the evening, however, Daniel had remained quiet and self-contained. Harold asked if he was feeling down.

"No, I've just been thinking about a lot of things."

"About what?"

Daniel shrugged. He was as yet unwilling to admit that the holiday was bringing up memories of times past and people lost to him. Just then, suddenly, the doorman buzzed the apartment.

Harold frowned at Irene. "I wonder who that could be?" he said.

Daniel went to the intercom. The doorman announced Gianni Scaravento.

"Oh, Jesus," Daniel groaned to himself. "I don't know if I'm ready for this."

"Who is it? Who is it?" asked Irene.

"It's not Sylvie, is it?" Harold said, faintly hopeful.

"No. It's Gianni Scaravento."

The news was met with silence.

"Well, ask him up," Irene said finally.

Daniel relayed this to the doorman, who came back on to say that Mr. Scaravento wanted Daniel to come downstairs.

Daniel turned to his parents. "Is that okay with you—if I go talk to Gianni downstairs?"

"Sure, all right," Harold said. "But don't stay out too long."

"Go on." Irene smiled mysteriously, as though she already foresaw the significance of such an unexpected visit.

Daniel grabbed his leather jacket and scarf and then in a burst of feeling threw his arms around both his parents, kissing each of them on the cheek. In the hallway while waiting for the elevator, he wondered why he had displayed such sudden emotion. It almost seemed as though he were going away and never coming back. However, he did not feel unhappy.

Gianni had declined to wait on one of the guest sofas provided in the lobby and was sitting on the vinyl bench in the passageway where the doormen usually sat. He was wearing a peacoat and a pair of rawhide gloves. He was staring down at the white and black tiles of the entryway floor.

"Hello Gianni," Daniel said flatly.

"Daniel," Gianni said, standing up abruptly, in his momentary awkwardness forgetting to shake hands. He beckoned to the cold, empty street. "Can you take a walk?" he said, unable to look directly at Daniel.

Daniel hesitated.

"Please, I need to talk to you."

Daniel now looked at Gianni as carefully as though he were looking at a map. Gianni's complexion had never been so clear. It gleamed with health, as though in secret agreement with college life. He had become one of the most handsome men Daniel had ever seen, a closer match to that perfect image Daniel had dreamed up in the Triumph last winter.

Without another word they left the building, heading north

along Sutton Place, then turned up an easterly incline and followed a cement strip that bordered the East River, a footpath busy during the day with joggers but deserted this Christmas night. They passed the heliport where a helicopter was loading passengers bound for Kennedy Airport. Daniel thought how awful it must be to travel on such a cold, lonely night.

Gianni finally spoke. "I'm sorry I didn't tell you about—" he faltered—"my mother. I tried to. I even picked up the phone a few times. But I was afraid you'd blast me for never calling you."

"If you wanted to hurt me you succeeded," Daniel said stiffly.

"So much was happening, Danny," Gianni said with an ache in his voice. "Things were coming at us from different directions." He paused. "I didn't think I could take seeing you at the funeral. I had to keep myself together. Tony and my dad were a mess."

"So what's up, Gianni?" Daniel said, continuing to walk. "What's the point of telling me all this? I feel shittier than I did before."

"What's up is I needed to see you."

"And I'm saying don't you think it's a little late?"

Gianni shrugged.

Daniel stopped and glared. "I just can't believe you never called me, Gianni."

Gianni was unable to meet his accusatory glance. "I was ashamed to face up to it. I was afraid you wouldn't forgive me."

"A bullshit excuse."

"It's the only excuse I have."

"Then it's not good enough."

The conversation dropped off as they walked aways. "But I knew if I showed up here tonight you couldn't have refused to talk to me," Gianni said eventually.

Daniel shook his head in exasperation. Gianni had let him down, had failed him and yet still dared to be overbearing. He saw a stone in their path and kicked it away. "So why aren't you with *your* family tonight?"

After a wistful chuckle Gianni explained, "My dad's in Florida. I think he's seeing some babe down there. Tony is with my aunt."

Daniel grunted as he learned the grim coordinates of each of the Scaraventos. His eye was suddenly caught by a light sweeping around from a cutter out on the river and for a moment he was stunned. Angela's passing was never more distressing to him now that Gianni told him the Scaraventos were split apart for the holidays. It was shameful of them to forgo Christmas, but then again perhaps celebrating without Angela would have been too difficult. Only now did Daniel realize yet another reason why he had been so drawn to her. For although Angela understood how couples ended up in divorce, and sometimes even applauded it, her own life had been rigorously channeled toward keeping her family together.

"Ah Jesus, Gianni," he said finally, "you should've told me. I'd have fixed you a plate. We have tons of food."

Gianni waved him off with a sad smile. "Na," he said. "I'm not hungry."

"*You* not hungry."

"Can't you tell I lost weight?" Gianni opened up his peacoat, which revealed a bulky fisherman's sweater.

Daniel appraised his friend as best he could in the darkness. "It's hard to judge. But, yeah. You look good. Don't you need to be big for football?"

A silence wedged its way between them, a silence that eventually ended with a burst of ironic laughter. "I'm not playing football anymore, Danny."

"What?"

"I quit. I would've only been second- or third-string q.b. anyway."

"Well what do you want for the first year? I mean Michigan is a Big Ten."

Gianni's shoulders gave a jerk and his gloved hands pulled at each other. "I'm lying actually," he finally confessed. "This is the lie I tell people back in Houghton, the lie I tell people when they come up to me at the Oaks. But I guess I can't lie to you," he said, pausing for a moment, preparing his next statement. "They just didn't want me on the team after they heard about the accident. Which is all for the better. I've decided to get the best education I can. That's what Angie would have wanted."

Daniel was silent for a moment, digesting this. They heard an explosive whirring of blades and turned to watch the helicopter lifting off its cement pad, making a beeline across the river and then rising steeply over Roosevelt Island. Daniel was surprised at how disappointed he felt that Gianni would never again play football.

"I don't even know if I would have lasted four years on that football team," Gianni went on. "Now I'm majoring in communications."

"Communications?" Daniel said grudgingly. "Sounds great. You've got the personality for it."

"What about you?" Gianni said. "How do you like college?"

"I like it."

"You decided on a major yet?"

"Philosophy."

"Any girls?" Gianni asked, grinning slyly.

Daniel hesitated. He described a brief affair he had had with a biology major. "But we didn't get to see each other that much because she went to a different school. I met her through Patrick Riordan."

"You're hanging out with him again?" Gianni asked.

"Yeah, I am," Daniel said. He knew Gianni would feel a little jealous, and felt satisfied at the thought.

"So what happened with this girl?"

"After a while it sort of fell apart. I guess maybe it was my fault." Daniel hesitated, trying to find an explanation. He was, he realized, confounded by all relationships these days.

"You can certainly be a bitch sometimes," Gianni said.

This annoyed Daniel; it reminded him of Gianni's ultimate remark that was made during their last phone conversation. He stopped walking. "Repeat what you said!" he snapped.

"You can be a pain to get along with is all I'm saying." Gianni turned defensive when Daniel felt he should have just backed off.

"Look," Daniel said, "You obviously haven't realized something you've done. You're obviously too stupid to understand—"

"Hold on a second," Gianni said. "I'm sorry about what I said to you on the phone. It was the shittiest thing I've ever said to anyone. It's unforgivable. And I should've apologized a lot earlier. Okay? But sometimes you can be difficult to take. That's what I just meant by calling you a bitch."

Daniel sighed. It all seemed so pointless now. Too much had happened, too much time had gone by.

They had continued walking and were now passing Sixty-ninth Street. A barge decorated with holiday lights came gliding down the East River, its huge whalelike body rolling with the currents. At first it seemed as if a freight company were having a little holiday fun by stringing up the decorations, but then Daniel heard music drifting in off the water and saw people dancing on board. It was a floating Christmas party.

"Now that must be a blast to do on a night like tonight," Gianni said.

Daniel was silent. He suddenly felt wary of continuing this conversation with Gianni and wanted to be back home with his family. He was feeling nostalgic and vulnerable and blamed it on the amount of wine he had drunk. And yet Daniel knew that even when sober, he had a tendency to feel out of control and enthralled when he was around Gianni Scaravento.

He stopped strolling again. "You're apologizing now. But you really hurt me," he said.

Gianni looked at him fervently. "That's what happens when people get close. They hurt each other without meaning to. Maybe you've never really been close to anyone before. Besides your family."

Although Daniel deplored the sound of the words he knew he was unable to refute them.

"I mean, look at me and Debbie Lerner," Gianni said with deliberation. "She's okay now, but she'd cross to the other side of the street if she saw me. Her mother still writes me nasty letters how her daughter will never be the same." He slapped his gloved hands against his thighs. "The girl can walk just fine. I've seen her in town. I've seen her with all her little friends laughing. She hangs out at the Oaks when she's not at college."

"I don't think her mother meant her health as much as she meant what Debbie went through."

They were now under a street lamp, and Gianni stopped, drawn to the light as though it would bring greater understanding to their conversation as it was also affording each of them a more vivid view of the other. "Debbie was the one who wanted to go out and lay against that windshield to begin with. She insisted on riding out there cause she couldn't stand being inside the car. Okay, so she went through thirty seconds of complete fear, she was in the hospital for a week and then home recuperating. Just in time to go to college. But she was as drunk as I was. Her judgment was as bad as mine. Except *I'll* never live it down. I got charged with reckless driving. Everybody at school found out about it and people assume I'm dangerous. . . ." He paused, his face haunted in misery. "And then my mother dies in the middle of it all." He shook his head vigorously. "No, I can't feel bad for Debbie Lerner anymore."

"It must be a difficult thing to get through, Gianni," Daniel said.

Meanwhile, tears had welled up in Gianni's eyes and he had to close them and compose himself before saying, "I didn't mean to take out my frustration on you. I meant to apologize right away. I realized I couldn't expect you to get off work and come out to Michigan. I was ashamed. But then . . ." Gianni took a deep, tremulous breath and blew out a billow of anxiety that condensed into frosted air. "My Dad arrived in Michigan and I was caught up in explaining everything and taking *his* heat."

"Then at least you could've let me continue to see Angela!" Daniel cried out.

Gianni hung his head. "My father refused to. When I told him it wasn't fair to her, he threatened not to help me get out of all the legal stuff with the accident. First, Debbie's father wanting to sue and the police breathing down my neck. It was bad for me, Danny. But no matter what, I never would've prevented you from seeing Angie."

"You'd only threaten to," Daniel pointed out.

"Understand that I wouldn't have done that for her sake." Gianni was shaking his head and tears shone on his cheeks in the lamplight. "I loved her, Danny. I miss her so much." For a moment he looked up at the night sky and then pivoted toward the river to hide his weeping. "And now she's gone and I never even proved myself to her."

Daniel approached his friend from behind and rested his arm on his shoulder. Feeling Daniel's touch, Gianni turned and hugged him. The embrace lasted longer than Daniel felt comfortable with, and eventually he tried to break free.

But Gianni wouldn't let go of him and with a quick maneuver he suddenly held Daniel in a headlock. "I missed you, my best buddy," he whispered in a broken voice close to Daniel's ear.

"Okay, Gianni, but let me go," Daniel said.

"I will in a minute." Gianni continued to hold him.

The moment was so ridiculous, Daniel started laughing. "Come on. Let up."

Gianni slackened his headlock and when Daniel made a quick move to extricate himself from it, he tightened up again. "Would you let go of me!" Daniel insisted, getting angry.

A clopping of shoes on the pavement told him people were walking by. He tried not to be embarrassed by their pose of intimacy.

"Why won't you let go of me?" he finally implored Gianni.

" 'Cause I haven't seen you in while," Gianni spoke softly. "But I'll make a deal with you."

"What kind of deal?"

"Promise you'll still hang out with me, sometimes."

"I'll hang out with you, Gianni. You know that."

"And I wouldn't mind something to eat if you got anything left over."

"I told you before we have plenty of food. Come on, now. Let go of me."

Gianni maintained his grip. "You got to promise me."

Gulping back his anger and his pride, Daniel managed to nod his head. "Okay, Gianni," he said. "I promise."

Joseph Olshan
Clara's Heart

From amongst the highly accomplished finalists in *The Times/
Jonathan Cape Young Writers' Competition*, Joseph Olshan
was awarded first prize for his outstanding first novel, *Clara's
Heart*, a magnificent portrayal of the bond of intimacy which
grew up between a young boy and his family's Jamaican
housekeeper.

When David Hart's mother Leona brought Clara Mayfield from
Kingston, Jamaica, to live in their affluent household, David told
the exotic intruder to go back where she came from. His life
had been disrupted enough by the death of his two-month-old
sister and the consequent grief of his mother, from which he
felt excluded. But indomitable Clara would take no nonsense
from David and within a few hours of her arrival she began to
capture the boy's affections. David's reluctant acceptance of
Clara's presence gradually grew into a rare and powerful form
of love, whose constancy helped him accept the erratic
attentions of his mothers.

'An extraordinarily mature range of sympathies'
IAN McEWAN

'*Clara's Heart* is a fresh and involving novel. Joseph Olshan has
remarkable empathy with his characters and writes some
scathingly funny and perceptive scenes. As I read this novel I
kept thinking this is a story I have never read before but I believe
these people totally' GAIL GODWIN

'*Clara's Heart* is an exceptionally fine study of love and growing
pains' THE TIMES

'In giving us a detailed child's eye view of the world. *Clara's
Heart* occupies similar territory to *The Catcher in the Rye*.
Olshan's achievement is to have created a separate and entirely
believable world, carefully, comically and humanely drawn
without literary self-consciousness. It is held together by much
tension and contains many excellent recognizable scenes and
embarrassments. *Clara's Heart* is successful on its own terms
as one of those novels that illustrate Gide's resonant phrase:
'Families I hate you.' It is a fine debut' TLS

Bel Mooney
The Windsurf Boy

'In the distance, floating effortlessly among the moored boats and gliding out and away with perfect freedom, was a small, blue and white sail . . .'

This is Matthew, the *Windsurf Boy*, and to newly-separated Anna, holidaying in Devon with her seven-year-old son, he represents all that is young, strong and free.

In a nearby nursing home, Anna's mother is dying of cancer, calmly accepting impending death with a dignity her daughter cannot begin to understand.

Faced with the dilemma of many conflicting emotions — guilt, grief, nostalgia, and an increasing infatuation with the teenage windsurfer — Anna struggles to come to terms with her life . . .

'Full of wisps of sadness and loss . . .' GUARDIAN

'Confidence and originality . . . a powerful sense of loss' TLS

'Strong but gentle . . . bittersweet' COMPANY

'A touching tale' THE OBSERVER

Bel Mooney was born and brought up in Liverpool. As a philosophy student at London University, she met her future husband, the broadcaster Jonathan Dimbleby. They now live near Bath with their son and daughter. She has written a book about children and another for children, but *The Windsurf Boy* is her first novel. She has worked as a journalist for a wide variety of publications and has appeared regularly on television and radio. She is now a regular columnist on the *Sunday Times*, and is the new book reviewer for *Cosmopolitan* magazine.

Grace Ingoldby
Last Dance With You

Witty. skilful and sparkling with originality, *Last Dance With You*
generously fulfils the promise of Grace Ingoldby's acclaimed
first novel, *Across the Water*.

Difficult and impulsive to the bitter end, Richard Francis Fox
leaves home at the age of eighty-two to drown himself in the
oily and quite unspectacular waters off the Isle of Wight. The
suicide of this once eminent man creates a hideous gap in the
lives of his dwindled entourage left stranded at The Round
House in Wiltshire: Joyce, his elderly secretary; Ralph, who
lives on Fox charity in the family cottage; and Peter, his forty-
year-old son, who returns for the funeral and, despite his better
instincts, finds himself staying on.

Last Dance With You describes Peter's year at The Round
House following his father's death – among people who have
all seen better days and who cling with desperate obstinacy to
carefully edited memories. Here conversation has reached the
point of inconsequential small talk; here, in the circular rooms
and passageways, the dead apparently hold sway. Dominant
women both dead and alive exacerbate Peter's state of shock
and loneliness until he can only describe himself as 'emotionally
incontinent' or 'technically dead'. Unease is heightened by the
arrival of Kate, his father's young protégée, and Nicola, who
eagerly and efficiently sets herself to tackle the muddle his
father has left behind. Shunted out of the spotlight, Peter
struggles to regain his sense of humour and perspective, to
make sense of both his father's life and his own, and to throw
off the black dog of the past.

'Grace Ingoldby's style is sharp and ironic, but she looks at the
futility of the games people play with compassion as well as
wit' DAILY TELEGRAPH

'If Peter learns anything about his father, it's that he went to
his death irascible, opinionated, fully himself. Grace Ingoldby is
a shrewd and stylish analyst of emotion' OBSERVER

'An assured book, strong and sensitive and deeply
moving' COSMOPOLITAN

Junichiro Tanizaki
Naomi

The long-awaited translation into English of Tanizaki's first major novel, the story of one man's obsession with the woman of his dreams.

Joji, a twenty-eight-year-old bachelor, sets up house with a fifteen-year-old café hostess, with the intention of giving her an education in return for her company. But she is not as naïve as she seems; she does not act as his housekeeper for she is a 'modern' girl, ready to defy tradition. In Tokyo of the 1920s she embraces wholeheartedly the avant-garde western ideas. She enjoys dancing, dressing in European clothes, and flirting with many men. Joji's dreams are shattered. Obsessed with his love, he cannot give her up: the master becomes the servant.

'Tanizaki says a great deal about a traditional Japanese culture both intoxicated and subverted by the shock of the new'
OBSERVER

'There is an intoxication and energy about *Naomi* that proves refreshing . . . *Naomi* is both a sad story about accepting humiliating compromises with a relationship and a clever, oblique evocation of a neurotic period'
TIMES LITERARY SUPPLEMENT

'A fascinating study in the unfamiliar and all-to-sadly familiar . . . some sharp comedy in the transfer of power in the marriage bed' GUARDIAN

Nicholas Christopher
The Soloist

Max Randal is in trouble. A superb pianist, darling of the critics, he has not performed in four years. The proficiency is there, but the magic is not: his playing is flat. Two wives have left him; so has the mother of his only child. And he is afraid. The summer of his thirty-fourth year, he schedules a major tour, daring himself to revitalize his career – and his life. It is a summer fuller and more challenging than any he could have imagined. Max's first wife is dying in a Boston hospital; his second wife wants to remarry him; his daughter's mother takes off for Europe, leaving him their child; and his current lover wants to move in with him.

Rich and exuberant, *The Soloist* transforms a musician's dark night of the soul into a brilliant adventure. In a wild romp through New York and Boston – a renewal of relationships with every important person in his life – Max Randal discovers what he needs to know about himself and about the people he thinks he loves.

Terry McMillan
Mama

Mama is a gutsy first novel which takes the reader into the heart of an American black family as it passes through the 60s and 70s, with all the social changes that era promised and finally delivered. It is a tale of survival – of gumption and weakness – and of dogged self-reliance in the face of poor odds.

'Marrying a man is a way of letting him know you want to be with him forever. It don't make no difference if it don't last but two weeks.' These are the words of Mildred Peacock, mama of five from Point Haven, Michigan, who, for all the men in her life – including three husbands – never had one she could really rely on.

Mildred's tempestuous drama takes its courses with compelling realism, humour and undampened high spirits.

'Terry McMillan tells her story with an unforgettable combination of compassion and sass.' OBSERVER

'A remarkable first novel . . . a brilliant description of life – noisy, destructive, earthy but not without comedy – among a poor black urban family' DAILY EXPRESS

'Terry McMillan has written a very engaging and funny first novel, an invitation into a world that would have remained unknown to anyone not of it' LITERARY REVIEW

Geoffrey Wolff
Providence

Providence, Rhode Island, is a mean city with a festering colonial past, a corrupt no-hope present, and the biggest organized crime racket on the Eastern seaboard . . .

From the moment that Lieutenant Corcoran of the city's Police Department fishes the slashed, bullet-ridden body of a minor hitman from the river, events conspire to change the lives of five of Providence's citizens forever.

Skippy, a would-be monster, his good-time girlfriend Lisa, Adam Dwyer, an honourable lawyer who has six months to live, his beautiful wife Clara, coping with her own private terrors, and the Lieutenant, who is about to sacrifice everything for the coked-out Lisa, discover that Providence is just murder.

'The atmosphere is entertainingly breezy and sleazy, with a wise-cracking, side-of-the-mouth narrator and some of the tightest, meanest dialogue this side of Elmore Leonard' TIME

'Stylishly and scatalogically written, with pace and wit' LITERARY REVIEW

'Absolutely dazzling' NEW YORK TIMES

All these books are available at your local bookshop or newsagent, or can be ordered direct from the publisher. Indicate the number of copies required and fill in the form below.

Send to: **CS Department, Pan Books Ltd., P.O. Box 40, Basingstoke, Hants. RG21 2YT.**

or phone: 0256 469551 (Ansaphone), quoting title, author and Credit Card number.

Please enclose a remittance* to the value of the cover price plus: 60p for the first book plus 30p per copy for each additional book ordered to a maximum charge of £2.40 to cover postage and packing.

*Payment may be made in sterling by UK personal cheque, postal order, sterling draft or international money order, made payable to Pan Books Ltd

Alternatively by Barclaycard/Access:

Card No.

Signature:

Applicable only in the UK and Republic of Ireland.

While every effort is made to keep prices low, it is sometimes necessary to increase prices at short notice. Pan Books reserve the right to show on covers and charge new retail prices which may differ from those advertised in the text or elsewhere.

NAME AND ADDRESS IN BLOCK LETTERS PLEASE:

Name

Address

3/87